In the Shelter of Each Other

Aberdeenshire Library and Information Service
www.aberdeenshire.gov.uk/libraries
Renewals Hotline 01224 661511

In the Shelter of Each Other

GROWING UP IN LIVERPOOL IN THE 1930s AND '40s

JACK MADDOX

ISIS
LARGE PRINT
Oxford

First published in Great Britain 2008
by
The History Press

Published in Large Print 2009 by ISIS Publishing Ltd.,
7 Centremead, Osney Mead, Oxford OX2 0ES
by arrangement with
The History Press

The moral right of the author has been asserted

British Library Cataloguing in Publication Data
Maddox, Jack, 1932–
    In the shelter of each other growing up in Liverpool
    in the 1930s & '40s. - - (Reminiscence)
    1. Maddox, Jack, 1932– - - Childhood and youth.
    2. Liverpool (England) - - Biography.
    3. Liverpool (England) - - Social life and customs
    - - 20th century.
    4. Liverpool (England) - - History - - 20th century.
    5. Large type books.
    I. Title II. Series
    942.7'53084'092–dc22

ISBN 978–0–7531–9536–9 (hb)
ISBN 978–0–7531–9537–6 (pb)

Printed and bound in Great Britain by
T. J. International Ltd., Padstow, Cornwall

It is in the shelter of each other
that the people live.
Old Gaelic Proverb

Acknowledgements

My thanks to Sue Wiseman for typing the manuscript, and to the following for kindly donating photographs and for offering general assistance with the compilation of this book: Mark Sargent and Sefton Libraries; Roger Hulse and Liverpool Record Office; Anne Gleave and the Merseyside Maritime Museum; Stephen Done and Liverpool Football Club; Alan Boyle; Peter Woolley; Frankie Connor; Euan Blackledge; Bill McMahon.

I'd also like to thank Hazel Shaw and Trinity Newspapers for publicising my search for photographs; Alan Wilkinson for manuscript criticism and guidance; Brian Plumb for records of the Archdiocese of Liverpool and *Catholicism in the Workhouse*; Jill Wallis for *A Welcome in the Hillsides*; The *Liverpool Daily Post & Echo* for their many reports of happenings of the time; Dame Beryl Bainbridge for her foreword and generosity, and finally to the city of Liverpool for providing the inspiration.

Contents

Foreword
by Beryl Bainbridge

This is the story of a boy, Jack Maddox, born in 1932, growing up in Liverpool during the war years. Told with vigour, its depiction of the lives of family and neighbours touches the heart. I can vouch for the authenticity of this portrayal of a world long gone, for though I was born into a more privileged family, my own father experienced the same background and talked with emotion of its lost values.

Liverpool in his day was a powerhouse of the shipping trade. Often he took me into town and pointed with pride at the offices of the Mersey Docks and Harbour Board, at the vast edifice of the Royal Liver Building, its twin towers set with clocks glowing like full moons and those giant birds, wings raised, tethered beneath flying clouds. And yet, Disraeli's "Two nations" existed in Liverpool in a more real sense than anywhere else in England.

Jack Maddox lived mostly in Bootle, a scruffy area boasting a grand town hall. His house was crowded with siblings, and with relations returning home on leave from sea voyages. He too wandered down Lime Street with its illuminated hoardings, scuttled beneath the Overhead Railway, travelled by train along the coast to Ainsdale, Formby and then exotic Southport with its fairy lights sparkling in the trees bordering the picture palaces. He too was told that William Joyce, Lord Haw-Haw, the Nazi sympathiser, went to school at Merchant Taylor's School in Crosby, and that Adolf Hitler stayed for three months in Toxteth with his half-brother Alois.

By the values of today, Maddox had a deprived childhood, and yet his use of words, his ability to describe past events, both humorous and sad, is exceptional. The odd thing is that sixty years ago, some people could learn to express themselves, whatever their backgrounds. Not so now.

This book deserves to make an impression. Compelling, important, utterly lacking in sentimentality, it is above all, the history of a city.

CHAPTER
ONE

Timon Avenue and Tom

"This man is dying. He must go to hospital immediately." May looked at Tom in the bed, distressed, sweating and restless.

"Which one?" she said to the doctor as he closed his bag.

"Walton." Walton, the old workhouse! They called it a hospital now. The change was recent but memory dies slow. That's where they took her mother. She never saw her again. It was really a reception room for the cemetery and the memories of the burial in a paupers' grave on a dark, cold and rainy day were strong. She thought of the picture in her grandmother's kitchen — a boat of souls crossing the river to Hell and the words above the entry gate, "Abandon hope all ye who enter here". Yes, Walton was like that. May was afraid. Walton had previous. She wasn't letting Tom go there.

"No, Bootle," said May, "or he stays here."

Dr Turnbull grunted, he didn't like his decisions challenged, but he knew May was serious, so when the ambulance arrived later, off went Tom to Bootle. It was all so sudden. Yesterday everything was fine when Tom returned on his bike in the heat of the still summer

3

afternoon. The sewer in the street had become blocked and the grid was lifting and leaking excrement, and all the children had been called in.

"The smell is terrible," said Tom. "Yes we're waiting for the council to send someone to clear it", replied May. Tom was not a man for jobs around the house, but he was fastidious about hygiene and collecting a mop he went out to the street lifted the grid and pushed and shoved until, with a loud sucking noise, the obstruction cleared and the flow resumed. He put the grid back and returned to the house, a bath and a meal and then it was time to go back and open the Glebe for the evening, the pub on County Road where he worked. Later that night when he returned, he was not himself and was unable to eat his supper. "I don't feel right," he said as he went upstairs to bed. During the night May, lying beside him, was conscious of his high body temperature, sweating and disturbed state, and by daybreak he was drained and unable to rise for work. And now he was at death's door in hospital fighting for life — all in the space of twenty-four hours. May was finding it hard to adjust to the rapid change. She sent a boy from the street to the Glebe with a note and busied herself with household tasks and the three children in the house. She uttered silent prayers, "please God, he'll be alright."

The road outside our house was empty and the arrival of any vehicle was an event — especially an ambulance. Most of the front doors were open with women standing on the steps wondering what was happening. The questions to May would come later.

Bootle Hospital was near the docks and quite new, with an excellent reputation for its accident and emergency work. Numerous casualties would arrive there daily from the miles of docks and ships on the river.

The initial diagnosis was difficult. The sickness was acute, severe and terminal. It could only be related to a lung infection from the blocked sewer and treatment would be difficult. There were no antibiotics in 1934. Tom was put on an "urgent note" meaning he could die quickly. He was twenty-six years old.

When May's mother died, her five children were consigned to the care of her mother-in-law, a hard, if good woman, who was aged, ailing and embittered by the loss of two of her own beloved sons. May's father, her eldest son, was in Australia. He played no part in the children's upbringing other than transmitting money for their keep to his mother in England and so it was that the children grew without father or mother on the streets of Liverpool.

May was taken out of school at eleven to help at home and she became the surrogate mother for her brothers and sister. It was early in life for such responsibilities, but it taught her that life goes on whatever difficulties it presents to the living. Only the dead escape. You can't hold back the dawn, and so it was that May returned home from the hospital to our little house in Timon Avenue well aware of the difficulties both present and to come, as well as the uncertainties of all our futures, and Tom's in particular. The only way forward was to get on with things, and do the best she could, particularly for the three little

5

children in the house. We would just have to carry on for now without Tom, whose absence could be temporary or permanent, we just didn't know.

Protected by mother from the worry and stress of the situation, we adapted quickly to life without father and then Tommy, May's youngest brother, appeared. He had arrived home in the night, docking on the tide after midnight and now here he was singing in the morning sunlight as he dressed. "Empty saddles in the old corral, where are you riding tonight?" Then a last stroke of the brush to the hair and turning from the mirror, he was ready. A tall, well-built twenty-year-old, mother's youngest brother. Home from sea and flashily attired in a pale silvery grey suit — a real "Cunard Yank". We looked up at him and he smiled. "Come on then Fran, let's go," and he grasped Fran's hand and led him out of the house, down the path and off to the shipping office on Strand Road to collect his pay. It was his big day — the payoff from his first trip to sea. I was left behind, being too little at the time for the four-mile trek there and back. Fran was five and hyperactive, a great walker or runner, though likely to break away at any time — usually in the direction of any action or danger which attracted him like iron filings to a magnet.

I didn't feel left out as we waved them off and was happy to be left behind with May, to whom I was much attached. Meantime, May was washing Maureen's face. Maureen was her sister Alice's child and lived with us. She was four months younger than I. Alice was a cook who lived in. She had no husband. May lifted us into the twin pram and strapped us in, and Maureen

(Biddy) kept reaching across and trying to pull off my bonnet as off we went.

There wasn't much to be bought — just essentials — bread, potatoes — a little meat, milk. Times were difficult, and like shipwrecked mariners, the city waited for the dawn, a ship on the horizon, and salvation. Hope — the greatest of all virtues — sustained everybody.

May wheeled the pram down the street and at the corner where she turned into Aintree Road, stood the usual cluster of men, a dozen or so, talking. They made a passage to let us through. "Fine day ma'am," one said. "It is so," replied May with a smile. They were there every day. "What are they doing?" I wanted to know and asked May as we moved on. "They have no work, son," she said. Each day they congregated, talked, dispersed and met again. One subject only occupied them — work. They met to exchange information and experiences — each spent the day going around employers asking for a job — anything. Any news of even a day's work gave hope; and enquiry as to "any chance for us?" The men were a mixture of young and old, skilled and unskilled, but work of any kind would have been gladly taken by any of them. The man who swept our street for the council each week was a former ship's captain and happy to have the job. Many like him were serving as ordinary seamen. One ship numbered six captains all signed on as Able Seaman. What does a ship's captain and his crew do when they have no ship? There is little call for their skills on land. What does a docker do when there are no ships to load or unload?

What does the carter and his horse do when there is no cargo from ship to warehouse?

They do nothing, or stand on the corner, or walk the city knocking on doors. Even that becomes difficult as the boots wear out along with hope. Cardboard was much used inside the boots, as the sole wore down. Hope was more difficult to substitute.

I thought about what I'd seen and had been told every time I looked at the men on the corner, and I resolved never to let it happen to me. I would never forget it. From such events character and values form though memory and recall can rarely define the moment when the mark is made. For me the moment was seminal.

The journey to the little parade of shops, which like the houses were also new, was only a couple of hundred yards. Biddy was still attempting to pull off my bonnet and throw it into the road. It was a regular activity and she seemed to actively dislike the bonnet which covered my whitest of blonde hair. To bring peace, May removed the bonnet and put it in the shopping bag as she stopped the pram outside William Ross the greengrocers, one of a chain of over 150 shops which competed with the even larger Waterworths — both now long gone.

The value of the pram was now evident as May entered the shop and left Biddy safely secured. I was totally occupied viewing the window of the shop which was piled with fruit and vegetables, but also a strange new arrival I'd not seen before. It looked like a bar of chocolate but it was so big. I thought it was chocolate because of the shape, the silver paper at each end and the distinctive bluey purple of the wrapper, but it also featured a picture of fruit and nuts. I was confused, the size of the bar was enormous. I wanted to know the answer — an early sign of the curiosity which would lead me later in life to some strange places and not a little trouble. When May came out and put the bag on the pram between Biddy and me, I asked her, pointing, "What's that in the window?" She told me it was indeed chocolate with fruit and nuts, a half-pound bar from Cadbury's. My natural sense of order was offended and I still thought it an odd place for a bar of chocolate. It was clearly a strange place, this world. Fruit shops were for fruit and sweet shops were for sweets, or were they? I was confused.

A couple of hours after we got back from the shops, Tommy and Fran returned bearing gifts — for themselves. Tommy had two new ties and Fran had a red pedal car which he insisted on driving home most of the way. May was happy at the delight on Fran's face but disappointed as the household was badly in need of money. Tommy had spent over half of what he had drawn from the pay office — most of it on Fran's car. He had a couple of pounds left and gave May one to help with the housekeeping. That was Tommy. He had a sweet and generous nature and was always in good humour, singing softly around the house. He would play with us for hours and make little carts out of matchboxes and an even bigger cart with shafts which he hitched to Mick, the dog, to carry us around the garden. But if he had money it burnt a hole in his

9

pocket. All May's brothers lived with us when they were home from sea and waiting for their next ship. This could often take some time. A seaman's employment contract finished when the ship docked. No money when you were at home, and back to sea when it was all gone.

Fran came back from school at four in the afternoon with all the other children in the street. All the houses had young children as this was the basis of housing allocation by the council which was advanced in its thinking. The small estate had a resident lady manager who attended to any housing difficulties or problems. She also saw to it that all tenants kept the houses and gardens in good order. This was a condition of the lease and the tenancy and ensured that standards and appearances were maintained and the housing stock kept up to scratch. "Tool sheds, trellis fences or other fences, or any other erections" were not permitted and sub-letting was "strictly prohibited". The rules were printed on the tenants' rent books and enforced. They sound severe, but they averted disputes and preserved harmony. Reuben Herd and family were new arrivals — gypsies who had forsaken the travelling life and embraced urban domesticity — but not completely. He was a totter with a pony and cart who went out every day collecting and selling scrap, mostly old oil drums. The day they moved in, he could not get the cart into the house but the pony came and trotting up the path at the side of the house was left grazing in the back garden. The estate manager arrived the same evening and told him to take the pony elsewhere or he would be homeless very soon. She also had a quick inspection of the house and found the bath filled with coal. Reuben said he thought that was its purpose. Put straight on city life, he stayed with us but remained apart. There were others with similar wishes. Many wanted to keep poultry, and others pigs and pigeons. The possibilities for discord offered by the keeping of livestock were obvious, and the council ban was total.

The street was transformed when the children came home from school. In the pre-car age, the whole street became one large playground. The only vehicles which entered were ice cream and lemonade salesmen and the rag and bone man with his handcart. His arrival was always announced on an old bugle which he blew as he entered the street. His main trade was jam jars, which he collected and sold to the nearby Hartley's jam factory. Jam was a staple in the diet of the working class at the time and the standard jar was the 2lb size. Smaller sizes were rarely seen. The 2lb jar has vanished and with it went its companions, margarine and the 4lb loaf. These, with tea, were staples for breakfast, dinner and tea.

Where food was concerned, Fran was almost an absentee. He was a quiet, thin child with an independent spirit. He was a loner. He arrived in the world at just 5lb, with the doctor's comforting words, "You won't rear this one." Being so small at birth, May had tried to build him up, but he had little appetite and she was concerned. When she put food in front of him, he would make no move to eat and she decided not to force the issue. The food would be left on the table and over the next few hours he would pick away at it until he'd got through most of it and it was then time for the next meal. This persisted until I arrived at the table for the first time to join him. A plate of little sandwiches was placed on the table between us and May, who knew what she was doing, watched.

Fran watched as well, fascinated as I attacked the sandwiches. When the number was much reduced, Fran seemed to realise that if he wanted any he'd better start now — later would be too late and so he started. He ate normally from then on.

May had realised early on that the firstborn is in status "an only child" until others arrive and the change in status from "only" to "elder" requires adjustment and management. When she was alerted to my future arrival she told Fran that he was going to get a little brother or sister and he had to look after them when they came. She kept telling him this and as she increased in size, she would put Fran's ear to her abdomen and ask him if he could hear the little heart beating inside. Including him in the arrival of his sibling gave him an early interest in procreation and all through childhood he kept asking May "where do babies come from?" He already had half the story but he wanted to know the rest. Maybe he could produce them too. In 1932 most babies were born at home. My arrival was difficult owing to the unwillingness of the midwife to call the doctor when difficulties arose. I was a big baby — over 11lb and the midwife was castigated for her delay in calling help. Mother and child could have been lost. As an infant I fed well and slept long from the start, unlike Fran. He waited impatiently for me to walk and play and felt quite proprietorial with none of the first-born's resentment often felt at such times — he had been conditioned. It was this sense of ownership which led to his wonder as he saw his "property" threaten to eat both their teas at the first sitting. Fran was a very protective elder brother and combative. Sitting in the road quietly playing one day I was subjected to an attack by the Faircloughs who lived opposite. They were two boys about the same ages as us, handsome lads with dark curly hair. My locks were blonde and attracted their attention. They pulled my hair and followed it with a kick when I complained. Fran, who was some distance away, was alerted by Biddy and followed the Faircloughs as they ran off back to their own house. All the doors were open front and back when the children were in the street and the oppressors ran in the back door into their kitchen. Fran, followed by Biddy walked, not ran, behind them, straight into the kitchen where two smiling boys each received "a puck in the gob", right in front of their mother. He was gone before she could intervene and she was left to comfort her baby boys, now both crying. Biddy looked on and stayed for some minutes — eventually emerging eating a butty. The boys had been given a piece to cease their tears and Biddy was included too, and then left.

Fran took his defensive duties very seriously and was not in the least averse to thumping any other boy who he felt threatened him or his brother and this made things much easier for me. I, for my part, realised that an elder brother was valuable and was worth deference, and subjection even. He was too big to fight and like all authoritarians, felt no aversion to keeping his subjects in order. From all this I learnt early not to confront superior forces openly. This included mother, who never laid an angry finger on me in the whole of my life. It was not that I never deserved punishment or retribution, but simply that May could never catch me when I'd been naughty — as all boys are. Fran was different. He would defy anybody and just stand in front of them looking them in the eye. This tactic disturbed May, who just wished he'd run away. She'd shown she was cross with him — that was enough — she didn't really want to do any more. In the classroom this behaviour got Fran into trouble and later at work it incurred the hostility of some superiors who considered he was looking upon them as inferiors. He probably was, but would have been better off hiding it. At school it incurred the dislike and retribution of those teachers who thought all children should be deferential and act so. Following behind, I would inherit these hostile forces at a later date and particularly so in the persons of Miss Leamy and Miss Lee. Form mistresses and strong women, but very different. The surname would invite retribution for fraternal offences and those not yet committed. The name was in deficit.

CHAPTER
TWO

May and Fran Show Their Mettle

For weeks Tom clung to life tenaciously through delirium and intervals of quietude. The infection spread from the lungs and the fear was septicaemia, which would mean the end. The crisis came quickly one evening as the infection spread and his right lower leg swelled and doubled in size in hours. A surgeon was called and the leg was cut in a 12-inch line to drain the pus and disinfect the cavity.

It was successful and a tribute to the skill of the surgeon in the dockers' accident hospital. The leg would always thereafter be thinner than the other, but otherwise perfectly healthy and strong. It was to be some months before Tom was ready for work but he had come through — that was the important thing.

At home, May was having a difficult time. No wages coming in, almost non-existent social security payments and too proud to ask for charity, three growing children and the daily visits to the hospital, but she managed, as always, and never complained to anybody. To the rent man (10s 6d a week) and all the others she could not pay, she quietly explained her position. They understood. They knew she would pay them in time and she did.

Her position was not unusual in those days and there was a toleration and humanity by many about money owed by those who couldn't pay. Many shopkeepers allowed "tick" — goods on credit to families simply because they would not turn them away knowing they would starve. This brought some almost to the same level of penury themselves.

In these circumstances May showed her mettle — producing much from little. No one in the house was hungry or in rags. It was a time when neighbours were borrowing all the time from each other: a cup of sugar, a bit of marge.

The Wharton family next door, new arrivals and nice people, were of great interest to Fran who spent much time there with his new friend Billy. "They sleep on the floor with coats over them and they drink out of jam jars. Can we do it too." The lifestyle was appealing.

May smiled at his earnest supplication, thinking how easily children accepted things. It's harder for the grown-ups, she thought.

Tom had now been in hospital some months and winter had come. May put the babes in the pram and taking Fran's hand (for he would run off if left free), closed the door and started the two-mile walk to the hospital. Tom was getting stronger all the time and in a few weeks would hopefully come home and start work again. The thoughts made May forget that Fran was only five as she quickened her pace while she pushed the pram with the other hand. A shout of complaint brought her back to reality and she smiled — she had always walked quickly, but she slowed the pace but still retained his little hand. She had been a victim of Fran's dashes for liberty too often. If he got away he could only be recaptured by abandoning the pram and the other two, a real quandary. It's like cowboys and Indians she thought, their journey was similar to that of the stagecoach in the new cowboy films everybody was talking about. You had to keep your wits about you and your eyes open all the time to travel safely. She was glad she had no Indians to contend with — Fran, for his part, would probably have been one of them.

At the hospital Tom was in good form. His popularity with the nurses was evident and his long stay had led to preferential treatment — he made them laugh, never complained and was always well groomed. He was an attractive young man. Visiting him one day, he reached to his bedside locker and fumbling, produced a matchbox.

"Look at this," he said, as he held the box in his left hand, gingerly opening it to reveal a bloodstained finger top in cotton wool.

"Ooh," said Fran, "whose is it?"

"Mine!" said Father, as he pulled his finger out from the bottom of the box.

We all laughed. I was totally taken in and thought it somehow natural that he'd found a finger in the accident hospital. It would be just the place to find such a thing.

He was eager to get out as soon as possible but his brush with mortality had made him more cautious. He would be patient. He would go when they said he was fit to go.

The return journey that evening was exciting. It began with a loud thunderclap followed by lightning which illuminated everything brighter than the brightest of summer days just as we started the journey. Then the rain followed — it was tropical in character, uninterrupted streams of water rather than sprinkler drops of the usual fall. It pounded the empty street, which ran like a valley between the dark hills of the black, sinister, smelly gasometers on either side. The rain bouncing up as it struck the pavements — then pitch black again, and then more blinding light and a fury of thunder and flashing skies before the black curtain dropped again. I was enchanted. Everybody and everything was quickly soaked. Going up the steep hill on Linacre Road by the gasworks was the worst part, but eventually we all reached the top and continued on the kinder, but still upward, gradient of Aintree Road. Not long now, thought May, just about half a mile.

May had always liked the rain and she was in her element. She didn't like the lightning, but realised if she showed concern it would affect the children. When the thunder and lightning started, she decided she would treat it as an exciting event and with us looking to her for explanation she said, "Oh good, God is going to give us all a bath. He wants lots of rain and light to see us all." Reassured, we remained unafraid. No panic, no fear, though all a little alarmed — often a necessary ingredient in the enjoyment of pleasure.

The storm was an epiphany that remained in all our memories for ever. None of us would ever thereafter be afraid of thunder, lightning and the elements.

We seemed to laugh the rest of the way — even Fran who was never one to enter into the common consensus easily. Back home, all towelled and dried — we'd had our bath and bed — an exciting day.

May decided to wash all the wet clothes right away after she'd put us to bed. We didn't have much in the way of wardrobes and the wet garments would be needed soon.

After putting them to dry on the fireguard, she banked down the fire ready for its burst into flame in the morning when she inserted the poker into the slowly smoking, slumbering slack.

There was great excitement in the street — we were going to have a party — or at least the children were. Young Father Anderton, one of the curates at St Monica's, the new church and school parish, had won a prize on the Irish Hospitals' Sweepstake (tickets were regularly on sale in Liverpool). With the money, he bought a motorbike so he could get round the parish quicker and the rest he donated to summer afternoon street parties for the children throughout the parish. All the children, not just the Catholics. What a show all the mothers produced. Long tables borrowed from the schools with white tablecloths in the middle of the road, laden with jellies and trifles, cakes, sandwiches and lemonade. Everybody lent chairs, plates and glasses and organised and served the children at the tables. We all had our faces washed and hands and knees scrubbed and clean clothes, and for some it was the first time they'd had such largesse on the table before them. We gave a good account of ourselves — even Fran, who I noticed was developing a strong liking for cake. The sun shone, there was no wind and we all hoped that the good father's luck would continue.

Uncle Jimmy arrived that day on the afternoon tide and as usual he had with him lots of baggage and good things. Most of it was piled on a handcart outside in the street. He'd just been paid off from his voyage to South America with Lamport and Holt and he'd brought back something for everyone — as usual. He was the most generous of a generous family and now being unloaded from the cart were two armchairs, a dressing table and a bedside table all in yellow wicker, or rattan as it's called nowadays. These had been acquired when the ship called at Las Palmas in the Canaries on the way home and the ever-thoughtful Jim knew they would be well-received by his sister who was still getting together a home for all of them — husband, children, brothers, sister and any others in need. We would be joined by her father later on. Ships docking in Liverpool were always met by handcarts — they were an early form of taxi, but capable of taking far bigger loads and sailors always brought things home. To this day most homes in the city display evidence of these sailings, for nearly every family had someone at sea. The handcart owners also had the return trade and were regular carriers of the kitbags, paliasses (each man brought his own new straw mattress for the voyage — price 2s from Duthies) and other gear wanted at sea, including tools if you were an engineer. The coastal trade was covered too for both seamen and passengers, and the family were regular users of the service, it being particularly needed on the return journey from Ireland for the accompanying sacks of potatoes, sides of bacon and other produce from the rich Wexford countryside. Ships and shipowners had a very relaxed attitude to this carriage trade. It never seems to have been a cause of difficulty for either party, nor Her Majesty's Customs and Excise. May's father had used this concession fully and brought all the furniture for his new bride and home from New York to Liverpool (many handcarts required!) courtesy of his employers — the White Star Line in 1903. It could be seen as a wedding present. His father also worked for the White Star Line, but he'd come ashore some years before and was by then well ensconced in the Liverpool Head Office.

Besides the furniture there was fruit, some quite exotic like kumquats (which we had not seen before), sweets, tobacco and souvenirs and Jim himself.

Jim was of medium height and different in appearance from the rest of the family. Brown eyes and complexion and dark, wavy hair. Always on the move, very fit, quick-witted and sharp and an excellent footballer. In those times, many ships' teams could give a game to the leading South American clubs, like Boca Juniors, and did so. A crew would often be signed with this in mind and everyone benefited. Good PR for the shipping line and the ship, and good for the crew including the non-players. The ship's agent at the ports of call arranged the fixtures and a social function followed the game. This was why Jim liked the South American lines with their regular and fixed sailing and departure itineraries. Games could be planned, prepared for and advertised, and this was how the game of football came to South America where it developed as the breeding ground of exciting players wanted by clubs all over the world. That time had yet to come and would be preceded by the mistaken signing of English players by South American clubs in the belief that they were better than their own. This fiction had a short life as a few months after the first signings, the World Cup was held in South America and England were beaten 1–0 by the USA in 1950, who until that time weren't even known to play the game. Besides the football, Jim liked dancing. Being quick on his feet, he was good at it and always very smartly turned out. He always had fancy good-lookers for girlfriends and he brought some of them home for a cup of tea, often before the dance. One girl he had, called Lucy, has remained with me in a picture ever since. A very pretty, well-put-together redhead. Her hair was magnificent — a rich deep chestnut and thick and shining. I could not take my eyes off her. I remember my disappointment when another took her place. I would have liked her to have been Aunt Lucy.

Dancing was a very popular activity and when May's brothers were home from sea, they would dress up and go off dancing to the County Hall, or one of the numerous venues for an evening of adventure. Tommy and Jimmy were not shy and very easy in female company, unlike their elder brother, Jack, who was of a more serious nature. He found it more difficult to chat with girls and to ask them up to dance. He was talking with May over tea one day about this when home from sea. "It's hard for the men, for we've got to ask the girls to dance and they might say no." It was clearly a confidence thing and a fear of rejection he had. "Well, have you considered it from the girl's side?" said May.

"No, but it's easier for them. They're supposed to accept unless you're unfit and they won't let you in unless you pass muster." (Collar and tie and not drunk).

"But they can still refuse. Tonight there was a girl I really liked the look of, and I asked her to dance and she said, 'I'm sweating, ask me mate' — and you should have seen her mate!"

May laughed.

"Well, what about this. Here I am in the dance hall waiting for some of the nice tall men I fancy to ask me to dance."

"Do they?"

"Well, it's a big problem for a girl, particularly if you're tall like me, because all the little fellas want to dance with you and it's embarrassing as you go round the floor with their face in your chest and your friends laughing at you. You don't know whether to sit down or stand in the hall because if you sit the tall men can't see you're a good height, and if you stand you attract all the little fellas. It makes you feel like a lighthouse in the night. You lose either way."

Jack drew heavily on his cigarette and thought about what May had said. "Yes, I suppose that's difficult."

"Many an evening before I was married I came home without a single dance with one of the men I liked. Men have the option at least of asking those they fancy and you get nothing unless you ask. Refusal is the price you pay for that. 'Faint heart never won fair lady'."

The diffident Jack gave a wan smile. "Yes, I suppose we have the best of the bargain after all."

"As usual," said May, smiling as she refilled his cup. They were very close and May had been his closest confidante since childhood.

Nobody got serious about marriage in those days until they knew each other and their families quite well and "going steady" usually only started after going out with a number of potentials. There was a lightness of touch about going out together and relationships generally. Marriage had to be planned and saved for and it usually started with living with the bride's parents until the new couple could afford their own place (rented not bought). There was little credit available at the time. Mostly you saved up for things or did without. Tough, but nobody got into trouble through owing money. Short-term difficulties were covered by the local moneylender or pawnbroker where the amounts were small.

Jim liked a bet and was a keen student of form. When he was home he bought the *Sporting Life* every day, which he studied before a short visit to the Aintree, a brand new commodious and grand hostelry to place a bet with the local bookie's "runner". Betting was illegal in Britain unless you had an account until the repeal of the Betting Act in the 1960s. Bookies existed for the better off and were called Turf Accountants, which is a strange euphemism, particularly in Irish

Liverpool. Turf (peat from the bog) being the main fuel for cooking and heating in Ireland at the time.

Nevertheless, the bookies were many in number and none starved, for betting is endemic in Britain and nowhere more so than in the cities' working classes. Being banned, it operated by an army of "runners", who worked from vantage points in the area. These could include the gents' urinal in a public house, a back entry, or a shop. Runners would often have lookouts on watch for the local constabulary, which carried out regular pogroms. All concerned knew each other well and often word was passed to the usual suspects to be out of sight for the next week. Runners were arrested on sight at such times and brought before the magistrates and fined. The evidence was always in the pockets of the accused: the betting slips and money they were carrying to deliver to the bookie. The slip was essential for from it was made the "book". The slip contained little information, but it was all that was required. "6d E.W. Faragosto. Macca. 1s", i.e. 6d for a win and 6d for a place on Faragosto (a horse running that day) and Macca, a *nom de plume*, or should I say, "nom de turf". The final figure was the total amount paid. The slips and the money always had to balance and the runner was paid a commission on the money taken.

The system worked well and was extended during the war, which brought full employment and government direction of labour. Runners were illegal and not recognised as a reserved occupation, and so were sent by the Ministry of Labour to local jobs in

25

factories and plants. They naturally offered their services to their new workmates and takings increased as everyone was working overtime, had nothing to spend their money on because of war shortages and they now had the facility of service in-house and no threat of arrest on factory premises.

The betting industry boomed but it caused problems for the runners for they were now working fixed hours and under the surveillance of management. At this stage, technology was invoked and the business made a great step forward — the telephone. Had not Lord Leverhulme, that other local lad, declared that the telephone had made the location of head offices unimportant? That was in 1922 — this was 1940. Public telephones near the factory were monopolised and the bets phoned in. This caused other troubles as there were few public phones and the runner would go in his lunch hour and occupy the booth for most of the lunch break. As each bet was transmitted, the runner dropped the slip on the floor of the booth and left it there. Freed from incriminating material, he returned to work, safe from arrest, but unfed and hungry. Everyone liked the *Sporting Life* and I noticed May would also read it. She would write out pretend bets and check next day to see if she'd "won". The slips were put under the tea caddy in the kitchen and May played this game all her life. Betting with real money and the bookie only took place years later and, for her, only on big race days like the Grand National or the Derby. She was a better and more successful tipster and gambler than either Jim or Tom.

Jim stayed at sea longer than either Tommy or Jack, his brothers — sailing all through the war in the Pacific, Indian and Atlantic Oceans. One trip was over two years long. For a little variety he was also in the invasion fleet for the Sicily landings. When he finally came ashore, he became a successful publican in south Liverpool at the Albion in Llanwryst Street off Park Road. He was widowed three times, had two daughters and worked till he was eighty-five. He died at ninety in full possession of his faculties and still trying to run everywhere. The house was always lively when he was home and he was constantly playing tricks and jokes on everyone, particularly on the children. We loved him. Dick, the canary, was one of his earlier presents and was eyed longingly at the time by the cat, Ginger. Every day this was a ritual and then one day it all became too much for the cat. May's elder brother Jack had just come home from Australia where he'd been for a few years, working — for there was nothing for him here. Suddenly, the cat leapt up and grabbed the cage. Swinging drunkenly it came off its hook and crashed to the floor.

The cat, in shock, ran out the back door while the door of the cage came open and out flew Dick.

Jack grabbed for the bird and caught it by the tail but Dick kept flying, leaving his tail in Jack's hand. Poor Dick landed on the picture rail and looked minute and it took some time before May was able to coax him back and into the rehung cage. Everyone was concerned about the tail and whether the loss was permanent, but a new one grew, though it took some weeks. The shock stopped further leaps by the cat, but it didn't stop Dick singing, fortunately, for his serenading was a feature of the house. Only if there was complete silence, which was rare, would he become quiet. I, "little Jack", was always singing, or trying to, and Dick always responded and joined in. May loved our duets and noted the little boy's voice — she listened as it developed as mothers do, and would do something about it later on.

Fran was his own man from the day he was born and May's feeding and attention had brought his weight and size up to a normal, healthy level. Like all good things, it had a reverse side. Fran, though not big, was strong and wiry, and could run fast. He was also possessed of a wish to see the world — now. He wanted adventure and external activities and most of these involved a quick departure from the house. He had run off countless times. It only required a momentary lapse by May and he was gone. She always tried to keep the front door closed, but there were always callers like the insurance man and while paying him the weekly pence at the only partly-opened door, Fran ran between her legs and was off. He really needed a ball and chain, but once school began he ceased these escapes and settled somewhat. But other forces were running and one day he announced to May that he wanted to break up all his toys — though he never had many. May listened to him and asked why, but no clear reason came forth. She pointed out to him that he liked his toys and played with them and if he broke them up he'd have nothing to play with. He listened to this and went away thinking about it. Over the next week he repeated his request. Eventually May decided to let him have his wish. She asked him how he would break them and he told her he'd use the axe under the mangle which father used for chopping firewood, and so it happened. Fran was about six at the time and needed both hands to lift and wield the axe but he made a good fist of it and finished things off with the back of the axe flattening any metal bits which were sticking up so that everything ended flat like sheets of paper. His great work done, he stood axe in hands, with his trademark half-smile registering his satisfaction. Biddy and I didn't understand what was going on. "He is strange," I was thinking and then May appeared and interrupted my reverie.

"Well now you've done it, you've made a right mess so you can put all that rubbish in the bin — and put the axe back, now you're finished." Fran disposed of his debris and well-pleased, gazed at us with a "what shall we do now" look. We found out a few days later, when he suggested that we offer our toys for similar treatment. Neither Biddy nor me were enthused with the idea, but such were his powers of persuasion that we both finally agreed. May only allowed the destruction when we both said we really wanted to do it and so Fran gave a repeat performance and we were toyless. I was the only one to express regrets. I was very fond of my dark green wooden van and now it was gone. There were no replacements and other amusements had to be found, but that was never a problem for Fran.

When out shopping, Fran needed handcuffs. It wasn't possible with three young children to keep hold of him all the time. One day he found an old nail in the gutter as we walked towards the shops on Stanley Road. We stopped at Inch's, the pork butcher, and May went inside to buy some bacon. Outside, a variety of groceries were displayed, including a tray of two dozen jars of pickles with their waterproof paper lids tied on with string. He proceeded to puncture each in turn and as May turned to leave she witnessed the last "holing" before he put the nail in his pocket with a smile. May grabbed his hand and walked rapidly away. On another occasion he appropriated a new pushchair on display outside a shop and May forced him to wheel it back nearly 100 yards. If pirates are born then Fran was one, though when he went to sea years later it was in the merchant service rather than the fighting branch — a real waste of talent.

Tom had finally come home and was soon back at work and everything became easier. The world was moving towards war, and re-armament and the uplift in trade were providing more jobs. Fewer men stood on the corner, but the king was sick. The heir who would become Edward VIII was unmarried and the Woman in his life — the twice-divorced Mrs Simpson — was causing great concern in government circles. Locally, and abroad, there were important events including the opening of the first Mersey road tunnel under the river and the construction of the East Lancashire Road, a new dual highway linking Liverpool and Manchester. In the budget, a penny a quarter pound was taken off the tea duty and a reduction in the fleet would pay for it. A strange piece of fiscal politics in troubled times. Adolf Hitler had come to power in Germany and reoccupied the Rhineland, and Roosevelt was in the middle of the "New Deal" — a public works programme to revive the American economy. Things were on the move but none were certain where it would all lead. The world was anxious about the future.

CHAPTER
THREE

A Reckless Class of Inhabitants

"I'm being called for an interview — it's about a house [a pub]!". Tom came home elated. The Outside Manager, as he was called, had made his weekly visit to the Glebe, the pub where Tom worked. These visits were the main management activity by the brewers to ensure everything at their licensed public houses was in order. Sales, stocktaking audits, housekeeping — everything that mattered in the business was discussed with the manager. Any serious failings would result in an instruction to present oneself at the brewery to explain. The system worked well and managers could rely on the weekly visit to report anything requiring attention at the premises including the structure of the building, quality of the beers supplied during the week and any ideas for improvement. The staff of barmen, barmaids, cleaners, etc., was left totally to the pub manager who worked on a clearly defined pay scale. In those days and for many years after, the difference between the lowest and the highest paid in any business or trade in Britain was far less than it later became in the 1980s when the self-awarding salary and bonus schemes of the controlling managers provoked national scandals and demands for government action.

Examining the books of Tom's employers, Threlfalls Brewery, at the time is very revealing on this matter. Threlfalls was a public company until taken over by another brewer, Whitbread, in the 1960s. The salary of Threlfalls Chief Executive around 1940 was £20 per week and the salary of one of his pub managers was £5 — a rough multiple of four and the manager also lived rent-free (including rates, gas, electricity and water).

Generally most people were in agreement with how companies apportioned their earnings — particularly the shareholders who as "owners" of the company did not witness the later appropriation by executives of large pieces of both the earnings and also the ownership of the company — these later acts, often rewards for very poor performance and results. But all this was yet to come.

Tom's elation was the result of the Outside Manager's discussion with Mrs Carver, the manageress, as to Tom's suitability for a similar position. She had spoken well of him and then Tom was spoken to about the idea. At this time in his life he was ambitious and in great need of a higher income and he expressed great interest and a wish to be considered for any vacancy available, now or later. He was told he would receive a letter from the brewery inviting him to attend for interview. May was delighted at the news but wondered where they might be sent. She was very happy in Timon Avenue.

Tom returned from his interview the following week and told May, "We've been offered a house and we'll get £3 15s a week and rent, coal and gas." When he told her which pub, her heart sank. The Marine was located in the roughest, toughest location in the great city — right on the Liverpool/ Bootle border, close to the waterfront. The decision would affect May and the children more than Tom negatively, but she agreed that they must accept and the die was cast.

"Bootle — the enormous area once owned by the Earl of Derby that straggles down to the Liverpool Docks via some of the most appalling slums in the Western Hemisphere." This was the description of the area by Arthur Christiansen in the 1920s. He was then a local reporter for the *Liverpool Echo* and later a national figure as the long-serving editor of the *Daily Express*.

An earlier, fuller description went thus:

As docks, warehouses, timber wharves and railway depots mercilessly obliterated Bootle's golden bay, Lyons Street, Dundas Street and Raleigh Street on Derby Road, south of Miller's Bridge, were the town's scarlet badge of infamy.

The houses there were appallingly constructed — and into ready-made slums flocked harlots and every conceivable brand of villain, looking for easy money from "soft touches", of whom there were many among the construction workers on Bootle sites and the Jacks-ashore from the ships.

Mayhem and murder, booze and bawdiness, along with child neglect, made these streets and their environs a by-word in Merseyside notoriety in the closing decades of the last century and at the beginning of this century.

In 1878 the Inspector of Nuisances reported to the Health Committee that on inspecting the cellar of 99 Dundas Street at 1 a.m. he had found three loose women. It was a place "much frequented by sailors and others," the committee were told.

There was a reference in the Health Committee in 1882 to "the reckless class of inhabitants" of Lyons Street, Dundas Street and Raleigh Street.

And Raleigh Street is where we went. The Marine Hotel at the top of the street where it meets Derby Road to be precise. Little had changed over the years and so we joined this "reckless class of inhabitants". The description was not inaccurate and our successful absorption into their number would not leave us untouched.

The brewers in Liverpool knew their market and their customers very well and they practised policies involving active ethnic and religious discrimination in most areas of hotel staff policy. All the pubs along the north docks and waterfront had Catholic managers. Their customers were mostly the descendants of the "poor Irish" who had been arriving each year following the famine ninety years earlier. The clientele was solidly Catholic and ministered to by a large number of schools, churches and pubs. The latter served as many things including "offices" for trade union officials and a meeting place for every sort of business.

A pub manager was in occupation described as a licensee. It had a nice ring to it and directed attention to the fact that he/she held a licence from the magistrates to manage the place. Not something any Tom, Dick or Harry could aspire to. Licensees were regularly asked by customers to sign important forms, documents and passports, as men of rank and status in the community. That was nice for the ego but didn't help very much when there was trouble, and in pubs there's always trouble. Managers had to be able to nip it in the bud before it developed into full-scale combat. The first sign was the raising of voices.

When this occurred, the manager would invoke his powers to pacify or eject the warring parties and restore peace for the rest of the customers. The preference for either pacification or ejection as the favoured solution by managers varied widely. It was always helpful if the manager was of the same religious persuasion as the customers and if they knew each other through the church or school as well as at the bar. If they were offended, as often happens when people are asked to leave, they were never able to invoke the manager's religion as a reason for his action. If religious differences existed, a favourite early expression of sentiment was likely to be:

"You were never any good you Catholic/Orange bastard."

This was never known to help resolve matters quickly. So the brewers, aware of these things, put each with his own in terms of religion. On the heights of Netherfield Road (behind the city) all the managers were Protestant and probably members of the Orange Lodge — a body set up to combat Catholicism in all its forms and manifestations. The area was solidly Orange — people, churches, pubs.

This open discrimination would be frowned upon today. Without it, however, there would have been many more difficulties and disasters and many casualties. The brewers knew their business. Discrimination could be good as well as bad.

Law and order in pubs was essential. The police didn't wish to get involved unless they were forced to, and if any manager could not keep his customers from fighting, he lost his job. It was bad for business. Men wanted peace and quiet when they were having a pint. The Magistrates' Licensing Committee met regularly. Any manager who had required police attendances on a regular basis was considered as being incapable of running an establishment and preserving law and order. The decision of the magistrates was final. He lost his licence. His renewal application was refused and he lost his job. Every police attendance had to be recorded in the management book by the manager and this was examined each week by the Outside Manager on his visit. The manager would then be questioned as to what had occurred.

It was natural that the brewers looked for men with "authority" when they appointed managers and it was equally natural that the customers looked for the same thing when a new manager arrived. Weakness would be probed for and detected, and confrontation from the more aggressive drinkers would follow. New managers are always an easy target for the bums and those who disliked paying for their drink and a total refusal to offer any credit whatsoever was essential. This tied in with a need to observe the drinking patterns of the customers closely. All drinking establishments are beacons for those who like to drink and socialise but have an aversion to paying. Their method of operation is to arrive early in the pub, buy a half-pint of beer, and station themselves in a prominent position at the counter. Now being "on station" they greet all arrivals with a smile and a few opening words of light conversation. Words are often followed by the offer of a drink by the new arrival and this is never refused. The favour, however, is not returned and this way a man may drink long and well with little expense. These creatures are known as "bums". Nearly all managers operated a veto on this type of customer — they were formally "banned", i.e. they would not be served. The banning was at the total discretion of the manager and was "sine die" (without end), particularly appropriate Latin terminology in a Catholic pub.

A change of manager was an opportunity for the bums to return and widen their area of operations and they would be early arrivals to see the new man. It was rarely successful, for the bar staff were quick to inform the new manager and the ban would then be implemented again. The act was significant and had a regular form. The barman would report to the manager the presence on the premises and the manager would nod. The bum would be drinking very slowly his half-pint, now down in the glass to the one-inch level ("the bummers' mark"). It would stay at this level until the arrival of a new full glass — courtesy of a new arrival. The bummers' mark could be sustained for up to an hour and in that time it was usual for reinforcements to arrive.

The barman on the manager's instructions would act. Going to the till he would remove coins to the price of half a pint and present these to the bum with the words, "Please take your custom elsewhere".

The ban was complete. Mild words, but like a sentence of death for the bum. He was now "banned" or "barred", the latter word seeming perhaps more appropriate.

Banning could take place for a variety of offences besides bumming. Fighting, bad language, disrespect to the manager or his staff, causing disharmony, gambling, etc. The manager's word was final as disorder could lose him his livelihood. He had to be strict.

Bumming is a particularly heinous sin in Liverpool and a man's reputation is greatly affected by how he is seen in terms of his generosity. Those with the least always seemed the most open to the needs of others, particularly in those years when few had much. You paid your corner or were ostracised.

Tom was well suited to management — he was always calm and I never saw him show fear in his whole life. As a youth he had been twice honoured for bravery for saving from drowning a boy and later a woman in the Leeds & Liverpool Canal. This was a busy highway in between the wars and it carried much traffic. It was also used for recreational purposes and swimming and claimed lives (mostly children) on a regular basis. He never talked about things like those awards from the Liverpool Shipwreck and Humane Society, though his second rescue cost him dearly. He was wearing his first new suit and ruined it by diving in fully clothed as the drowning woman came up for the last time. The woman was saved but the suit wasn't. It shrank. He always laughed about it if his brothers or sisters mentioned it. He was not worried by the physical challenge of managing a pub in a rough area. He was twenty-eight years old and very fit, slim and could handle himself. Streetfighters are not easily intimidated and his sense of humour was a great asset in defusing disagreements and tempers.

The van came early. We didn't have a lot of furniture or possessions and May had finished packing the previous night, so in no time the job was done and the goodbyes completed and we set off on foot for our new home. Dick the canary was put in the care of one of the removal men and Ginger the cat was put in a box in the back away from avian temptation. Mick, our Airedale, trotted beside us. It was exciting, and eager to see our pub, we started at a good pace. It was a bright, sunny July day and as we came to Bootle village, we heard the strains of fife and drum which increased in volume as we reached the main street and there it was all before us. It was Orangemen's Day, 12 July, the anniversary of the Battle of the Boyne, which celebrated the victory of Protestantism over holy Catholic Ireland in 1690. The parade was lining up behind a man with a broad orange sash and a massive sword. He led the procession and was followed immediately by a man on a white horse dressed as King Billy (William) the victor at the Boyne. Then came the band. Mostly drums, fifes and tin whistles and behind them the marchers carrying banners aloft declaring their provenance and origins "Sister Sorensen's Own — Daughters of the Boyne". Most were dressed in Sunday best and many of the men wore bowlers and had orange sashes across their chests. There were a number of floats and tableaux bearing a variety of exhibits including a pig's head with the words "Cured at Lourdes" underneath, and a statue of Our Lady holding a rosary of black puddings. The street was crowded and we stopped to have a good look. I didn't yet understand the significance of the day, but all children like a band and we dallied, then after a minute or so the Parade Marshall called them all to order and the columns moved off. They were headed for Southport to celebrate the day and were marching to board the train at Bootle station. We were going in the same direction and followed on the pavement along with lines of children on each side of the road, who, if they were not going on the outing to Southport could still follow the band and parade to the station. I kept asking May questions about what was going on but apart from, "I'll tell you later," she maintained a discreet and diplomatic silence. We all got to the station quite quickly and once outside, the Marshall called the parade to stop and after a few words telling everyone to enjoy the day he stood down the ranks and they broke up into small groups of friends and family and entered the station going under the subway to a special excursion train awaiting their arrival.

Our Lady, the white horse and the pig's head were left forlornly outside the now-deserted station.

We were now close to our destination and my attention shifted once more from the now-departed parade to the Marine, for I now knew that was the name of our future home. I had enjoyed my first encounter with the Lodge and in later life would claim that I had marched with them. "Nearly there," said May, as we marched down Miller's Bridge and turned left into Derby Road. There was activity and movement everywhere with shops on both sides intersected by streets of small houses on the left running up to the canal. On the opposite side were tall Victorian dwellings running down to the docks and Harland & Wolff's ship repair workshops. In the centre of the road trams were running to and from the city. No. 17, I saw, was for the Pier Head and no. 18 was going to Breck Road, wherever that was. Then — there it was — the Marine, on the opposite side facing a huge bakery which filled the air with the lovely smell of baking bread. It stood on the corner of Raleigh Street. Three floors high and a cellar beneath with three entrances and tiled on the ground floor exterior in blue and cream — the house colours of Threlfall's brewery.

I liked it. "Interesting," I thought, my four-year-old mind running ahead, waiting to view the inside. Tom had gone on ahead and had now assumed command. May pushed open the door of the outdoor department and Fran, me and Mick entered. Two men were standing at the counter and turned as we entered. Tom saw us immediately. "Welcome aboard," he said, smiling as he raised the counter flap to let us in. "Come this way," he said, leading us up the stairs to the large kitchen. "I'm going to like it here," I thought.

The rules of the brewery stipulated that only direct family could occupy the house — unless one also worked in the pub below. Poor Biddy didn't qualify and despite all father's efforts, she wasn't allowed to come with us, and we were all sad about losing her. Alice, her mother, working away was "living in" and was unable to take her, so she was taken to the nuns at Nazareth House Orphanage and deposited. Alice paid for her there from her meagre wages and although Biddy seemed happy whenever we visited, we were not. She was to be there for three years until grandfather returned from Australia and set up home with Alice and Biddy in Bedford Road.

For Tom, the adjustment from barman to manager appeared seamless — a natural progression. He had a casual confidence, was good with people and a quick learner but he was also the immediate recipient of much guidance and help from the Irish Catholic Managers' Mafia. The Godfather of this family was John Hargadon, the manager of the Old Toll Bar at the intersection of Miller's Bridge and Derby Road. This was another Threlfalls house and John, some twenty years older than Tom and long in the trade, took the new arrival under his wing. He taught him all the things that managers need to know in dealing with their staff, customers and employer — particularly the latter. Barmen learn how a pub runs, but they are not privy to the secrets of the operation and its economics, for on these rest the manager's livelihood.

The contract between manager and brewer was detailed and, looked at from today, it would appear harsh in its terms and unbalanced in favour of the brewer. But things are not always as they seem, and like all such documents what was not in the contract was just as important or more so, than what was.

All beer glasses used in public houses by law had to bear the mark of the king (the current sovereign) and certification of the volume from the weights and measures authorities. Any glass without the imprint could not be used and glasses were one of the things checked on the government Weights and Measures Inspectors' visits. Any beer glasses found in the pub not bearing the king's imprint would result in a heavy fine and dismissal of the manager. To avert such events, the brewery supplied all glassware appropriately marked. Pubs would also often refuse customer requests to drink from their own tankards or favourite pots because of the regulation.

This was an early example of consumer protection and government entry into the world of consumer affairs which had for centuries relied on the principle of *caveat emptor* or "buyer beware".

Under the legislation a pint or half-pint glass contained, when filled, exactly a pint or half-pint. That is — filled to the brim, which is rare in public houses because the drinker always demands a nice frothy top — without such a head the beer will usually be returned, and critical comments made on the barman's inability to "pull a good pint".

So the king's glasses were rarely filled to the brim and a good pint was seen as between ¼ and ½ an inch below the rim, which allowed the carriage of a nice head of white froth on the pint. This made the customer happy and the publican especially happy, for the froth was his bonus.

A barrel of beer contained then 288 pints and, depending on the diameter of the rim of the glass, ¼ or ½ inch depth at the top amounted to a volume of 1fl oz or 5 per cent of the glass filled to the brim. The customer always got less than a pint. The foaming glass was more important than the full. The breweries knew this, but would do nothing about it. They were aware that knowledge and recognition of the fact would lead to a public outcry of the wicked brewers robbing the poor working man, so they had long accepted that what they expected from managers was the money for 288 pints from each barrel and nothing less. They then made no further comment.

Then there were the spirits — whisky, gin and rum. "Don't tamper with them," said John. Traces remained of earlier discredited practices of adulteration (adding water or potable alcohol for example). There was also the substitution and "passing off of inferior brands as the real thing — Haig Whisky, Gordon's Gin or Lemon Heart Rum, for example. Both practices had been common earlier in the century when spirits were supplied in bulk — in large copper jugs — bottling and labeling came later but they had by now mostly died out as detection led to instant dismissal. Some managers continued to try to beat the system by buying spirits privately, which they would display openly next to those supplied by the brewery. This was risky as although the clandestine spirits were from the same distiller, of the same quality, and identical with their legitimate fellows they carried different identity codes. The breweries' stocktakers would pick these up immediately on their regular visits. The temptation was there, however, for spirits, though a drink for the minority, were expensive and the profit was excellent. A bottle of Haig or White Label Whisky cost 36s — most of the price was duty, and there was no discounting. A small whisky, however, was twice the price of a pint in the pub, 1s 10d, and a bottle contained thirty-two measures. Measure is the word, for all the spirits were measured by hand with small metal pots, again stamped with the sovereign's mark and the quantity held. Such a method of dispensing is by nature inaccurate and sometimes a bottle would yield more than thirty-two glasses or measures. Thirty-two at 1s 10d yielded a profit of a few pence short of £2. For the manager who bought and sold spirits for his own account there was more profit from a bottle of whisky than from a whole barrel of beer, but in the brewery's eyes one was legitimate — the other was not.

Then, of course, there was the hazard of the Weights and Measures Inspectors. When they visited they would check a number of things, including the spirits. A whisky would be ordered by a customer on entry but, on it being put before him on the counter or table he would declare his credentials as an inspector. He would then open his briefcase, take out two small sample bottles and pour the whisky equally into them. Then he sealed and labelled them — each bearing his signature and the date, gave one to the manager to hold safely and taking the other, bade farewell and departed. At the end of the day all the inspector's samples were handed in to the government laboratory and assayed and checked. Any deviations or suspicious findings were reported to the brewery — distillers and manufacturers themselves who probably knew more than the laboratory. Anything "non-standard" demanded a strong explanation, which was never forthcoming. Spirits gave plenty of other difficulties for managers as the brewers wished to sell their own brands rather than those of the national distillers as the profits were so much greater. This meant staff always gave customers the house brands unless others were specifically ordered. The "own label" brands, like Golden Glow whisky, were generally held to be inferior in quality, although they cost the same.

All this esoteric pub lore and guidance was passed to Tom by John, along with instruction about what the brewery looked for and didn't look for in the manager's weekly reports, and the visits by the Outside Manager. Tom was particularly lucky with his mentor, who was not only experienced, but intelligent and wise in the ways of the trade. They were both managers for the same brewer and overseen by the same Outside Manager — Mr Powell, so John's guidance was particularly relevant. Pat Lee, the manager of the

Washington (Smarts), in between Tom and John's establishments, was also helpful but he was with a different brewer and each had their own peculiarities and different ways of doing things.

All the managers had an interest in "not rocking the boat" and new managers were taken in hand to ensure that their performance and returns to the brewery were par for the course. Any newcomer producing outstanding figures could lead to questions to the other managers from the brewery about why they weren't doing better. "If he can do it and he's new as a manager, why can't you?" A difficult one to answer. Equally, a manager in trouble over his stocks and returns would be helped by his fellows. A manager getting into trouble always led to questions, and a general tightening up for everybody else, which was unwelcome. Par was the thing all managers aimed for but, unlike golf, no birdies, eagles or going into the rough. No one sought to be top of the leader board. Being a manager was as far as a man could go. There was no promotion to higher positions in the brewery and so each ensured that they made the best of their position, and in those harder times there was also a pension to think about. Most brewers provided such pensions which, though not huge, were very welcome and some including Threlfalls provided retirement homes, for living in pubs all their life, they had no home to go to when they retired — much like the army and navy. Brewers and managers were united in keeping things as they were — it had been a system which worked over a long time. Why change it? The status of licensee or public house manager was much higher pre-war than now. This was a result and recognition of the importance of the pub in the community and the high standards imposed by the law and their employers on those who managed them. It was an envied position and usually very financially rewarding. The Marine, from memory, was selling about twelve barrels a week, for it was a very busy pub. This meant that Tom's share of the take from the king's glasses was in the region of £8 a week, every week and tax-free. The money was all made on the draught beer — that's what everyone drank, including the women. Bottled beers and soft drinks offered no profit opportunity at all. Managers realised this and paid great attention to how their beers were kept and served. A "good pint" was critical to their income, and trade and custom was soon lost if standards dropped. This was the way things were until the 1960s. Then everything changed owing to a combination of brewery mergers, television, cheap beer from the new supermarkets and the brewers abandoning in great part traditional brewing. It was ironic that the changes everyone in the industry didn't want finally arrived but from places and in guises they could never have imagined.

CHAPTER
FOUR

Mr Cohen and the Commodore

Mr Cohen was the family tailor. In those days, suits were the thing for men and most possessed one for "best" occasions and Mass on Sunday. Few possessed two. Suits were "made to measure' — the description "bespoke" was never used. "Ready to wear" and "off the peg" lay in the future. Strangely Mr Cohen was found by May rather than father, for his business was mainly men's tailoring. Out shopping one day, she looked in his window opposite Woolworths and there was a ladies' raincoat which she liked and it looked as if it would fit. While she was looking, out came the man himself, Mr Lewis Cohen.

"You see something you like," he said. Mr Cohen was very short — around 5ft 2in, balding, about forty, comfortable in shape. In shirtsleeves, wearing glasses, tape measure around neck with chalk-marked black trousers.

"The raincoat."

"You come in and try."

"No, I can't afford it at the moment."

"No matter, you try," and he inveigled May in and reaching to his full height held open the coat. It was a

50

nice fit and May really wanted it, but there was no money.

"You like?" said Mr Cohen, and before May could say the obvious yes he continued, "You take it now, you have an honest face, pay me when you can," and with that passed the coat to Tom, his tall, quiet, Irish assistant, who without a word folded and packed the coat she'd been wearing into a paper carrier bag as Mr Cohen insisted she carried on wearing the new raincoat.

"It suit you very nice." It was the beginning of a lifetime relationship which would lead to him making suits for our large extended family for the next thirty years. When I was an adult and visited him regularly, his first question was always "And how is Mutter?"

Dress was distinctive — all the women, both young and old in the poorer parts of the city, wore shawls. Black, always black, never any other colour, and made of wool. Wrapped around the shoulders with the hands holding it close to the body inside, away from the cold, they were very serviceable. If it rained, it was pulled up to cover the head and usually there was a baby wrapped snugly warm and close to the mother's body inside with just the little happy face visible. The women had amazing dexterity and could hold baby and shawl with one arm while they manoeuvred purse, basket, purchases and often another small child with them when out shopping. I never saw or heard of a baby being dropped. Shawls were also used at night on the beds for additional warmth and were donned and removed in a second. Being simply a large woollen square, they would fit anybody and a single shawl, although belonging to "the Ma", was used by all the girls in the household. Who grabbed it first could go out — but check with Ma before you leave.

Boots were worn by both sexes more than shoes. Women's boots were often high and laced. The men wore flat caps all the time — often even in the house. Shirts had separate collars and these were generally ignored and missing and the shirt was fastened at the top usually by a brass collar stud. So attired, this is how they presented themselves for the evening pint.

A visit to the tailor for a suit was a rare event — usually provoked by a wedding or christening. Suits, like collars and ties, were for special days. Status would often be indicated by the observation that "He had a collar and tie."

As life proceeded, everything seemed to be moving faster — people, vehicles, news. It was as if the world had moved up a gear. The king had abdicated and there was a new king — all because of this American woman. I listened to the grown-ups chatter, being already a professional listener and learning that the more you know, the more questions you have. What was it all about? She was not a nice or respectable woman, they were saying, and quite unfit to be the wife of a king — and that was that. His brother George, with that nice homely wife, would be king. Respectability and morals would be upheld and everybody would be happy it seemed, except the retiring king and "that loose woman". What was a loose woman? Was there a tight woman, and if so, was she approved? I wished that grown-ups would speak in words I could understand.

The new king was to tour the nation and Liverpool was to be an early stop on the journey. The route for the royal procession was printed and illustrated in the Liverpool evening papers, the *Express* and the *Echo* and came the Saturday and the whole of the city it seemed went off to see our new King George. The crowds were immense and we found ourselves in a dense crowd outside the gates of the park on Smithdown Road. Father placed Fran and me on the window-sill of a house so that we had a fine view of the procession which passed and was gone in seconds. Everyone was cheering and waving flags. The route was decorated for miles with flags and bunting, of which there was never any shortage in Liverpool because of the shipping trades. All the people were dressed in their Sunday best just like when they went to Mass to honour that other king. It all seemed right and proper. Everyone was happy, the sun was bright, the day was warm and somewhere nearby a band was playing as the crowds all in good humour dispersed and went home to tea.

The green Liverpool Corporation trams ran all over the city and in no time the crush had cleared and we were on our way home. The no. 18 tram dropped us 20 yards from our door. Cost of journey for four — sixpence. May had prepared the tea before we left and she immediately put the kettle on and removed a slightly damp tablecloth covering the table already set revealing a wonderful sight of sandwiches, salad and cakes ready for our enthusiastic reception.

May was a great cook and always there was something in the oven. Cake features very strongly in my childhood memories. Cake in wide variety. Sponge and Madeira cakes, apple and pear pies, jam and lemon curd tarts, currant buns and scones. I cannot recall seeing a bought cake on the family table. It was similar with the savouries — meat pies and pasties, and then there were biscuits, dumplings and puddings — baking to a high standard and delicious to eat. Meals were always an event particularly for me, for I had an immense appetite and was always asking May what exactly she was doing when she was baking and cooking. We lived nearly all the time in a large kitchen with a high ceiling facing south and very sunny, in full view of each other, and children miss very little. Observation is a great teacher and I became very interested in how all this lovely food was prepared. May was happy to explain the principles of cooking and allowed me to assist — like stirring the cake mixes with a large wooden spoon. I particularly liked this job because I was allowed to scrape the bowl and eat the remains. Later she would encourage me to prepare something by myself, which I was often keen to do. She would let me make mistakes, as she knew I would learn more quickly that way than if I was just told what, or what not to do. She was full of artifice and greatly impressed one Saturday afternoon when we came back from the children's matinée at the Commodore Cinema. This was a fine new cinema on Stanley Road, very close to where my grandmother and Aunt Emily (two houses) lived on Wolsey Street.

The cinema, or as we called it "the pictures", was producing ever bigger and better films. Everybody wished they were a film star. Cinemas or picture houses were everywhere and the *Liverpool Echo*'s front page was devoted to small advertisements listing what was showing at each of the hundreds of cinemas in the metropolis. Programmes changed three times a week. Monday to Wednesday; Thursday to Saturday and Sunday. Missing a film was rectified by looking at the paper and seeing where it was now on. Films were classified as "U" — suitable for children, "A" — for adults and "X" — horror. All the children, of course, wanted to see the horror films and the monsters of Bela Lugosi and Boris Karloff, but it was difficult. Children were only allowed entry if accompanied by an adult and there were only two alternatives. The first was to "bunk in" (sneak in via the emergency doors at the back and avoid detection by the ushers, who were always alert for these intrusions. The second required the price of entry and the complicity of an adult. Out of sight of the box office would be boys and sometimes girls coins-in-hand waiting for an adult cinemagoer. "Take us in Mister?" They would usually co-operate and in we'd go. Today this common practice would probably result in the adult coming before the court as a child molester and the child being taken into care by the social services. I can't recall a case of anything untoward occurring ever. Kids were more streetwise and once inside, they separated and went to different parts — ushers and

55

their torches were ubiquitous and even courting couples were forced to behave or risk expulsion.

Bob Murphy, under age, undersized and underfunded, 2*d* in hand accosts a heavily petticoated and black-shawled old woman to assist entry. Now the petticoats were several and all reached the ground. Smiling, she took the coins and said, "get under there, son" and lifted her petticoats. Bob was small and, keen to see the film, he did as he was bid. "They" then approached the paybox and from somewhere under the shawl she produced tuppence. "Just one, love," she said passing the coins over in return for a single ticket to the cheapest wooden benches nearest the screen. Progress to and from the box and into the cinema seats was slow and understandable, it appeared, because of the poor woman's age and physical condition. Bob was released from the tent in the dark interior. "It took my breath away," he said. Perhaps that saved him from "death due to inhalation of noxious gases." His deliverer liked the film and Bob's 2*d* bought her a glass in the snug of the bar on Byrom Street later on. Benefits for both, bonded by necessity on each side — each needing the other.

Every Saturday all of us children queued for entry to an always exciting children's matinée bill of Buster Crabbe in *Journey to Mars* and Johnny Mack Brown in some western serial. In addition there were the Dead End Kids and the Three Stooges all for tuppence. Order was maintained outside and inside by a uniformed commissionaire with a huge moustache. The screening was an event involving total audience participation. This involved cheering, booing, hissing, warning shouts, encouragement and abuse all through the programme directed at the on-screen characters and action. "Look out, he's behind you!" It was noisy, enjoyable and cathartic; everyone had a wonderful time and we emerged released of all emotions and not a word of foul language to be heard in the whole performance. This was the training ground for supporters of Liverpool FC. The Saturday cinema was its nursery. Audience participation came naturally — they wanted to play too.

After the Commodore, we ran all the way home slapping our backsides as though on horseback just like Johnny Mack Brown, and when we arrived we were ready for tea. Mother opened the oven and brought out a large crusty well-done loaf. I was impressed and consumed with admiration for both the loaf and mother, and I decided I would wait till it was cool enough to eat with lots of butter before having tea. Much later she told me that the loaf was one that had gone stale and she'd put it under the tap and into a very hot oven, wrapped initially in a towel — another of the tricks she had picked up in her years in the hotel trade. It impressed itself indelibly and the technique has been much used since.

This shared interest in food was later of great benefit for from it I learned so much. It assisted a lifetime of good eating, both at home and outside and gave me an insight into restaurants and catering and how the professionals do things — a great benefit in later life. When May was in her eighties we were still regularly discussing food and such questions as the competing merits of butter or oil for frying an egg, and which produced the better result. One day I was despatched in search of rye flour to make black bread which we both fancied — this, a memory from her work for a Jewish family in the city. The mission was unsuccessful, though I journeyed to the best Jewish grocers in the Holyland (Menlove Avenue), a residential area much favoured by the Jewish community. Her knowledge was wide and included many ethnic influences. Curry was widely used (Abdullah's 8oz tin 4s 10d) and olive oil. The only place one could obtain the latter locally was Boots the Chemist. She used it widely and often — particularly in salad dressings rather than the ubiquitous Heinz Salad Cream.

The Marine was a very busy pub, with no private entrance. We had to push our way through the legs of the men drinking at the bar and go under the counter to get to the door leading upstairs to the living accommodation. The latter was quite good. There was a large kitchen and adjoining sitting room and two bedrooms on the first floor. Above was a bathroom and three more bedrooms. Heating was provided by large pipes from a boiler in the cellar. This was surrounded by large heaps of coke and coal to feed it. It was always lit for constant hot water for cleaning and glass washing. This boiler came in for our close examination and was soon being used for melting lead and shaping metal picked up around the streets. It was a wonderful toy. Access to the cellar was from the stairway in the living accommodation and we could come and go as we pleased.

Neither parent objected to these pursuits, though they warned us (when they knew) to be careful. Often we met father or the barmen in the cellar doing "cellarwork" — tapping and connecting new barrels to the twelve beer engines (hand-drawn pumps) in the bar above. All the barrels (36 gallons each) were oak with steel hoops holding them together. In the centre of the long, curved side was a round wood plug which was opened for breathing when the barrel was broached and in place on the stillage. On the flat side at the bottom nearest the rim, was another wood plug — the keystone. To tap (broach) the barrel a brass tap was hammered into the keystone with a wooden mallet. The inner core gave way and the tap entered the barrel which was now connected to a brass adjustable pipe linking it to the beer engine through a ceiling connector above. Being a busy pub, barrels were emptied at a rapid rate and empties had to be removed and replaced from the stillages where they rested to await the weekly collection and a new delivery. It was heavy work — a full cask weighed around 500lb. A barrel had to settle on the stillage for at least twenty-four hours to allow the sediment to settle. All beers had to be crystal clear when served. Anything cloudy would be refused by the customer.

This was sometimes a problem, particularly in hot weather when the rise in temperature often led to the beers becoming cloudy. When this occurred the barrels were cooled by hosing them down with water throughout the day and cellars were constructed with this in mind, having sloping floors and several grids.

Wet sacks were also placed on the barrels and these were quite effective as water jackets. Other brewers, like Walkers, provided all their managers with "finings". These were added to the barrel and settled all the sediment to the bottom, restoring the beer to a crystal clarity. For some reason Threlfalls would not countenance the practice. Their managers in times of need relied on their fellow managers in other brewers' pubs to help them out.

Bottled beers were supplied in heavy wooden crates of twenty-four, 12oz bottles. All the brewers made their own stouts, pale ales and stronger winter beers. Draught beer could only be supplied if a jug was brought to the outdoor department for filling. All outdoor sales for parties, etc. required a deposit on each bottle to ensure return. This custom applied to all drinks — even the lemonade sold in sweetshops. All empty bottles were prized by children as they were a source of pocket money and eagerly collected for the return and "money back" to the pub or shop. Beer in cans or plastic containers was twenty years away, as was its sale in grocery shops. The sale of alcohol in any form was confined to pubs and a very small number of wine stores and licensed grocers. Most restaurants were without a licence to serve liquor. Wine with meals was confined to the best restaurants and would not become common until the educational influence of the package holiday to Spain and the easing of licensing in the 1960s.

In the cellar was a special room, the "Spirit Cellar". This was always locked and it contained wines and spirits, tobacco and snuff. It was a magical, spotless, white-washed place with a wide range of spirits, wines, pipe tobaccos and cigarettes stacked on shelves. It had a rich aroma and induced in me the feeling of pleasure and good times and wealth and riches and great men smiling as they talked happily together. This association has lasted and was probably strengthened by watching films regularly and it gave me an interest in wine and tobacco particularly cigars (the leaf) which I pursued avidly when I became adult and possessed of funds. I followed my father into the spirit cellar at every opportunity, for it was usually he who went, because of the value of its contents. I began to look at what people drank and smoked, for the cigarettes themselves told much about the smoker. Woodbines were the cheapest and the smallest and the Greys the biggest (thickest) and dearest, Capstan, Senior Service, Craven A, Players, Flag, Gold Flake and a host of others all with their devotees and a whole range of exotic other brands not all of which were stocked. All tobacco and beer was cheap (a long-established government policy to keep the people happy). Spirits were dear (also government policy). The smallest measure (less than 1oz) was twice the price of a pint of beer. This differential remained substantially intact until the 1980s and Mrs Thatcher.

Pipe tobacco was a world unto itself. Most brands were sold in 1 or 2oz bars. Some were sliced, others were solid dark brown bars smelling of treacle and then there were the plug tobaccos wrapped in tarry rope. For those liking easier smoking, there were the packet varieties, already cut, rubbed and flaked like cigarette tobacco and here Erinmore led the field. The bar tobaccos were the most popular, though they were hard and unyielding like the name of the leading brand — Battleaxe. You needed one to cut it, they used to say. The preparation for the pipe was important and all devotees carried a sharp penknife with their tobacco pouch for cutting thin slices from the bar which they then rubbed tightly in both hands before filling the pipe. If the pipe was lost or forgotten a white clay pipe was usually on sale in most pubs for a halfpenny and a fill of tobacco would always be available from cronies. Some of the tobaccos were named after saints and this intrigued me. St Bruno and St Julien were very popular and everywhere, and then there was the Three Nuns brand in round tins but there were no religious cigarette brands. Were pipe smokers more religious? Certainly they were more into ritual with all the cutting, rubbing, mixing, pressing and filling — perhaps that was it. It was a bit like getting Holy Communion prepared at Mass, there's an awful lot of "get ready", I thought. It didn't finish there either, like some religious ceremonies. There were often add-ons like Benediction and for the pipe-smoker there was knife-sharpening. The penknife for the tobacco had to be kept sharp and small wetstones were often carried for this purpose. Once the pipe was lit, attention was then given to the stone which was applied to the knife blade after being lubricated with spit in between puffs of the pipe and testing the edge against the thumb. All this often preceded the first sip from the glass of dark foaming mild before them. And then there was the

62

lighting up. Lighters were rare: matches were the thing, made locally at Bryant & May's matchworks in Litherland, a mile away. Many pubs, including the Marine, had a gas jet on the wall of the bar always lit for smokers, and beneath it was a container holding spills for lighting — just like the candle rails in church. The gas jet was just above the head for safety and rightly so. There was an altercation one evening and to get out of the way a woman jumped onto the bench beneath the jet. Lizzie had a wide and frizzy hairstyle and lost the whole of one side as it touched the naked flame. She gave a loud scream as it flared like a forest fire emitting an unpleasant smell of burning hair. The fire was quelled by a pint of Threlfall's Best Mild from one of her duo of admirers and Lizzie, descending and looking at herself in the mirrors behind the bar, exclaimed "Will you look at me", then as she caught sight of the damage, "No, don't!" and she fled through the main door to go and get her coiffure evened up. Everybody was laughing and thought it great sport and the disputants were now the best of friends once more and drinking together. Lizzie wasn't long gone and soon returned, but this time to the ladies' parlour. Whoever had wielded the scissors had done a good job and the consensus was that she looked better than before. "I think I'll have a port and lemon to steady me nerves" she said to the beau as she sat down. It was not a night for drinking mild beer.

After the Coronation the focus changed. War seemed inevitable and preparations were beginning to become visible. New bodies were being formed, the Home

Guard, ARP, AFS (Auxiliary Fire Service), new buildings, factories, air raid shelters, ARP posts were springing up in every city, sandbags were all over the place, steel water tanks on the street with the letters EWS (emergency water supply) printed in yellow on the side. Stirrup pumps, buckets of sand and long-handled shovels for extinguishing incendiary bombs were in mass distribution and every factory and office block was drawing up duty rotas for rooftop fire watch service during the expected air raids.

The government issued gas masks for everybody and these had to be carried at all times of the day in their brown hard cardboard box with strings for carrying on the shoulder. Hand bells and rattles were also issued for warning of gas attacks. These were happily never required in the war but were very popular and much used afterwards by football supporters when fixtures recommenced. As the supply was limited, they eventually died out but were a big feature for a long time.

Tom was called up and instructed to present himself for a medical — he was now thirty-one years old. He failed, because of the leg wound sustained in hospital when his leg was lanced, which left it thinner than the other. What would have been the future if he'd been drafted? May would probably have replaced him, and as she proved later, would have done so successfully. Tom was annoyed at this blow to his vanity and immediately joined the nascent ARP. This gave him a uniform, a steel helmet and a whistle. The uniform was "clothing" and precious clothing coupons had to be surrendered when it was issued — just as in the services. The newly constructed ARP post was 100 yards away, across the road at the bottom of Sheridan Place. It looked like a small air raid shelter — the same industrial brick, thick windowless walls, narrow entrance and a flat roof of 8in thick reinforced concrete. Inside a telephone, a table, benches, a kettle and a street map on the wall with their area of operation outlined in black.

The Chief Warden was Charley Dash, an engineer. This was a full-time and paid position and there were six others part-time and unpaid including Tom, his friend Harold Brown (from Duthies), Dolly Kelly the telephonist and Messrs Burke, Courtney and Porter (Dick). Their job was to locate and rescue bombing casualties, summon the ambulances and get them off to hospital and everything had to be done in the complete darkness of the blackout. They were also required to assist the police and fire services generally. Duty commenced when the air raid sirens sounded and lasted until they rang the "all clear". During the heaviest attack periods in May and June 1941, raids lasted on average from 6p.m. until 4 a.m.

After a night digging people out of the rubble of collapsed houses, the ARP wardens had to go to their regular jobs as usual. It was hard, but it was like that for everybody. I don't remember hearing anybody complain about their lot while all this was going on.

CHAPTER
FIVE

Sandwiches and the Chinese
Parcel Service

The Marine Hotel was very different from Timon Avenue and for each of us it represented and evoked different things. For Tom it was opportunity and status amid the maelstrom of humanity where he was happiest. Fran got the space and opportunity to slip away and play silently by himself in a big house unobserved and I was immediately totally fascinated and occupied with the bustling busy life and characters all around me. "This is better than Timon Avenue," I thought. I was, if studied, clearly my father's son. For May it was a less attractive scenario. In distance we were only a couple of hundred yards from William Henry Street, which though not far, was divided from us by Miller's Bridge. It was a nicer and better class of area on that side and the place where she'd first met Tom when he was a young barman at the Blue House at the bottom of the street.

It was also the place where she'd been happiest with her beloved mother and brothers and sister and unhappiest with grandmother after her mother's death.

So for May the move was a return to the scene of sadness and bad memories. We had only been in Timon

Avenue four years and it was only ten years since she'd left her street of memories when grandmother died. She did not renew any of her childhood contacts and wished she was elsewhere. The Marine was just too close.

I never heard her complain, but was made aware of her feelings by how she spoke of Timon Avenue. That was where she would have liked to have remained. She was a strong woman who realised that progress requires sacrifice. Talking with her elder brother Jack one day, drinking tea in the kitchen, she summed it up.

"It was a good move to get the pub so soon," said Jack.

"Yes, it was. The right time but the wrong place," replied May.

"I suppose you can't have everything."

"No, you're right, but a little bit further away would have been nice."

"Well you won't be here for ever, Threlfalls have lots of pubs and hotels all over the city and in North Wales and Lancashire — North Wales would be a nice move — say Llandudno."

"Yes, I'd like that, and as you know I worked there in the Grand, but I think it would be too quiet for Tom."

Jack drew heavily on his Capstan and emitted good smoke.

"Well, you know him best and I suppose it's much less busy than here."

May smiled.

"Part of the problem is pubs in places like that only do about a quarter of the barrels we do here and that means far less money for the manager."

I was having my breakfast while they were talking and Father arrived to join us from his morning toilet and admiring himself in the mirror. He sat down at the table, smiling, and May put two boiled eggs and toast before him — mine was coming. Fran called me from upstairs.

"Don't be long, your breakfast will be on the table in a minute," said May.

Fran just wanted to show me a new game he was evolving in our playroom at the top of the house. When I got back, my egg was in position in its cup. Father had finished his and was talking with May and Jack. I took the spoon and removed the top of the egg. Catastrophe — no egg — just shell. I roared and was near tears.

"I've got no egg — he's gone."

At four I'd already developed a love affair with egg, which to me was almost a person. I had one every morning and now — disaster. Father was laughing and, reaching across, removed the eggless shell and replaced it with the egg from his own cup. He'd eaten his and replaced mine with his empty shell turned upside down. My face lit up and everybody laughed. You had to be alert with Father around.

All Threlfalls pubs in working class districts were tiled on the ground floor exterior in blue and cream. These were the company colours and their most popular bottled beer was Blue Label. Modern marketing would have approved of much of the "marketing" activity of the brewer, but the word had not yet been invented and specialists in selling and branding were probably only found in the two national and international brands of Bass and Guinness.

Neither of these owned any pubs and this meant nearly all brewers stocked both brands in limited quantity giving a little variety to the "tied" (own brewers' products only) range on offer in each of their pubs. Many brewers like Threlfalls also operated their own distilleries and own-brand whisky, gin, rum, sherry and port were always served unless another national brand such as Haig (whisky), or Gordon's (gin) was specifically asked for.

Tobacco was purchased locally from wholesalers by the manager. Pipe-smokers were everywhere and pipe tobacco brands were as numerous as those of cigarettes. Cigars were very expensive and only common in the city among the financial, shipping and insurance sectors. Specialist importers and factors such as Durandu maintained large emporia with a magical aura of wellbeing, comfort and pleasure. Here the leaf was reverenced and stocks were maintained in large humidors. The staff were highly trained and exceedingly knowledgeable. To them, like Rudyard Kipling, "A woman's a woman, but a cigar is a smoke."

Food in pubs was the responsibility of the manager and his wife. It was their decision whether to offer it or not — the brewery was interested only in the sale of beers, wines and spirits. The majority of pubs at this period offered very little in food for most of the customers lived close by and went home for lunch and dinner. Those who did not usually brought sandwiches to work in a tin box together with sugar, tea and tinned condensed milk — often all mixed together requiring only the addition of boiling water to the mixture in the tea can. The cup was also the lid of the tea can which was carried by a thin round steel handle. A spoon was not required for the can was swung around in vertical circles with the lid closed after the water was added. This produced a rapid intermingling of contents and an excellent brew of tea. There was little demand for food in pubs generally in the 1930s, for most of the workers in our area were on the docks where they were catered for by a chain of canteens and "cocoa rooms" which offered good, cheap food around the clock. These were the establishments of such companies as the Liverpool Workingmans Public House Co., later to be renamed as Liverpool City Caterers. As trade picked up and war loomed even larger, the workforce everywhere increased rapidly — particularly on the docks — and the canteens were unable to meet the demands of feeding the enlarged working population at lunch time. The docks were also dry and if you wanted a pint you had to leave the dock estate, cross the road and go to one of the dockside pubs. The dockers were a hard-drinking crew.

Tom began to mention to May the number of requests they were receiving at the bar for food and May saw the opportunity and decided to use some of her skills learned earlier in her days working in hotels.

Men who'd been labouring heavily for four hours needed a drink — particularly the coal heavers. These moved coal cargoes from ship to shore and on again to carts and wagons manually with large shovels and each man had his own — highly polished by the coal and standing flashing in the sun against the wall of the Marine while they slaked their thirst and cleared their throats inside. Lunchtime from 12 to 1 o'clock was announced by the firing of a gun which was audible for miles. Work ceased and restarted immediately in response. When the gun's roar signalled 12 o'clock, the coal heavers left the coal, each carrying his shovel and hurried and sometimes ran to the dockside pubs close by. They were a fearsome sight — face and body black with coal dust advancing en masse with their silver blades, money in hand. The Marine was close to Canada Dock, where most of the coal came in or out and it was one of their favourites, so preparations for their arrival began early. May would have been working since 5 a.m. cutting sandwiches — around two hundred or so — and these were strategically placed behind the bar. At around ten minutes to midday the bar staff started drawing pints of mild beer and placing them on the counter, and by the time the gun went at noon the counter was full. It was the only way to deal with the rush and it worked well. Nobody had to wait and everybody got what they wanted immediately. Most drank two pints very quickly to clear their throats of coal dust and then settled for a more leisurely pace for the rest of the hour.

The sandwiches received short shrift and were all gone in the first fifteen minutes. May would have liked to have sold more, but she did not have a caterer's kitchen or oven and this limited the size of the piece of beef she put in to cook every night before retiring. She was also limited by wartime regulations which allocated a rationed supply to all caterers. The piece of beef filled the oven and in it went every night as May retired. There were sometimes problems with delivery and Fran and I were called into service to collect. Straight up Bedford Place to Stanley Road, turn right and Holdens was 50 yards along. Carrying it was a struggle and we eventually devised a way to transport it together. It was too heavy for one, but difficult for two. Although we were small, we were strong, and I was regularly carrying 20lb of potatoes from Cissie Clarke's greengrocers so the beef must have been a lot heavier.

Blackledge's bakery was opposite the Marine on the other side of Derby Road and at around 4a.m. each morning twenty-four hot 2lb loaves were placed on the doorstep. Sometime around 5a.m. May would arise, take the beef from the oven and go downstairs to collect and start thickly slicing the bread by hand. Hot fresh bread is difficult to slice and can't be done quickly. It is an arduous affair for there were no sliced loaves in those days. After the bread was cut and then buttered (with margarine), the beef was sliced and the sandwiches salted and made up. They were then placed on large oval meat plates covered with a damp cloth and taken below to the bar. It was always a race against time but the reception they received was always enthusiastic and made it all worthwhile. Better than a vote of thanks. May felt a great sympathy for the dockers and never attempted to cash in on the popularity of the sandwiches. The laws of economics dictated a price rise to bring supply and demand into equilibrium, but she would have none of it. Fourpence was her price and it never increased in the six years she catered.

What it did do was increase the lunchtime beer sales, for although the beer was always good and worth the custom in its own right, the sandwiches were an added attraction. The brewery was pleased. Coming home from school for lunch (sandwiches), we had to squeeze through the crush to get under the counter to the stairs to the kitchen. This often led to encounters with sailors, dockers and other customers and occasionally presents of a penny and sometimes even a sixpence. I liked these collisions and saw it as an advantage that other boys didn't have. It also gave a perspective to things. One day, aged seven, I rang the doorbell after school around 4.30p.m. (the pub was closed from 3p.m. until 5.30p.m.). Father opened the door almost immediately and there was the deputy headmaster, Mr McDonald, having a quiet glass with Father. Friendly greetings all round. Father and Father's mother had both been to the same school, so there was a family tradition there of sorts. It impressed itself on me. Teachers were normal like everybody else — just like the sailors and dockers in fact who'd be in later. Everybody liked a drink and a chat, I could understand that.

May was looking out of the kitchen window. It was a beautiful sunny afternoon and the pub had just emptied the last of the mid-day customers, but there were still voices in the bar and she assumed that it was the local constabulary calling in for a little refreshment. This was a regular happening and could only take place at such a time as the place was closed as drinking on duty was strictly forbidden. Across the road, speaking into the recently erected emergency telephone stand for the security and rescue services, was a man. She recognised him as a "bad egg" and thought it odd for it was a quiet afternoon, and then she remembered the voices below. Descending, she looked into the bar and there were two of Bootle's finest enjoying a pint on this warm day with Tom. She told them what she'd seen and looking at each other they decided it was time to go, and finishing their pints they exited by the back door into the narrow entry. This took, in all, probably about five minutes. The police often patrolled in pairs as it was necessary because of the resistance sometimes offered in the course of their duties. Emerging from the entry they walked the short distance to Derby Road and there was the inspector at the door of the Marine, just arrived by car. Caught in the act it was, "Hello boys, I'm just going in to have a word with Tom — come with me." Publicans and the police worked very closely together and so there was nothing unusual on the surface about this call, but though unspoken, all knew it was the result of an anonymous malicious call to Bootle police station a quarter of a mile away. Tom immediately drew three pints, smiling and saying at the same time that he hadn't seen any of them for a little while. After a quick dispatch and the briefest of chats, the three policemen left — all by the front door. The informer, "Farragher", was now a marked man. The constables would have lost both their job and their pension if they'd been discovered by the inspector.

Some weeks later on a Saturday night, coming down Miller's Bridge in the dusk was Farragher. Coming up the same side are PCs Bailey and Conlon, returning to the station. Unaware that his snitching had been found out, he was totally off-guard as he was attacked, felled and handcuffed and dragged back to the station where he was charged with assault, resisting arrest, being drunk and disorderly and injuring a constable. Into the cells he went before being put before the beak on Monday morning. In the interim he was the recipient of visits which did little for his comfort or physical appearance. The magistrate was severe. "Far too much of this behaviour going on", he said, and attacking the police was a serious matter. It had to be stamped out. An example had to be made — twenty-eight days in Walton and a fine of £10.

Justice had been done.

About half a mile away in Bankhall — quite close to our school — lived the Larneys, where they kept a general store. Bessie was May's mother's sister — a Pepper. She'd married John Larney who was also Irish and they'd been busy — producing a big family and opening and running a general store which was open from very early to very late. John was the brains behind it and it was very profitable, though from appearance, not obviously so. The store seemed to sell everything and John operated a foreign exchange bureau and parcel collection facilities as additional services for his clients who were mostly seamen from ships in the nearby docks. He studied the exchange rates in the newspapers and took them as the basis for his own rates — plus of course an added commission for the service, just like the bank. His relationship with Martin's Bank on the corner of Derby Road and Bedford Place was good and doubtless there was also a profit contribution when he paid in the different currencies.

The day's rates were chalked on a blackboard in the shop and they covered quite a number of different currencies. He did particularly good business with the Chinese who also used the parcel collection service a lot. The Dangerous Drugs Act was passed in 1921. Up till that time class A drugs were legal and freely available, and cocaine was widely used in the First World War by soldiers on leave trying to relax from the horrors of the trenches. This was a factor in the legislation which outlawed all the major "recreational" substances, including opium, much used by Liverpool's long-established Chinese community. The shop seems to have been a regular delivery and collection point for the substance. Parcels arrived regularly, always tightly wrapped in brown paper and string with the knot sealed under a large blob of red sealing wax. To John they were just parcels — he never asked what they contained and the service continued right up to the end of the Second World War. He had his suspicions, but was unwilling to act as a policeman, feeling he had no right to interfere in their business by refusing to continue a service which he'd been doing legally for years, purely because of suspicions.

I was in the shop one day when a Chinese man arrived with a parcel. It was the size and shape of a small library book. He looked like Son Number 1 in the Charlie Chan matinée serials at the Commodore and he just smiled and handed the parcel over to John and then left immediately. John put the parcel under the counter saying to me "they'll be in for it soon." Being convinced by Charlie Chan of the fiendish, devilish cunning of the Chinese Tongs (gangs), I was intrigued by the mystery of the unaddressed anonymous parcel and its silent carrier.

"How will you know the right man, Uncle John, when he comes? You've got a few parcels there."

He picked up the parcel and pointed to the neat wax seal which featured an intricate Chinese logo.

"He'll have a ring on his hand the same as the seal when he pays me."

"Wow, it's really secret isn't it?"

He smiled. "Not when you think about it. We don't speak each other's language and the seal and matching ring make everything simple. There's no chance of a mix-up and the parcel going to the wrong person."

"I see." I was impressed with the system but disappointed that it was based on utility rather than some secret ritual of the Tongs.

In the 1920s he was hit by the Inland Revenue with a massive income tax demand which was reported in the *Liverpool Echo*. If the subject arose in later conversation he would smile and say that it was a misprint in the paper and they had printed one (or was it two) noughts incorrectly when reporting the size of the fine and payment. Whichever it was, he paid and carried on as before. He seemed to be always in the shop quietly reading if there was no customer requiring attention.

Uncle John was of course hag-ridden. The boys had left home but the three daughters were still there — all unmarried, and of course his wife Bessie. It wasn't for lack of effort. The handsome room above the shop with its grand piano had hosted many parties and guests and handsome young men over the years but the girls were still at home and all quite pretty. It was possibly something to do with contentment and the joy of home. It was a house of *Bon Accord* and we never heard either a cross word or the slightest disagreement in all our visits. Each of the women had a cat and when talking together and seated, a cat would be on each lap.

"Isn't that right, Cissie?"

"Yes, it is, Mollie," this was how the conversation progressed in the living room behind the shop. There was total agreement and satisfaction with everything that arose in discussion and unpleasant subject matter never entered the place and the atmosphere was lovely and happy. On my first visit I remember being presented to Great Aunt Bessie, and smiling at me she opened her mouth where there was not a tooth to be seen. I was about four at the time and had never seen such a sight. "You're gummy," I said, and she laughed before going to the blackened kitchen range and producing a meat pie from the oven which she cut in two and sitting me down gave me half. May told me off and said it wasn't a very nice thing to say to somebody, but Bessie thought it very funny. I liked the Larney household very much. Many years later, Cissie, the only

78

survivor, finally married, it was to an odd-job man she got in to fix the fence. She died shortly after and the odd-job man and his crony drank themselves to death on the inheritance. Would John have spent his life as he did if he'd known how it would all end? He or the family didn't benefit very much and it proved lethal for the beau and his crony. A moral tale for all concerned. But learned too late for use in this world.

CHAPTER
SIX

The City: the Irish and the Welsh

The Marine was much larger than Timon Avenue and the benefits of the extra space were appreciated by all — particularly Fran. He would play happily in our playroom at the top of the house for hours all by himself, mostly soldiers or ships with the bathroom next door available for sailings. The bath was constantly full and would always have to be emptied and refilled with fresh warm water before our bath before bed. May bought us two tin motorboats from Woolworths which worked from a solid fuel block burning under a boiler at 4*d* each. They steamed around the bath over a long time. Less successful were the toothbrushes. Our first. They had a golliwog on the handle and we'd clean our teeth before we got out of the bath. Fran left his toothbrush in the water and Golliwog vanished down the plughole. The fireplace in the bathroom had been closed off with hardboard and when this was removed some years later during redecoration there in the fireplace was a child's rag doll. An arrival down the chimney from a bomb nearby. When Fran needed an opponent in his games, I was summoned. I never remember my side winning. The floor was wooden

80

boards and the battles featured defences of long stretches of barbed wire made from nails hammered into the floor and strung with cotton from May's sewing basket. The weaponry was varied and on one occasion included "poison gas". It didn't harm the soldiers but we had to open the windows and door to clear the air when we started coughing as the room filled with smoke. Eventually we had to leave the room. I don't know what triggered Fran to produce this, but it may have been the gas masks we'd all been issued. And I don't know where he got his supply, but one day he called me upstairs and showed me a roll of ciné film. He cut a piece off, lit it with a match and as it flared up he blew out the flame and the film continued to burn with an acrid foul-smelling dense smoke. I surrendered immediately.

Our interests were different and May realised this. One bright summer evening before the start of hostilities she said, "Would you like to come with me to the library, I think you'd like it." This sounded interesting as I'd read everything in the kitchen bookcase (constructed by May) that was of interest.

Off we went to the grand Bootle Library next to the Town Hall and Museum. They were together and very imposing, and built some fifty years before, when civic pride and Bootle's new status as a county borough, demanded recognition. The development also featured the police station, the Municipal Swimming Baths (two pools) and a post office — all in the same style and by now blackened by the smoke of the ships and the town.

When we arrived at the library I had a surprise of the most wondrous kind. As we entered, we turned right into the Children's Library and May said, "Now this is your library and mine is on the other side." She presented me to the lady at the desk and we filled in a membership form and I was given two tickets. May then said, "I'll pick you up on the way out," and left me as she went off to get some "whodunnits" for herself. For me this was one of the most wonderful and memorable things that had ever happened to me. I was not even aware that such things as children's libraries existed. I gazed at all the well-laid-out shelves of adventures, history and knowledge of every sort and all for children. "If you need any help, just ask," said the lady librarian, smiling. I was transfixed. All this pleasure and for me! I didn't know where to start, so I just began opening books and glancing quickly at how they were written. None of it was too hard and there was so much that was appealing. When May returned I was still absorbed in wonder at all the delight and pleasure on the shelves around me but I selected a couple which looked promising and handing over my new tickets took my books after the return date had been stamped on the lending record gummed to the first page. Feeling very grown up with my books under my arm, I prattled away and enthused and extolled the wonders of the library and this new experience all the way home.

It changed my life, for it was a new interest with an infinite capability for progression and pleasure. There were books on so many subjects and discovering the writers one liked was like finding gold nuggets on every visit. Winter nights became idyllic, sitting in front of the fire in the kitchen with the cat at my feet on the thick rug May had made out of old clothes. I think finding the books by myself without any guidance probably invested the experience with even greater pleasure. It added a personal dimension and somehow deepened the feeling of contact and relationship with the authors. I had found them — I felt quite possessive. May with her innate comprehension and keen eye had realised I was ready, though still very young. She was, as usual, right.

I think it began on our trips to town before I started school. These carried on until I left to join the army. There was a regular pattern. Tram to Lime Street if we were starting at Rushworth and Dreaper or the no. 17 to the Pier Head if we were going to Castle Street. We seemed always to spend a long time at the many second-hand bookshops in the town and the one on Castle Street was the favourite — down the steps from the street into the semi-basement. Most of the stock was beyond me, but I could read before I started school and limited as I was, I enjoyed looking inside all sorts of books on strange subjects of which I had no comprehension — or even of the title. Books just appealed and May noted this and took me to the library when she judged I was ready. Fran, for his part, was not interested in books and naturally was bored by such visits. He preferred to be at home playing, though at this time he was at school except in the holidays.

May was a quick mover and all the other shops we needed to visit would be covered quickly. She didn't dawdle, knew what she was shopping for, and got it. Then we had tea. This was the best part of the outing for there were many teashops and cafés all over the city. A recent survey on family outings and shopping showed Liverpool holding a clear lead in this activity — often the eating and drinking being the first event after arrival. I liked the ritual of finding a table, looking at the menu, ordering and being served. Usually by older women or the very young. Those in between all had children and their hands full with life at home. The waitresses everywhere wore black with a white pinny and cap and were always very friendly. We never had much to eat — just a pot of tea in a shiny silver pot with nice white cups and a cake or two or even a savoury like mushrooms on toast or Welsh Rarebit, but it was an event. We'd discuss what we'd done so far and where we'd go next and May would take advantage of our one-to-one situation if she wanted to mention anything out of earshot of the rest of the family. I always read the menu completely and asked May about any offering of which I was ignorant, like Welsh Rarebit, Brown Windsor Soup and Bath Buns. She, with her background, was always able to respond and explain and this, added to my expanding store of food knowledge gained in the daily kitchen. I have always liked eating out and restaurant ritual, particularly where the service is not rushed and perhaps, it all began there, with May, on our shopping and teashop visits to town.

Like most mothers, May quickly noticed how we responded to new experiences and things and encouraged us where she perceived an interest. One Christmas we both received a child's tool set. The tools were small but real and we both quickly became adept in their use. There was a small wood saw, a tiny claw hammer, a plane which used razor blades for a cutter and an archimedean drill with six bits in a hollow handle. The cellar had lots of wood — mostly wooden orange crates for chopping into fire wood for lighting the fires in the bar and the house. We set to immediately trying to make boats and forts and other boys' toys and in time our capabilities improved. I think we got more pleasure and value from these little tool sets than any other presents we ever received. It gave us a keen interest in tools and what they were used for and how each craft had its own "tools of the trade" which had been designed by its artisans for specific works in their calling. I particularly liked the leather-headed hammer (mallet) I saw in a coppersmith's bag one lunchtime. He was having his pint and I stopped momentarily on my way in to look at this strange tool in his green canvas bag. He had moved aside to let me through and saw my interest.

"You like my tools, son?"

"What's that?" I replied, pointing to the hammer.

He pulled it from the bag and gave me a playful light tap on the forehead. "It's for bad boys."

I looked up at him unconvinced.

"It's for flattening and shaping sheets of copper and lead — soft metals. If I used a steel hammer I'd mark and damage the metal and it would be no use and I'd have to start again."

"U'mm — I bet Fran doesn't know that. Wait till I tell him," and I crawled under the counter and ran up the stairs looking for him as the coppersmith smiled and returned to his pint. By manhood we both had large tool collections and a wide capability in their use.

Would our skill development have been the case without the child's tool sets? Perhaps not, for neither of us ever had a woodwork or metalwork lesson at school. I still have the small saw and hammer from the set, and surrounded now by a large workshop with a tool for everything, I think "this is how it all began" as I look at the little saw. That was the start and starting is always the hardest part of everything.

Fran was fond of drawing and showed promise, so May bought him a paint box. He used it enthusiastically and revealed a strong tendency towards the modern schools in art in his use of colour, which was appalling. May was interested in this and thought it might change as he advanced but it never did. He was little interested in reading, though capable, and not at all in music, despite encouragement. He had a fondness for animals and "creatures" and kept in his pockets various beetles from time to time which he would bring out and play with on the table and then put back in his pocket. They seemed quite happy with the accommodation where they would remain until the shorts got washed. Animals and insects are quick, but Fran was quicker, with very fast hands which caught flies and mice without difficulty. Mice he was very fond of, and though we had plenty living with us, Fran decided he wanted more for his birthday. May was aghast at his request as she disliked them intensely.

It was all the fault of visiting Lewis's Pet Department, for that was a great mistake. Most boys would opt for perhaps a rabbit, or a guinea pig where there's already dog, cat and canary, or even a parrot. Not Fran, he wanted a pair of rats which he saw and despite his entreaties, May would have none of it. We had thousands of them already, all around us in the sewers, drains and warehouses as well as our own cellars. She hated them — enough was enough. No rats and that was final. So the mice came as a concession. Two white and one dark brown in their small cage with their exercise treadmill. Naturally they were placed in the playroom — on the mantelpiece where he fed them daily with occasional outings for each — in his pocket!

When we moved to the Marine our pets came too, naturally. Dick, the canary, liked the bigger kitchen and the higher ceiling but his sparring partner Ginger didn't like any of it and promptly left home and went back to Timon Avenue. The new tenants brought him back to us, not once but twice and then he went again so it was clear he'd made his mind up. May obtained a replacement, another ginger — called Rust. She would only have ginger cats — favouring men again for all gingers are toms. Rust was a wonderful cat and we had him for many years and when we moved later he settled into his new surroundings immediately. Mick, our big Airedale, slept on the half-landing between bar and bedrooms usually with Rust lying on top of him. He was an excellent watchdog, alert immediately to the slightest sound. He was not excitable and barked little. If he sensed danger he would give a low growl which would continue until the threat receded or he sprang to his feet and then barked loudly. During the day he roamed free like the rest of us, but even further afield. He was a clever dog and always hungry. He discovered that ships had galleys and food, so he spent much of the day on the docks visiting ships and canteens, but he was always home for his dinner in the evening. May had reared Mick from birth. He was one of a litter of six and she decided very early that he was the one she would keep. She chose well. I have never seen a bigger Airedale and he combined a sweet nature with a fierce combat ability. Shortly after arriving at the Marine he was out with Father one day and walking up Bedford Place when he was attacked by a guard dog which leapt out as they passed the yard where the dog was usually confined. This day it was off the leash and the gate had been left open. Mick, unaware and taken from behind, was savaged but saved from worse by Tom who knew how to deal with such situations. He punched the guard dog on the nose (a dog's weak spot) and squealing, it let go of Mick and ran off back to the yard. Mick was taken home and the injuries treated and that we thought was that. At this time Mick was still growing and was really just a pup, but he remembered. It must have been around a year afterwards that Fran and I met him on our way home from school — sitting quietly outside the yard.

The encounter was repeated every day for some weeks and we wondered about it and then one day things changed. The gate opened and his aggressor, off the leash again, came out into Bedford Place. Mick was at him in a flash and in no time was revenged. His attacker, torn and bleeding, was only saved from worse by two men in the yard who drove Mick off with wooden staves. Fran and I arrived at the scene as Mick was driven off. He was unmarked and with tail wagging, came with us, as we continued home.

On Sunday afternoons we often walked Mick around the docks with Father or one of our uncles. Mick liked these expeditions and roamed free off the leash once we were on the dock estate. He rarely ran and usually proceeded at a walking pace which allowed much sniffing and examination of all the odd things found on the quays. We usually encountered men who knew Father — customers or others, for publicans know many people, and we would stop often for exchanges of pleasantries and information. For Fran and me, these walks were adventures and sometimes we'd be invited onto ships and this gave us a good idea of how seamen lived. This was important to Fran who was obsessed with the idea of a life on the ocean wave and all things maritime. Alongside the Canada Dock one Sunday we were hailed from a small boat in the dock.

"Hello Tom — would your lads like a sail? We're going up to the lock gates." These were a couple of hundred yards away. The boatmen were collecting floating debris — one sculling at the stern and the other picking up the rubbish from the water.

Tom looked at us and Fran said, "Yes please!"

I said nothing — it didn't appeal.

"Right Jim, Fran would like a trip." With that we moved towards the steel dockside ladder a few yards away as the oarsman moved the boat towards us. The water was about 20ft below and Fran moved quickly to the side of the dock and started the descent. Mick didn't like it and grabbed Fran's collar. Father was unable to get Mick to release his hold, so Fran didn't get his trip. The men in the boat were amused and impressed by Mick's protective instincts. He only released the collar when Fran began his return to the quayside and satisfied with Fran's return and himself the tail started to wag.

"Well if you ever want to go to sea you'd better do it when Mick's not around," said Father, smiling. Fran was looking at Mick and Mick at Fran, and the situation resolved, we resumed our walk. It was full of interest — each dock with different lines, cargoes and character. In the Alexandra Docks, the quays were littered with cases of oranges and other fruits which had gone bad in transit, now dumped and awaiting removal. In those days Yeowards, McAndrews and other shipping companies ran fast passages from the Canary Islands and Mediterranean ports with all the local fruit and vegetables as they came into season. On arrival they were met by their agents from the Fruit Exchange in Victoria Street. Cases of each item in the shipment were broken out, loaded on trucks and taken to the exchange and sold. Wholesale and retail buyers examined the fruit from the opened cases and made bids as each lot came up for sale in the theatre saleroom with its stage and staggered rows of seating.

By lunchtime the shipload would all be sold. Around the exchange and close by in the surrounding streets, all the wholesalers had their depots from which they supplied markets throughout the country. The prices paid were all recorded and listed in the following day's national newspapers. The streets around were packed with horses and carts and trucks delivering and removing the newly arrived produce. There was a particular concentration in Queen Square right next to St John's Market and the Stork Hotel. The latter was the favourite for all visiting theatricals and also the centre for the city's homosexual socialising. St John's Market nearby in Charlotte Street always had the freshest and the cheapest produce for it was only a minute away — by handcart.

The fruit trade brought with it many who decided to stay as the prospects were more attractive than back home in Spain, Italy or France. The Ferrignos came with a cargo of their own lemons from Sicily in about 1890 and stayed. The Cheminais came from south-west France and stayed too, and there were many others. The trade was linked with blood as well as produce all over Southern Europe.

Then there were the Irish. The night crossing from Dublin on the open decks brought handcarts piled high with cabbages, potatoes, carrots, turnips, eggs, butter and all sorts of other edibles securely tied down under tarpaulins. Their owners — all female, arrived at first light, sold everything and left on the night boat, returning for restocking of the empty carts. They disembarked and wheeled their carts to the open public markets on Scotland Road, and the rest of the city where they were in business by 8a.m. Much effort for little money, but it was a living. They were strong women who could push the heavily laden handcarts for miles. It seemed effortless. Their cries and shouts in the open markets to attract custom were tuneful and had an element of song. Although they were from outside the city they were not regarded as intruders but thought of as "our own". The language of the two groups was almost indistinguishable and years later in Moore Street, Dublin, I closed my eyes and listened to the cries of the Saturday market. I couldn't tell whether I was in Liverpool or Dublin. It was not just the accent which was similar but also the way the language was used, "Well you wouldn't want to be hearing from that eejit (idiot). Sure he's only a gobshite and him with all the fine talk," and that put him in his place. And the words — many gaelic in origin in use in both places. "Ah he's very flucuric (generous)." Understandable when three out of four people in Liverpool in the year 2000 are of ethnic Irish origin. It was not "The Capital", as it was often referred to in Ireland, without a serious claim to the title. In the North "British Out" was daubed on the walls and underneath "Only if you give us back Liverpool".

Although the Irish element in Liverpool was dominant, the Welsh were always important too. They had not arrived in poverty like most of the Irish and with the Welsh border only twenty miles from the centre of the city, travel was cheap and maintaining family contact easy. There were local Welsh language newspapers *Angor, Bont,* and *Glannau* and the arrivals had established themselves strongly in certain trades and particularly in the grocery, housebuilding, printing, shipping and carriage trades. In some areas they were the largest ethnic group of the population and in Bootle, Everton and Toxteth, their presence was marked by their chapels, churches and street names. Sometimes builders acquire the right to name the streets they build which would account for the many Welsh named streets in the city — around fifty in number including Gwladys Street outside Everton Football Club. Irish streets in contrast are few. Dublin Street, outside the Irish Ferry Terminal and Roscommon Street, being the only two which readily spring to mind.

In Bootle alone there were nine Welsh churches with their affiliations and meeting and service times signposted in Welsh outside. There was a local Liverpool Eisteddfod and even the national event had been held in Liverpool on several occasions — 1884, 1900, 1929.

The railway companies ran excursions one day every week from North Wales to Liverpool for shopping and visits, and stores like Lewis's put on special promotions for them. Emlyn Williams, the great actor, author and playwright, describes in his autobiography his visits and living with his aunt in Bootle when he was attending drama school in Liverpool. His aunt lived just off Stanley Road, opposite the Kings Park, and these streets were heavy with Welsh. Queens Road included the dairy and store of Tudor Davies. This was an enclave and never empty where the talk was always in

Welsh. With Tudor licking his lips between his Celtic enunciations in a slow, beautiful deep voice, you'd enter and ask for a pint of milk. He would take from you the jug and dipping his ladle into a churn pour it slowly without spilling a drop, and all the while continuing his talk in Welsh with cronies in the shop. It was always a group. I don't think I ever heard him speak English, even when he served his customers. He just gave them what they asked for, took their money and kept talking. If he didn't have what you wanted he just shook his head and carried on talking. He was not bad-mannered or offensive, just occupied totally in the belief that he was still in Wales, which in reality he was. At the side of the shop was a yard and a cowshed where he kept two large cows which supplied his milk. The keeping of livestock was quite common in the city at the time and lasted until the heavy bombing of 1941 made it very difficult to keep and protect all animals, including the horses for cartage which were numerous, with stables and blacksmiths for shoeing all over the place.

The Welsh communities based on the churches were very active in preserving their heritage and many of them ran instruction courses in the language both spoken and written, and they celebrated national events, not just St David's Day, with fêtes and concerts. If anything special was required it was easily brought in from North Wales by train, bus, or ship. There was a strong tradition of Welsh schooner owner captains from the North Wales ports sailing into Liverpool and from there to far-off places which again lasted until the early years of the peace after the Second World War when transport of every sort was in short supply. These schooners covered a lot of the trade in and out between Liverpool and the Welsh coast for years and many captains, for ease of operation, lived in the city, leaving the Welsh end of the operation to relatives to manage. Most of the seafarers were native Welsh speakers who used English (if they had it) only when they had to. Connections like these kept Welsh alive in the city and then the war came and gave it a mighty boost.

The government had been aware of the dangers of aerial bombardment for some years before 1939. Realisation of the damage and loss of life this could inflict was confirmed by the Luftwaffe squadrons in the Spanish Civil War in 1937, notably at Guernica. That was the trial run. All of Britain was in range of the German bombers, and as most industrial areas were also heavily populated, with housing and industry cheek-by-jowl, any attack against industrial targets would inevitably lead to heavy loss of life. It would be unavoidable. Outside these areas, however, would be almost free from bombing as there was nothing worth destroying, and so the government designated evacuation areas for children and mothers for all industrial areas. For Liverpool and its environs, North Wales was the main reception area chosen. Smaller groups were sent up the coast to the Southport district. These offered proximity, easy access and established links, but the total North Wales population stretching down as far as Aberystwyth and Welshpool was less than that of the city of Liverpool alone, so there was not a lot of spare accommodation, even though the war had taken away many for the services.

Nevertheless, in 1939, Liverpool and district including Birkenhead, sent out around 130,000 children and mothers with children under five, plus teachers, and somehow they all found a home. Most of the children rapidly came to understand the Welsh language which was spoken by nearly all the locals, and being young, many were rapidly fluent and began to use it as their first language. It was harder for those older, including their teachers, and at the end of the war when they were returned to Liverpool many were talking and singing in Welsh as well as any of the natives.

One day, a party of schoolchildren were standing on a platform of Lime Street station, singing in sweet unison. Passers-by stopped to listen. They were attracted in the first place by the sweetness of the singing, but then stopped also out of curiosity. For the words of the song sounded like a foreign language. Where the children little French, Dutch or Belgian refugees?

No, they were Liverpool children all right, greeting their native city with a rendering of "Calon Lân". They were the first contingent of the children who were evacuated from the city to North Wales at the outbreak of the war and who are now being returned to their homes. Many of them had been living in areas where English is hardly ever spoken and they could now speak Welsh. A few of them had forgotten practically all the English they had ever learned!

The following day, a further 540 Liverpool evacuees as well as 120 or so Birkenhead children arrived home from North Wales, Cheshire and Hereford. The special train which brought the children from Caernarvonshire had started its journey in Portmadoc, picking up children at intermediate stations en route. A party of children from Anglesey had joined the train at Bangor and a mid-Wales contingent at Chester. The "train-marshal", W.A. Jones, Head of Heyworth Street School, had been in Caernarvonshire since September 1939. The children leaving Pwllheli and the Lleyn Peninsula were described as "like a typical Welsh colony conversing with each other only in Welsh when they assembled at Chwilog". Just before boarding the "Evacuee Special" they gave a rousing rendition of the Welsh national anthem.

So much for the warnings and opposition of the Welsh Nationalists in the period which were based on the belief that the evacuation of "aliens" into Wales would weaken the language and strengthen the hold of a foreign language in the principality. That the result was exactly the opposite of their predictions and in addition provided returning "missionaries" for their language to their alien neighbour was never commented upon. The humour of the situation was obvious and the children's immersion and capability in the language was a big boost to the later Welsh activities in their native city. As a language and cultural instruction course, it was certainly more effective than the "au pair" schemes of later years.

The North Welsh, with a good knowledge of "sin city", their neighbour Liverpool, perceived its citizens as immoral, with a weakness for drink and given to crime and bad behaviour. Being a rural community, what they saw was an industrial urban society different from their own. A place where the rules were different and the Devil was a popular member of the community with relatives and friends on every street all engaged in non-stop activities to fill that underworld of eternal flames and punishment.

The Welsh had prospered in the city and their peasant cunning and distrust had served them well in becoming established. The first half of the nineteenth century, however, had brought the Irish famine, mass immigration and appalling social conditions. These events were frightening but progress was made and things changed. But not the perceptions. Perhaps the Irish were to blame, for the English view of the city from both inside and outside, was not dissimilar from the Welsh, and the Irish were increasing all the time. Is the view today different? The answer must be no. The Liverpudlian then as now rejoices that he is "not as other men". What was the reverse view? How did Liverpool see the Welsh? Well they lived next door, were careful with a penny, just like the Cork men, and they drove a hard bargain. They were clannish like the Irish, but less gregarious. More temperate and reliable but less generous. They were considered somewhat mean or tight. "Welsh", as a word, was pejorative, both adjective and verb. Welsh tea (weak tea), and to welsh on a bet or promise — to run off and avoid payment or fulfilment.

Perhaps this branding was a reaction to their early business success in the city — and though denigration is a poor substitute for fair comment the view persisted. In the streets we chanted:

Taffy was a Welshman, Taffy was a thief.
Taffy came to our house and stole a leg of beef.
We went to Taffy's house but Taffy wasn't in
And Taffy came to our house and stole a silver pin.

One successful Jewish retailer with many branches throughout the country, when asked why he had no branch in North Wales, replied that they had found it too difficult to make money there. So close yet so distant — two peoples, neighbours yet steadfastly and contentedly apart, but it did provide humour for both sides in abundance. The graffiti on the gents urinal in Denbigh. "Ffuck off" — Scouse. And then the allegedly true story of the Liverpool holidaymakers on the seafront at Llandudno falling into conversation with a couple of the natives (a minister and his wife) one Sunday afternoon:
    "Are you coming to the service this evening?"
    "No, sorry, but we don't understand Welsh."
    "The collection is in English."
    One-nil to Wales.
    Yet both were there when they needed the other and threats from outside arrived — just like most families.

CHAPTER
SEVEN

St Alexander's and a Smoke

Aunty Rose was May's first cousin. Their mothers were sisters. Rose and her sister Lily had always lived nearby and the threesome had worked together in a number of places in the city before they were married — mostly catering establishments. Rose married George (Connolly) or "Con", as he was always known. He was of medium height, solid build with a rosy complexion and a ready smile. We liked Con, but he was not so popular with the men for he had a reluctance to put his hand in his pocket. In the pub that was almost a capital offence and led to a certain unwillingness to bring him into the company. He worked as a dock gate man for the Mersey Docks and Harbour Board and this was considered a good job. He had an impressive black cap and uniform which he decorated with a heavy chain across his waistcoat — one end attached to a large timepiece which he checked regularly (time for the authorised fifteen-minute break and a quick walk across the road to one of the many dockside hostelries) — gatekeeping is thirsty work. I don't know what the other end of the chain was attached to in his right-hand waistcoat pocket. I always meant to ask, but never got around to it so the mystery remained.

Each dock had a gatekeeper with a small hut inside the gate where he kept his things and sheltered when the weather was bad. Duties were not onerous: checking what was coming in and out, helping carters and truckdrivers to find the ship or warehouse they were looking for, and generally reporting immediately any events requiring attention or assistance — accidents, injuries or fire, from his telephone in the hut. The gatekeepers were not police, but they worked closely with them and gave them shelter and access to the telephone if needed. The Port Police were at that time independent from the local constabulary and employees of the company.

The government had enacted draconian legislation to prevent the emergence of a black economy for all items like food and clothing, which were controlled or rationed. Everybody knew about the laws and the penalties, and everybody with the chance of a little bit extra for the family probably ignored them. It was difficult not to when there were "orphan" objects all around, lying on the dockside, falling off carts, or thrown into the street from collapsing warehouses. In general the laws worked well, for they were intended to prevent the growth of criminal businesses dealing in stolen goods — particularly food, clothing and tobacco — and in that they were successful. It was however impossible to control every item and farmers, dockers, retailers, seamen, etc. — everyone in fact with access to these rationed items all indulged in a little evasion and acquisition of any item which would help at home, and that was what did for George. A docker friend passing

101

out on the way home gave George a tiny brown paper parcel. It contained a 12oz tin of corned beef and George, delighted, put it on the shelf in his hut — but unwrapped. Later in the day an incident brought a port policeman to his hut to use the telephone. He saw the corned beef, seized it as evidence and arrested George. Shame, degradation, reporting in the *Bootle Times* and three months in prison followed. On release he was called down to the Port of Liverpool building, that "cathedral", the third of the "Three Graces" on the Liverpool waterfront, and dismissed. Job gone after many years, pension gone (forfeited by his criminality), reputation gone — "a black marketeer and thief" and in their place a letter from the Ministry of Labour telling him to report for work immediately at a distant location. Back at Smollett Street in Seaforth, Rose, who was also working full-time buoyed up his fragile spirits and I never heard the subject mentioned again.

The punishment did not fit the crime, but the authorities were determined to make examples of those who benefited in any way from goods improperly acquired — it was postulated as taking other people's rations. Thankfully similar cases were few in relation to the area and its population. People were unwilling to inform on others, even if they disapproved of their actions. Authority was regarded as harsh and unsympathetic and the natural enemy of the people.

George was just unfortunate. Adam had his apple and George his corned beef, small things — big consequences, but they both got over their difficulties and Christmas found us with George unabashedly serenading the company in the Marine with the strangest of songs:

> In the land where they shovel no snow
> Shovel snow,
> Shovel snow,
> In the land where they shovel no snow.

Where was this place he was singing about? And why were they not shovelling snow? No explanation at all. None of the adults were curious. They were probably glad of the brevity, but I was dissatisfied — I didn't like stories with no ending. I hadn't yet realised that I had an excess of curiosity even for trivia like George's song.

St Alexander's was one in a line of Catholic schools which follow the waterfront going north from Liverpool city centre. It was the last within the city before the boundary with Bootle was reached. Following the Irish Famine in the 1840s, the influx of people into the city from Ireland was massive and continuous with over 4 million in fifty years. Most moved on mainly to America in the emigrant ships leaving daily, but many stayed. They had no money for the fare, only destitution. This brought with it the usual problems which come with forced migrations — starvation, cholera, typhus, unemployment and unrest. For Liverpool — the second city of the empire — it meant rapid, painful expansion, cholera epidemics, the first City Medical Officer of Health in the world and continuous construction activity. The docks were

103

expanding rapidly to cope with ever-increasing trade as they moved north along the river up to and into Bootle. The Irish came with them as the demand for labour increased. Their labour was all they had and they rapidly became the bulk of the workforce. Other industries avoided recruiting Irish for a variety of reasons, including prejudice and religious hostility, for the Irish were Catholic and this was England. They were not wanted, were a burden on the city and were a different people. But they were needed on the docks and lots of other places and they stayed, for there was nowhere else to go. There was nothing in Ireland, and they needed money to get to America. Some went later, but many stayed and they pitched their camps in the new cheap housing along the docks. It was natural, therefore, that the church should follow and it did expanding northward and following the line of extension of the docks. St Augustine's sprang up in 1845, St Alban's in 1849, St Alexander's in 1862 and St Winifred's in 1895.

The churches' establishment followed a set pattern. A hall would be found or built on a piece of land which had been acquired for future building. The hall was used primarily as a school to educate the children and take them off the streets. Education was not provided by the state and only became a responsibility with the first Education Act of 1870.

It was paid for by weekly collections from the men after pay on Friday at the dock gates and often in the pubs after mass on Sunday — for then as now attendance at Mass was never 100 per cent. The hall was used for Mass every day (before school) and in the evenings other church societies and activities met there, such as the Legion of Mary, St Vincent de Paul Society, choirs, etc. Then in time the school was built, followed by the church — always in that order.

So the Irish followed the work, and the schools and churches followed the Irish, and so did the pubs which were built for the growing population and on the line of docks they were nearly all managed by Catholics. And that was how we came to the Marine. In the roughest, poorest part of the city.

St Alexander's, the local school, for five- to fourteen-year-old pupils was licensed for 1,183 pupils which made it the largest in Liverpool for that age group. It is difficult looking at the site of school and church in retrospect to see where all the boys and girls went, but they were there, and now I was coming up to an age when I would join them, but not just yet. I was only four — six months to go and excitement all around me.

It was a wonderful hot, sunny day and I looked up at Alice as she appeared over my shoulder as I looked out the window into Raleigh Street. She was a wonderful sight, even for a four-year-old, quite statuesque. But she was always picking me up and hugging me tightly into her capacious bosom. I pretended to resist but really liked it, but it was disturbing. This day as I looked at her she was particularly resplendent in the sunlight. "What's that?" I said, as she smiled. "What?" said Alice. "That," I said, pointing to Alice's bosom. She smiled again, "Oh that, it's a cushion to keep my chest warm."

105

I was unconvinced. It didn't feel like a cushion when she hugged me, which she continued to do until she left to live-in as cook to Rileys, the coal merchants. I missed her when she went but she gave me a love of close physical contact which would be a great blessing throughout life.

Finally the day to start school arrived and May, Fran and I left for St Alexander's where I was handed over at the school gates. The cries from the schoolyard were loud and still audible as May and Theresa made their way home after the handovers. "You feel awful, just listen to them," said Theresa, another mother who May had just met. "Yes," said May "and the loudest — that's my son." They quickened their pace and parted by the subway under the railway at Bedford Place. "They'll be alright by lunchtime," said Theresa, who like May, had done it before. I hope so, thought May who had had a different experience when Fran started. When she handed him over to the school he was gone in seconds without even a word of goodbye. They're all different, she thought, and she was right. I, meanwhile, felt totally abandoned. How could she just leave me like that? A nun came up and took my hand gently. "Are you coming to my class? You'll like it there," and she led me slowly to the classroom with a group of other five-year-olds — some happily settled and others as bewildered and tearful as myself. The morning passed quickly and I liked the milk and tiny gingersnaps we got at playtime. I think I like the school after all, I thought, and then it was lunchtime and there was Fran waiting for me at the gate.

We arrived home for lunch, pushed our way through the customers in the bar, crawled under the counter and climbed the stairs to the kitchen. There was May, smiling and anxious to know how I'd got on.

"How did you like school?"

"The teacher doesn't like me."

"Why do you say that?"

"She called me John."

May smiled, "she was just being polite — your name *is* John."

"Then why am I called Jack?"

"It's a pet name, your Uncle Jack is really John, and the same with your grandfather in Australia."

I had never been addressed as John. It sounded strict and formal and I found this change of identity confusing.

May then had to explain that pet names and nicknames didn't feature in the school or baptismal registers and neither did school or church allow them. Satisfied, I sat down to lunch and we all chattered away. May was pleased I'd settled in, for she'd been suffering herself. She had missed not having a child around her feet that morning — it had been the first time for eight years that she'd been on her own. She could get more done, but it left a gap. The gap was the sense of loss that mothers feel when their child starting school opens new doors and takes them away into the outside world.

A place where they now belong. Distant, dangerous and attractive. Different values, influences and instruction which may one day take the child away forever. An exciting time for the child and a difficult one for the mother. Mothers know that successful parenting requires making children independent enough to stand on their own feet. May was very conscious of this and she also knew that she would have to breed "men" living where we did. This caused much anguish, for she had to decide whether or not to let us play in the dangerous streets outside with the children of the poorest, toughest and roughest of the city. Putting her faith in God for our protection, she decided not to restrict our liberty and keep us housebound. It was a brave decision and was to provide us with a rapid education in life at the bottom of society. Exciting, amusing, interesting and dangerous!

One of the dangers was the Leeds & Liverpool Canal, a busy waterway between the docks and the industrial heartlands of Lancashire and Yorkshire. Access to the canal was easy and it was a favourite recreational spot, particularly at weekends when the towpath was quiet and free from the passage of horses towing the barges. Around the turn of the century, wild great-uncle Bill had thrown a policeman into the water who'd interrupted his Sunday afternoon card game on the banks. The other players fled at the approach of the law, but not Bill. The constable couldn't swim and Bill had to dive in and rescue him. He felt contrite and allowed himself to be arrested. He got seven days from the beak and his mother took his lunch every day to Walton Gaol. No prison food for her son. Poor Peggy Daley was less fortunate. Eating fish and chips with her friend on the bank with their feet in the cool water one summer's night, she slipped in and drowned. She was

108

an attractive woman with no husband but a pretty daughter and a Swedish seaman admirer. When the Swede returned he was shocked at the news but in a short time the young daughter Peggy had replaced her mother in his affections. She was well below legal age for such association, but similar alliances were not uncommon.

We would often walk up Princes Street and onto the canal bank on our way to school. It was only a short section from there to the bridge at Bedford Place, but there were often things to see. Fran and I were following this route in the winter of 1942/3 one morning and it was cold. Very cold, in fact, with lots of ice everywhere. The canal was completely frozen and protruding slightly from the ice was the body of a seafarer, frozen in time with a box of matches in one hand and his pipe in the other. We wondered why he hadn't climbed out, ignorant of the rapidity of death from things like strokes and heart attacks and we felt very sorry for him, for he had a nice kind face — not distorted in any way by death. The blackout was responsible for many deaths of this sort, for nobody could see where they were going and once in the waters of the canal or the docks it could be difficult to get out. We told the policeman outside the school, and on our return journey the ice was broken and the body was gone but the memory remained for both of us.

At school, things were progressing at a steady pace under Misses Leelass and O'Neill and alliances were being formed in the class and in the playground. It had been an advantage to have Fran there, as an elder

109

brother is a form of insurance in such places. Family details are known early by all the boys and those seeking playground dominance in particular. We went to and from school together which was helpful to May as she didn't have to take and bring her five-year-old every day. The journey was quite interesting. First get across Derby Road in front of the trams and dock traffic, then past Blackledge's bakery and the wonderful smell of baking bread. Up Bedford Place with cotton warehouses on the left and some grand houses with gardens and a savage gated dog on the right. Over the canal bridge, turn right along St Johns Road and there was the school on the left.

In terms of events, the first couple of years at school were dominated by the adjustment involved in moving to a different life amid industrial activity and human poverty and squalor. As we mixed with the children around the Marine, we became aware of the level of deprivation of the majority, and how little most of our new friends possessed. As sailors left the pubs they would be surrounded by children asking for pennies. "Give us a penny, Mister? Go on, just one." It required a lot to refuse these pleas from thin, barefoot boys in torn shorts and darned wool jerseys, with pinched red cheeks, big smiles and uncombed hair. But if you gave to one it created turmoil among the left-out and a pursuit by a noisy ragged mob all the way back to the dock gates. Nevertheless, being sailors they often obliged although they had little themselves. Seamen from the East did not frequent pubs and the bulk of the custom was made up of northern Europeans, particularly Swedes and Norwegians. These were immediately identified by their blonde hair.

Tragedy struck soon after we arrived, when a Swedish seaman was surrounded by a group of urchins as he left the Marine. He put his hand into his pocket and flung a fistful of coins to them and proceeded on his way back to the ship. The children rushed for the bounty and in the mêlée one of their number, Tommy Allen, was kicked accidentally in the head. He went home, apparently none the worse, but died shortly after. Tommy was a nice lad — eight years old — who lived close by in Back Lodwick Street. He was laid out in his blue jersey in the coffin just by the front door of his mother's little house. He had lost his father at sea. All the children went to see Tommy. I had been playing cowboys and May told me that I should have dressed properly to pay my respects. To children, death happens to old people, not the young. We were shocked that it had claimed Tommy — and couldn't understand why. Even the blow that caused it — it had not been particularly hard and there had been no blood. How was it that a man's kindness had caused the death of a child? We were all to learn a lot about death and treat it as commonplace in the near future when Liverpool would be heavily bombed by the Luftwaffe. Even then they were flying reconnaissance missions over the city and photographing everything in preparation for the blitz to come. In those days an aeroplane in the sky was an uncommon sight and if one appeared, people would stop in the street and watch it as it coursed across the sky. These sightings were becoming quite regular and

111

people assumed they were just an increase in civil aerial activity. They were wrong — as the Luftwaffe records would show after the war. Poor Tommy would soon be followed by many more — the old and the young.

In those times, the loss of a close relative was marked by the wearing of a black armband or a sewn-in black diamond on the left-hand coat sleeve by almost everybody. It would be worn for up to a year and in some cases even longer, during which the bereaved would abstain from dancing, parties and merrymaking. Its presence always led to enquiry and commiserations by those they met who'd had no knowledge of the bereavement. It was a long-established and civilised custom which led easily to talking about the departed and eased the pain of loss. Even the worst were spoken of kindly, for you "never speak ill of the dead". There was no embarrassment in speaking of the departed, possibly because death was a more frequent visitor then than now. It was regarded as a natural happening and people were very open about it. This attitude would serve the people well in the near future.

Our playmates living close by were numerous and so were the dogs. Both species ran wild, unrestrained either by adults or the leash. Nearest was Jimmy White from the house on the opposite corner who lived with his parents and two sisters, Mary and Kitty, in the left-hand downstairs flat. This fronted onto a shop on Derby Road, where Mrs White ran a teashop. Next door, Stevie and Johnny Porter lived with a number of other brothers and sisters. The mother, Edie, was a very pretty, dark, petite woman with a gentle nature. Her husband Dick was a bully and the least popular of four brothers. He treated her appallingly. This culminated in her losing an eye and wearing a patch. The perpetrator was unpunished. Stevie and Johnny were not bad boys, but subject to bad influences. Mickey, the eldest was the nicest. I walked in one day, looking for Stevie, and there was Mickey, home from Reform School talking happily with mother and both smoking. He would have been no more than eleven at the time. Next door, Jimmy White seemed to be always sniffling and wiping his nose on his sleeve. This was a common habit. The noticeable stain it left brought with it the nickname "Silversleeves". Mary, his sister, was an epileptic, gentle and feminine. Kitty was ruddy in complexion, strong and a great worker. She worked for May for several years until the war and sometimes took us to the cinema in the holiday afternoons. George Cornwall lived next door to the Porters. His family was slightly better off and he always had shoes and socks. He was never without his dog, Rex, who went with us everywhere. Along the road next to the Victoria, another pub, but always called "the Clock" because of the large hanging clock over the main door, lived the Clarke boys in their mother's poorly-stocked greengrocers. I don't remember seeing a customer — ever. Gerry was particularly keen on trams and spent all his money when he had any, on riding round on them all the way as far as they went to the terminus or their turnaround destination. When not travelling, we would be made to sit on the stairs (pretend tram seats) while he made tram noises — starting, stopping, imitating bells and calling out for fares and issuing us with old tickets in return for payment with bottle tops for money. I hope his passion had diminished by the time the trams finished. It would be a hole in his life not easily filled. We lost touch with the Clarkes when the bombing started. They were early casualties and losing their home, they migrated to King Street, Garston, at the other end of the city.

Living in a constant cloud of heavy smoke, day and night, we all accepted it as a natural part of life. Even the constant strong breezes coming off the sea failed to clear the smoke, for they brought with them the emissions of all the ships and all the waterfront workshops and factories. That was a lot of smoke, for most ships still burned coal. Our bedroom at night was always full of smoke — drifting up from the bar below but we never noticed it until we went to Ireland. There, no ships or industry interfered with nature's good clean air. Nearly all the adults smoked and children got into the habit at around ten or eleven. Cigarettes were very cheap but money was very scarce and "stumps" (discarded cigarette ends) were picked up from the pavements and furtively pocketed by both adults and children. Fran and me for some reason were never interested in smoking cigarettes, though I liked very much the world suggested by cigars.

Most of our pals entered the world of tobacco via the "stump", but not Gerry Clarke. He surprised me one day when I arrived, for being obsessed with trams, we either went on a trip together if we had money or played trams on the stairs. This day it was different.

114

"Shall we have a smoke?" he said.

"If you want, but I don't really like it."

"Come on, let's have a go," he said, and with that tore out a piece from the *Liverpool Echo* and rolled a cigarette-sized substitute.

"You're not going to smoke that!"

He ignored my comment and striking a match from a box decorated with Captain Webb in bathing costume, he lit up and inhaled.

He immediately started coughing violently and passed me the smoking paper. "Your turn," he croaked. I put it to my lips and took the lightest of breaths. It was acrid, sharp, burning and totally unpleasant.

"It's terrible."

The coughing had not yet ceased but when it did he replied. "Yes, I don't know why, I had one the other day and it was O.K."

"You'd be better off with a stump — no one smokes paper."

"Well it was alright the other day — maybe it's the paper that's different — it was the *Evening Express* before."

Gerry was convinced that smoking paper was better than tobacco and also that the *Express* was a better smoke than the *Echo*. The *Express*, like the tram, went out of business some years later. He was unfortunate in his chosen pleasures.

Peer pressure provides an introduction to many things, particularly for children, and especially the younger ones. Fran, being three years older, naturally regarded me as test material and a valuable second

115

opinion. We would try out many things together, mostly at his volition. Not being interested in food and drink or smoking, unlike Gerry, he caught me unaware one day.

"Come upstairs," he said, and I followed. Instead of going to the playroom, however, we went to our bedroom and there, on the dressing table, he had a tray with two wine glasses and a collection of tiny bottles which I recognised from May's kitchen cupboards.

"We're going to have a drink," he said. I was suspicious and never replied. He then started mixing a concoction in a pint glass and finished his confection with a couple of drops of cochineal, which turned it deep pink.

He then poured the liquid into the two glasses and passed me one with a grin.

"Taski champagne," he said, touching glasses. I put it to my lips. The flavour was impossible to describe. It wasn't unpleasant, just strange.

"Do you like it?"

"Not bad," I replied as I examined the selection of tiny bottles — beside cochineal there were vanilla, lemon, clove, strawberry, peppermint and caramel.

"Does she know you've got her bottles?"

"No, but she won't mind."

He was good at clandestine removal and return, and I wondered how he managed it, for May was in the kitchen most of the time.

I had to stay till the "Taski champagne" was finished and realised I was fortunate that his interests did not lie in the kitchen. Our parents' bedroom received his attentions one day, for on the dressing table was a bottle of Eau de Cologne which had caught his eye. Fran thought this resembled the vinegar in the chip shop, for like the vinegar, it had an obstructed aperture for sprinkling, rather than pouring. He decided to play chip shops there. The cologne became the vinegar bottle and was applied liberally and removed all the polish from the dressing table top. Being out playing in the street, I missed inclusion in the transgression. I don't know what he used for chips but I felt I'd been fortunate to escape his certain invitation to dine.

Fran was not an inquisitive child, unlike myself, but there was one thing he was very curious about and he regularly pestered May wanting to know "where do babies come from?" May told him that she would tell him when he was older and one day, many requests later, she took him quietly into the sitting room and told him. I had to stay in the kitchen, which didn't displease me as I had no interest in the subject despite my usual all-embracing nosiness. He emerged some minutes later with a smirk of satisfaction on his face and went upstairs back to his soldiers. I think May expected me to ask to be told too, but I was much more occupied with weighty matters — was it a tram or a tran that passed our door every few minutes? I'd picked up an unusual-looking discarded tram ticket in the street and it was headed by the word "TRANSFER". At four, my vocabulary was expanding quickly and "TRANSFER" suggested "Trans Fare" — had I got it wrong and been calling a tran a tram? May listened to the question and explained as she went through the rest of the words on the ticket with me. These stated the conditions of issue and the ticket's validity for changing route (transferring) to different routes to reach a distant destination. Much more interesting than babies, I thought, and full of satisfaction I went out to find Gerry Clarke, our tram enthusiast to share my new knowledge. He liked it and we began searching for similar discards to add to Gerry's ticket rack.

We marauded in a gang, all over the place. Usually wherever there was something which seemed of interest — like Sam. Sam was a night watchman from the Gold Coast (Ghana) and he arrived one afternoon outside Blackledges with a team, who dug up the road for some distance and left a hole, barriers and building materials on the site. Sam had a shelter like a sentry box, a brazier and a pile of coke to keep him warm and illuminate the site at night for traffic. He immediately acquired a host of small friends who were with him every evening until bedtime. He was a tall, well-built man in a dark blue serge suit, collar and tie and a bowler, which gave him great authority and he became our main attraction after sunset, when he'd light his fire and his pipe and settle down for the night. He must have loved children, for he regaled us with stories about his life in faraway places as he sat puffing and smiling before his glowing brazier and audience. All a bit like *Uncle Tom's Cabin*. We never forgot Sam and were all sad when the work was completed and he left. Days were spent searching all round the area trying to find him — but in vain. I suppose it was company for him as well in the dark night, and he probably enjoyed it as

118

much as we did, for there were many questions which amused him because we were not a backward lot.

There were plenty of black men and women in Liverpool, but Sam was the first I met and spoke with. I think he conditioned all of us to regard his kind favourably. Many years later in Africa I would remember Sam as I experienced that wonderful sense of humour once again. In retrospect, I think I was fortunate to grow up in a place where there were so many different people. Different in colour, behaviour, dress, food, religion and humour — they all brought something to the party. Exposure early to these differences would prove invaluable later, though I was unaware of it at the time.

Unlike our peaceful earlier home in Timon Avenue, there was now something happening all the time and we were subject to all manner of influences and things which impressed themselves upon us. Sleeping at the front, our darkened bedroom was illuminated by every passing tram, and although only yards away from the tracks, the noise and the lights, we slept easily. The light moving from one side of the room to the other. Left to right for the Liverpool tram and the opposite way round for the Seaforth tram. The bedroom on the floor above was unoccupied and I spent lots of hours in winter sitting in the wardrobe with a lit candle and the doors closed and the room windows open as the wind blew noisily on the streets outside. This was my imaginary cabin in the Canadian wilderness and there were bears and wolves outside and no one knew where I was — including Fran. He, for his part, was probably occupied devising a new game. He was endlessly inventive. We'd had a large pile of sand delivered into our small back yard by the side of the toilet block. This was a new toy and had been provided to put out incendiary bombs. As they were still to come, we used it for playing soldiers and building tunnels and military fortifications. Fran (ever the vandal) thought it should be bombed and from a great height. We went to our playroom at the top of the house where we could do whatever we liked and leaning out of the third-floor window, we proceeded to drop the weights from May's kitchen scales onto the fortifications below. This was great fun but we had to keep running down four floors and into the yard to recover our bombs. Inventive as ever, Fran decided there was a better way of bombing and removing May's ball of string from the kitchen draw he tied it to another weight (a 2lb one), which had a looped handle. The new projectile was then lowered and the string measured and cut. The much reduced ball of string and all the other weights were then returned surreptitiously to May's kitchen. Ready for action, one holding the string and the other the bomb, down it went. The aim was bad and instead of the sand it hit the glass louvre of the toilet window removing a large piece. Action was suspended while we waited for adult shouts and enquiries. The bombing was immediately abandoned until further notice. By the next day nothing had been said, so we recommenced and had a great time until we tired of the game and sought something else. We were, however, careful to remove the broken glass in the yard to avoid later questions. Perhaps the broken louvre was listed on the schedule of war damage presented after the hostilities ended. How else could it have been caused? The "evidence" question once again. I was certain Father Coupe wouldn't like it and I didn't know whether I should tell it in a confession. It didn't appear to be covered by any of the commandments.

CHAPTER
EIGHT

Law and Order

Fran had left St Alexander's to go to St Martin's and I became aware of a change in the school environment. Gangs were emerging as the boys grew and started imposing their authority. This had been absent from the earlier, gentler years. Bullying was just one of these new manifestations. Gangs were usually, but not always, made up from boys of the same age, school year, and often the same class and often from the same street. This meant they operated as a group both in and out of school. You couldn't just join — you had to be chosen. The only defence or protection for us was to be a member of another gang or have a big brother. At this time at school I was now both gangless and brotherless and so began to attract attention as an easy target. The Dryhurst Gang was the worst and they started confrontations with me in the playground, which I avoided by moving and refusing any dialogue. They were determined to "get" me and eventually Dryhurst himself grabbed my arm and began threatening me, flanked by his followers. He was quite a big lad and was in the year above. I tried diplomacy — unsuccessfully — and then he struck me. Expecting attack, I was alert and moved my head and the blow glanced off. Being streetwise by now, I attacked him furiously and he was taken aback. The cronies did not intervene. This was the leader's show. Rushing at me, he ran straight onto a hard right. The blood spurted from his nostrils and with a handkerchief to his nose, the fight ended. I walked away unmolested and I was left in peace from then on — for most of the time anyway. Establishing a reputation for combat makes others wary of entanglement. There are always "easier marks" elsewhere. But reputation brings with it another danger and for me that was Tommy Grattan. Reputations attract, and there's always somebody looking to take the title in all walks of life. Tommy was actually a boy I liked. He was in the same class and the leader of another gang. The Dryhurst and Grattan outfits avoided each other. Stocky and strong with lots of energy, his playground importance was growing and he decided that my subjugation would add to his battle honours and esteem. He started by attempting to provoke conflict but I was quite adept in avoidance until the school emptied at 4 o'clock one summer's day. As we left together he struck me a blow to the side of the head as soon as we were out of the gates in St John's Road. I turned and retaliated and soon we were hard at it. His gang were now in attendance and I thought it was time to leave, as outside of school there was no certainty we would be left to settle matters alone. I took off and ran, and being swifter than Tommy, put lots of space between us. All along St John's Road, down Bedford Place and under the railway bridge. At the bottom and in the recessed entrance to the steps leading to Kings Road above, I waited. I had seen that Tommy had separated from his followers who were half-heartedly a long way behind. Tommy had seen me take the entrance to the steps and as he came round the corner I hit him right on the button — his nose went flat — he fell to the floor and started blubbing. I ran up the steps laughing, turned right into Kings Road and ran. Kings Road leads to Miller's Bridge and then Derby Road. I would be home soon. Looking over my shoulder to see if the pursuit continued, I ran straight into a lamppost. I saw stars and it stopped me in my tracks. It was a hard blow — a big bruise and swelling rose on my forehead, but no blood or further damage. I was dazed and in pain. I hoped Tommy felt the same. Back home, no comment was made about the forehead.

Every night we said our prayers kneeling at the side of the bed. In retrospect, I suppose our home and life was very stable in the sense that no matter what was going on around us there was order in when we ate, what we did, where we went to school and what times we went to bed and got up.

Four corners to my bed
Four angels round my head.
Matthew, Mark, Luke and John
Bless this bed that I lie on.

Before I lay me down to sleep
I pray the Lord my soul to keep

Make me safe by night and day
And bless this house, O Lord we pray.

After the prayers, May tucked us up in bed and kissed us and then went down to continue her work, which was never done. This is the time most beloved of mothers. The time to contemplate the joy of children. Now safely tucked in bed after another busy day. In later years when we had grown and fled she would return to the happiness of those times. Times when everything was harmonious and everything secure — or seemed so — for then the war broke out. It had been a long time coming. The nation believed it would all be over soon with Britain and France triumphant again. They were wrong. Fran and I were playing soldiers in the playroom when Neville Chamberlain, disappointed and sick, announced on the radio on the Sunday morning: "We are now at war with Germany." Fran was ten years old and the war would continue until he was due to report for military service. A longer struggle than its predecessor a quarter of a century before — so much for the predictions of a short, sharp engagement.

The Marine was on one corner of a block of three retail premises. The one in the middle was a cobbler and the other was the shop belonging to George — a grocer and a man of some mystery. He was probably an illegal immigrant — a Romanian seaman who'd deserted ship and set up a shop where he was hugely assisted by Eileen, an attractive redhead, who at eighteen was about twenty or more years younger than George. The shop was a goldmine for George who was our supplier for both family and catering requirements. When the shop was closed, business was at the back door and George was always happy to oblige — even for the smallest of purchases. In the war George would be arrested as a suspected spy and taken in for questioning. He was alleged to be under suspicion for signalling to Luftwaffe bombers on their nightly visits. Nothing came of the questions and he was quickly back at the shop. The Luftwaffe required no assistance in locating their targets in Liverpool (the docks — bringing in everything from America). Since 1936, German air reconnaissance had provided detailed maps of the whole area pinpointing key installations. These maps were to come to light only after the war. The heavy bombing of Liverpool between 1940 and 1942 was assisted by the signposts of Tuskar Rock lighthouse on the south-east Irish coast and the bright lights of neutral Dublin 100 miles north and 100 miles east in a straight line from Liverpool. The markers were infallible and always lit. After bombing Liverpool, the planes kept flying east to their bases in France and Holland.

George was arrested by Detective Constable Gene Harvey — a ladies' man, tall, handsome, a sharp dresser with a fine head of wavy hair. Talking with him in later life, one felt that the lovely Eileen rather than the Luftwaffe might have been the real reason for his arrest. With George out of the way the field would have been clear. Gene would always be able to visit — pursuing inquiries in the course of duty. The shop, of course, was another attraction. It was not to be however, and George was to return and keep his shop until his old age and the removal of his customers by the post-war planners. They all went to new estates but George did not go with them. By then he had enough and when he died Eileen got everything.

We knew many of the children who lived close by from school, but not all. Some went to other schools, but they were not many. Everyone seemed poor — the boys in old wool jerseys with holes, short trousers with no arse and bruised and cut bare, black feet with thick, uncut nails. The girls were also barefoot and many had but one cotton dress often patched and previously worn by two or three others beforehand. "First up, best dressed", was the saying — and the reality. This produced an unwillingness to attend school from the children and a refusal to enforce attendance by the parents, as they would be advertising their poverty and place in the world. These children attended school sporadically, usually in the warm times of the year for it is difficult, painful and dangerous to trek to school through snow and ice with no shoes or socks or overgarments, but that is how it was. The most notable of this group were the Porters. More a tribe than a family, all ruled by "Ma" Porter who was probably only in her late forties but seemed older. Girls married regularly at sixteen or seventeen. I do not remember any word or information about a husband, for he seems to have been either dead or absent permanently. "Ma" had four sons, Nish (Nicholas), Paddy, Stevie and Dick. There were daughters also, but being all married, they went under other names such as McDonald.

They were a rough, tough family and feared by others who were less aggressive and fewer in numbers. In a society like this, the only way to be paramount is to outnumber your rivals. In numbers the Porters were the greatest, but they never interfered very much with those outside the tribe — their main opponents were the police and each other, but nevertheless, they were best avoided in daily life.

On the top shelf under the counter facing the till at the Marine, Father kept a police baton and when he left the bar each night to retire he would collect the baton and take it to bed with him. Beside the bed, was the safe, which also served as a bedside table and each night the till was emptied, counted and put in bags for the bank the next day and placed in the safe. Safes were not the usual bedroom furniture, but May (it was on her side of the bed) had covered it with a decorated cloth and a vase of artificial flowers. Father, on the side nearest the door, kept the baton under the bed within easy reach of his right hand. He sometimes appeared with it at breakfast time on his way down and one day looking at it on the table waiting for my egg I asked him about it.

"Have you ever hit anybody with that?"

"Not yet," he replied, straight-faced.

"Would you if you had to?"

He chuckled, "What do you think?"

"I think you would. I've never seen you use it, but you always have it with you — in the bar and in bed."

"So far it's not been necessary."

"When would it be necessary?"

"If I were outnumbered or they had a weapon — it's the equaliser — it evens things up."

I looked at the baton with growing respect. "Is it that good?"

"This one is," and picking up the baton and pointing to the base below the handle and leather trap. "Can you see anything there?"

There was a faint circle shape about a half-inch in diameter in the wood.

"There's a little round shape there."

He nodded. "Well spotted, that's where they put the lead in."

"Lead?"

"Yes, lead. The baton was drilled out and molten lead poured into the hole — feel the weight."

He passed me the baton and I was surprised by how heavy it was.

"Wow! I wouldn't like a bang from that."

"No, neither would any of the baddies."

"Where did you get it?" By now I was really getting interested and holding the baton I felt great confidence in my ability to take on superior forces. I'd soon sort out Dryhurst and his gang with this, I thought.

"Bailey gave it to me — they used them in the Dundee Riots ages ago and he got it when he was in the police there. That was before he joined the force in Bootle. All the police there had one similar. They needed them as they were constantly under strength."

"So it's been tested in action then?"

"Not half!" he smiled, "we know it works."

I knew Constable Bailey — a no-nonsense red-faced Glaswegian. He was a regular visitor usually at night after closing when he'd arrive at the dark shaded side door in Raleigh Street if he was with a trusted colleague with a thirst as big as his own (always in pairs at night). Nobody messed with Bailey who was a disciple of the "get your retaliation in first" school. I witnessed him in action next door one day when the Porters, who'd moved in, started a barney. There was shouting and screaming, for the women were as combative as the men, and this brought a new young policeman to the back door to investigate the hullabaloo in the yard. He entered with a "What's going on?" and was immediately hit with a flat iron and semi-conscious, pushed into the toilet. He pulled out his whistle when his senses returned and blew as loud as he could.

Bailey, coming from the other direction and attracted by both noise and whistle, arrived on the scene. They were all busy fighting each other and he never announced his arrival or attempted to speak to them. He just drew his baton (new issue from Bootle with the Dundee modifications added) and entered. Everyone got hit, men and women — no discrimination, and having knocked six unconscious (four men and two women), the remaining three, hands up, surrendered. By this time the prisoner in the bog had emerged and Bailey sent him across the road to the newly installed emergency services phone for the "Paddy Wagon" which arrived in minutes. Business was slack that day. Some of the combatants had not yet come to and Bailey made those still standing act as bearers and put

130

them lying flat in the wagon and off it went to the lock-up. I had witnessed this with Johnny "Silversleeves" White from the entry and open yard door. We were impressed. The gladiator now turned his attention to the young policeman he'd rescued and gave him a severe castigation finishing with "Use yurr stick mon — dinna hesitate, it's no a job furr lassies."

With that he put his truncheon away and continued on his beat back to the station and the charging of all the Porters. He wasn't going to be delayed going off duty, however, and delegated the charge sheet construction to the young constable as he left.

"It's a gude exercise fur yurr laddie — we'll gah thru it later afore inspection and gannin on duty."

The children were numerous, ragged, hungry and broke. Always outside pubs, factories and workshops like Harland & Wolff. Many days there would be boys standing at the gate as 5 o'clock sounded and the men left their work.

"Any sandwiches, Mister?"

No one threw good food away and anything left in the tin rectangular lunchbox was taken home or given to the kids at the gate. Anything received was scoffed immediately with excitement and anticipation as the gifts were unwrapped.

"What have you got?"

"Corned beef — gear."

"I've got cheese — not as good as yours."

"Swap you one."

"OK" exchange of produce and cries of "Gis a bite!" from the non-recipients.

Fran got into trouble with May over this activity because one day he'd been observing the 5 o'clock feeding and a customer reported to Father that he'd been at the gate begging. May told Fran off.

"Don't you be anywhere near that gate or any other at 5 o'clock."

"I won't Mam," he said. Fran had his pride too.

Looking into Raleigh Street from the window one summer afternoon, there was a sound of disturbance from below and the pub disgorged a crowd into the street. They quickly formed a ring and two men removed their jackets and squared up to each other. No words were said — they'd had those in the pub. I recognised both as uncles of my friends the Porters. The action commenced immediately. There was no shaking of hands or Marquis of Queensbury Rules in this contest. Joe rushed at Stevie and unleashed a haymaker which would have taken Stevie straight back into the alehouse if it had connected, but it didn't and as he was off-balance, Stevie gave him the lot. A hard right and left to the head and one which sank deep into the midriff. Joe was down and then Stevie put the boot in and that was it. It was a brutal encounter that didn't last long. Two policemen walked by on the opposite side of Derby Road and ignored the event. They knew the customs and considered it outside their jurisdiction. The loser was in a sorry state — cut and bloodied and called to account for his hammer attack from behind in the pub toilet some months earlier. It was a family quarrel — Porters and McDonalds and now the score was even.

Stevie was generally reckoned to be the top man, or "cock" of the family. He was certainly the best physical specimen and was a regular drinking friend of May's brother, Uncle Tommy. Paddy was slimmer, but wilder and had done great damage to the glassware in the Marine on an earlier occasion. Alerted by shouting from the bar below one night, May ventured down to see what was happening. Paddy was drunk and on the warpath. He'd been elsewhere and was refused a drink when he entered the Marine. It was unusual for May to enter the bar, and as she did so, she saw the last of the customers leaving quickly through all doors and Paddy with a movement of his right arm sweep all the glasses on the counter in front of him to the floor with the violent off-key sounds of breaking glass. Tom was waiting for the right moment to engage in the combat as May spoke up. "Go home Paddy, you've had enough."

"Get out of my way, Missus," he shouted, as he attempted to lift and throw one of the cast iron and mahogany bar tables over the counter at Tom. It was too heavy and at that moment a voice behind him said, "that'll be all, Paddy". There was Jim Slowey, the biggest policeman in Bootle. Paddy went off with Jim and got six months. There were no hard feelings and when he came out his first action was a visit to the Marine to shake hands with Tom and say sorry. Tom shook hands and smiled but told him he was banned for six months, which he accepted. Upon expiry, he returned on the day to his usual position at the bend of the bar counter.

At the back of the Marine's small yard was a passage (jigger) and the walls of Campbell & Isherwood and Harland & Wolff. The latter's ship repair works were large and employed many, while the former, though smaller, was equally important as one of the leading shipping electrical contractors. Both companies' premises ran down to the Dock Road (Regent Road) and faced the gates of the dock estate. On the other side of Raleigh Street, on the corner with Derby Road, was a house divided into apartments for four families, including the Whites, and this was joined by a line of warehouses running down to the docks. On the bottom corner was another pub which had unique beer engines which produced a pint in a single pull — everywhere else required two pulls of the pump. Next door to Whites on Derby Road was a shop and a Cocoa Rooms (a workman's canteen). On the opposite side of Derby Road was Blackledges' Bakery and then a line of shops and a pub. Next to those was Ma Gleeson's "shebeen", chip shop and lodging house, where the sailors could always find a girl. All the streets ran into Derby Road and terminated at the other end by the wall of the Leeds & Liverpool Canal. All these streets Princes, Mann, Johnstone and Sheridan Place were of terraced housing, mostly occupied by dockers, seamen and port workers. Derby Road joined at the corner with Miller's Bridge with a children's recreation park with swings and roundabouts and an attendant park keeper with his little hut. Tom was very popular with all the children and was always on hand to help in accidents and incidents. Even the roughest of children treated him

134

with respect and I never heard him raise his voice when he exercised his authority. The opposite three corners featured John Hargadon's Old Toll Bar, another pub and a shop.

The whole area teemed with life and the population density was high. Derby Road, the main thoroughfare, carried trams in both directions to Seaforth and the city. In the war it would be in use day and night with traffic to and from the docks.

On the same side as the Marine and going towards Miller's Bridge, the streets had been truncated and flattened by the growth of Harland & Wolff, but Howe Street and Effingham Street still ran all the way down to the docks with a mixture of tall Victorian housing and warehouses.

The Derby Road frontage featured Dr Regan's surgery (no. 282), McConnell's Catering (nos. 286–8) and Ross & Alexander tool merchants. It also included Duthies, a small department store, and the Irish National Club. Both of these were of great importance in the community, though for very different reasons. Duthies provided, among other things, the straw mattresses required by sailors joining a new ship. All old mattresses were burnt at the end of a voyage to prevent infection and infestation. The Irish Club was open all hours and was always packed. Its political agenda of Irish Independence had just been advanced with De Valera's declaration of the Irish Free State in 1934, but the question in the North still needed settling. It had been a big player in earlier Victorian times in local politics where its strength in electioneering had been felt in both national and local elections. Liverpool was to return the only Irish Home Rule MP to Parliament: T.P. O'Connor. His successor, Dan Logan, was the sitting member in the Scotland Division constituency in the city centre. The anti-partition of Ireland movement was very active in Liverpool and provided a regular supply of candidates in local and national elections throughout the period.

At this time, the social side of the Irish club was paramount and it provided a haven at all hours for a large cosmopolitan clientele, including dockers, seamen and the local constabulary, when both on and off duty. Paddy McNally, the local bookie, also operated from the premises, safe from the hand of law. The club occupied a Victorian house with entrances in each of the two parallel short streets (Drake Street and Keppel Street) both truncated by the building of the Harland & Wolff yard. This was convenient for many, including Paddy with his clandestine operations, though by tacit agreement the club was "out of bounds" to the law. One of the entrances was literally "at the gate" of the Harland & Wolff works where it was necessary to be Protestant for all the good jobs. No religious restrictions existed at the Irish Club where the only rule was "no bumming, and buy your round". Every year, St Patrick's Day was celebrated with an outing to Southport. This had originally involved a horse-drawn omnibus for the fifteen-mile journey. The return was always slower than the outbound trip. On one occasion, the poor horse dropped dead on the homeward journey and the travellers had to walk, but it was "no sweat" as they would say, as in those days. Everybody was expected to and able to walk miles in the normal course of the day. There was from the late nineteenth century an excellent rail service between Southport and Liverpool with a station at Bootle only a couple of hundred yards from the club. This was eschewed in favour of the horse omnibus for a long time, though the latter had to stop many times on the journey to rest and water the horse. All the drinking troughs of course were situated at wayside inns which was a most fortunate coincidence. Discipline was required to arrive on time for the booked lunch at a Southport hotel. To be certain of this, the departure time from the club was very early, as the journey always took a long time — it was the horse of course — you must never drive it too hard.

Blackledges the bakers was a bit along from the club, directly opposite the Marine. A large building running along Derby Road between Princes Street (where Paddy McNally lived) and Bedford Place with its footbridge over the canal. The bakehouses were in the basement and when war came, the bakery had sufficient spare room to provide an air raid shelter for the dense surrounding population. Mr Blackledge, the head of the family firm, was a man of vision as well as ability. Selling bread was difficult like selling everything else in the Depression as money was short — even for life's essentials. Blackledges had their own shops and supplied a wide field of caterers, including mother, but the competition was fierce, particularly from the other big local bakers like Scotts, Sayers, Outrams and Taylors — besides the mass of small family bakers all over the city.

To get an edge, he advertised in 1938 in foreign newspapers for a Viennese Master Baker. The details of exactly how he got him is lost in time, but get him he did. He arrived in Liverpool to teach and instruct Blackledges in the making of Viennese breads. His contract was at £50 a week, an unheard of wage, and the result was Blackledges' Viennese Rolls. The success of these small loaves was instantaneous and the public couldn't get enough — everyone wanted them although they were no good for the sandwich trade — the baguette's moment had yet to arrive. A 2lb sandwich loaf cost 4½d. The much smaller Viennese Rolls were much dearer in relation, but everybody was happy to pay and it was hard to supply public demand.

> Blackledge's bread, hard as lead,
> Anybody eats it, falls down dead.

So sang the children playing in the streets. Blackledges had always been a popular baker, but street songs never respected anybody.

The streets around the bakery were always littered with pieces of dough. This was the result of the bakery staff pelting each other with the dough when they came out of the hot bakehouse for a break in the fresh air. Left on the street, it was picked up by the children and used again as missiles. It was a sticky dough, and would adhere to surfaces quite easily. I threw a piece at a passing sausage manufacturer's van (Brentons) and it stuck on the side window. The driver stopped the van, got out and chased me. It was no contest in the running stakes, and I couldn't understand why he was cross about it. Everybody else thought it an amusing activity — but not the sausage man.

I took to school very easily once I understood what was going on. The first class found me seated next to a diminutive imp of a girl named Frances Keegan from Bianca Street. She was quite bossy and as number three in the family, she felt she had to assert herself, which she did. We got on well and were to meet again twenty years later. Frances had two sisters and two brothers and the eldest girl, Phyllis, was particularly attractive, a scholarship girl and very calm, unlike Frances. The boys in the class were the usual bunch — mostly poor and from large families and great fun, though with some exceptions. There were other boys and girls from better-off homes and the children of pub managers and shopkeepers and these were all better dressed. Neagle, Saunders, Cloonan, McKeating and Joyce Cruikshank whose parents had a general store right next to the school were among this group.

In 1941 a bomb removed the centre section of the school, dividing it neatly into two separate tall buildings. Classes were large and discipline strict and when it was at recreation, the playground resembled an ants' nest in perpetual motion. The school backed onto the Liverpool — Southport railway line and all round it were houses — mostly small with iron railings in front of tiny gardens and doors surmounted by fanlights, usually featuring a china dog. All the steps were red local sandstone and washed and scrubbed daily — any unwashed would be commented on by the neighbours. Inside, the houses were comfortable and very clean. The front room was for visitors and for courting and there was always an excess of furniture. Most carried souvenirs from distant places, brought home by relatives who were sailors and many had pets who had arrived the same way. Parrots were particularly popular. All the children lived nearby and walked to school. Cars were a rarity and no member of the large teaching staff possessed one. Traffic accidents usually involved trucks or horses and carts coming and going to the docks. The streets were quiet and safe for play — only the main roads carrying the trams and commercial traffic were dangerous, though less than today as everything moved more slowly. Horse traffic was greater than motorised, and earlier in the century the horse numbers in the city exceeded those of the population. Horses were everywhere and remained important in the carrying trade up to the mid-1950s.

There was no school uniform. Most of the boys wore short trousers up to about fourteen years of age with a jersey top. This was wool with a collar and three buttons. The girls all wore cotton dresses. The boys wore boots, mostly with iron studs to reduce wear on the sole and make them last longer. The poorest were often barefoot, which meant that in winter they didn't attend. We all got milk (1/3 pint) at the break and were made to drink it and the regular visits of the school nurses kept a check on hygiene standards, illness and head lice. Teachers were highly respected and contact with parents was minimal.

Next door to the school was the church and presbytery, ruled by the formidable Canon Kelly and assisted by his curates — fathers Taylor, Maguire, Rigby and Coupe.

St Alexander's church was a wonderful Pugin edifice with a beautiful gothic heavily gilded altar and every four weeks the whole school would attend for confession on different days. Even with four or five priests this took a long time, as the only absentees were those under seven years of age who had not yet made their first communion. It involved shifts and the long wait allowed plenty of time for preparation which shortened the time in "the box" — but not always.

The canon was a short, stocky man with iron-grey hair. He knew everybody. He was a great settler of disputes, particularly domestic ones, and was both feared and respected. The church was completely destroyed by fire bombs in the blitz of Christmas 1940, along with many of the surrounding homes and post-war planning removed the survivors. It became an industrial zone which was probably sensible in view of its proximity to the docks but it destroyed a once vibrant community with four generations of history.

The canon had earlier been the chaplain at the old Liverpool Workhouse from 1907 until it closed in 1928. The workhouse features strongly in the history of the city. Set up by the 1834 Poor Law Amendment Act, it was designed deliberately to make poverty and unemployment unattractive and harsh. Inmates were allowed no personal property or possessions — not even a prayer book. It housed over 4,000 and was entirely self-contained from maternity ward to coffin-making, a vast receptacle for the unwanted poor, aged, infirm, infected and insane, of a rapidly growing port. When Florence Nightingale, the pioneer of professional nursing, visited Liverpool workhouse in 1860, she said that conditions were worse than at Scutari.

Husbands were separated from wives, parents from children, and boys from girls. Any protest that this was contrary to nature was rebutted by the reminder that soldiers and sailors had to endure long periods of separation, so paupers could not expect anything better.

Canon Kelly of St Alexander's, Bootle, was a powerful personality, a person not easy to approach. Whether he was sent to the workhouse on that account or whether he developed such characteristics during his long period of work among what another Liverpool priest once described as "the flotsam and jetsam of humanity", who can say? But my memory of him is still vivid. His years witnessed another great public health drama in the terrible influenza outbreak of 1918, when he anointed over a hundred persons daily for a week. In normal times he did so around a thousand times a year and he used to say that had there been an award for the number of times a priest had given the last sacraments, he would have won it easily. He was no critic of the system, pointing out that many a destitute person received a roof and a bed, and without the workhouse they would not even have had that.

One day in the presbytery, I asked him what it was like in the workhouse. He pointed to a volume at least four inches thick and said, "There are nine of those recording births, but almost no records of deaths. Evidently the task of writing out the names of the dead was too great," he said, and he lowered his head.

Everybody feared ending their days there and "You'll have me in the workhouse" was the usual comment on any expense considered excessive. As times improved, so did life at the workhouse, until it closed and the city sought to redevelop the site.

Archbishop Downey thought that the site of the redundant workhouse would be ideal for the new cathedral and offered £100,000 for it. Claims were made that it would fetch twice that amount and opposition to the Catholic Church acquiring it at any price was fierce, led by the Grand Master of the Orangemen, Alderman the Revd H.D. Longbottom. The site and buildings were offered for sale by auction but bidding only reached £70,000 and as that was nowhere near the reserve price, the sale was withdrawn. The City Treasurer then contacted the archbishop to see if his offer still stood. It did, but Longbottom and his followers continued their hostility. Eventually came the day of decision and the workhouse and all its emoluments became the property of the Archdiocese of Liverpool. Addressing the assembled gathering, Archbishop Downey said, "Well it's all over, the site is ours. This is where the new cathedral will be built. But," he explained, "don't think it was a resounding victory, it wasn't. In fact we only won by a short head." Then he added in his own inimitable style, "But I suppose it is better to win by a short head than to be beaten by a long bottom."

CHAPTER
NINE

Jimmy, Father Coupe and Liverpool FC

The school playground was an arena of relentless physical activity. Tick, hopscotch, British bulldogs, leapfrog, football, skipping all intruding constantly and momentarily invading each other's space. Falling over, bruises and cuts were common, expected and ignored — just like when playing in the street. School playgrounds today are bigger, less active, dynamic or fun. Many activities are banned — in case of objection and difficulties from over-protective parents and authorities. Unfortunate for the children who just have to get rid of the bursting energy in their growing frames. Skipping was extremely popular with the girls — all that was needed was a bit of old ship's rope or washing line. Apart from the exercise, it taught timing and co-ordination, which helped when they started dancing. Group skipping was common — two girls turning the rope and two, three or more skipping in the centre with different steps from one or both feet and constantly changing performances as everybody got their turn. Sometimes the boys would leap in for a laugh and jeers from the girls — but it was all in good spirit and we were never as good as they were. It was regarded as a girls' activity — not for boys though highly regarded in boxing training — clearly a case of male deprivation! When the boys and girls left school and went to work, the lunchtimes were occupied by football for the boys and skipping for the girls. The games carried on and it was a common sight in summer to see factory girls, with skirts tied up, skipping and laughing outside the factory. They were thinner than today and maybe therein is a connection.

All forms of transport were regarded as vehicles of conveyance by boys and sometimes girls. A passing horse and empty cart would be boarded while moving from the back and used as carriage. The carter would usually shout for them to get off, but most times he would be unaware of their presence. Motor vehicles were more difficult to board, for they moved faster, but traffic lights made things easy. If it was not possible to board as in the case of vans or a fully loaded trailer, the boys would secure a handhold and just hang on the back with their legs tucked up. It was a very common and dangerous practice and there were many accidents. Anything in the cargo was treasure trove and considered fair game. Tate & Lyle sugar and molasses tankers were regularly pillaged. This involved opening the tap at the back and sometimes in haste to depart the tap would be left open leaving a trail of molasses on the road, much appreciated by the numerous roving hungry dogs, collarless and leashless and like the children running free.

146

At school, things proceeded with the odd small disturbance. I read early and read everything — the labels on any sauce bottles or jam jars or beer bottles, newspapers, advertising posters, the print on cigarette and matchboxes and particularly cigarette cards. These were included in nearly every packet of cigarettes and were very popular with children who collected them avidly. They were usually printed in series of fifty or so, and we all tried to collect complete sets. The subject matter was wide — Ships of the Royal Navy, Uniforms of Army Regiments, Footballers, Flowers, Trees, etc. They were very informative — a picture on one side and information on the reverse. I had a particular fondness for the ships, and having a good memory, I could list the weight (displacement), armament, speed, builder and launch date for much of the British Navy — all from the cards. Other boys and girls acquired a similar knowledge of their own favourite subjects from the same source. The health dangers of cigarettes have been well-aired but none have ever referred to the educational value of the humble cigarette card, beloved of all children. The collection, swapping and reading were going on in our world all the time. Today, like much of the unconsidered trifles of the past, they are collectors' items.

And so I came to the class of Miss Leamy — and the "full stop". She looked like Olive Oyl in the Popeye cartoons. Long black skirt and white blouse, mousy hair, untidy and always tied in a bun at the back. I was seven and it was time to begin "Composition" — that backbone of the English education syllabus. This would have been a difficult time for me, even without the full stop, for Miss had had a run in or two with Fran three years before and she remembered the name with great displeasure as she took the register. When she called out "Maddox" and I answered "here, Miss", raising my arm she halted and gazed at me with obvious distaste before continuing. I knew then it was going to be a bad time and so it was. In addition to my carrying the baggage from Fran's open rejection of the great teacher, she was also a very poor instructor. Allied to this was a large class and very few of us could grasp what she was trying to tell us. If she wanted full stops she could have them, so she got them — a composition with a full stop after every word. She greeted this gleefully and abused me soundly for some minutes. For this she had waited for three years. I lacked Fran's ability to make her feel like something crawling out of the cheese (his specialty) and just had to take it. The bell sounded for the end of the lesson and we still didn't know what the full stop was, or what it was for. At home that evening, May explained it to me (and the comma) in a couple of minutes. Parents were rarely seen at the school and this was tacitly regarded as a good thing all round. The children didn't want any transference of information from teacher to parent, or vice versa. The teachers were well-regarded generally and parents deferred to them on education quite happily. All lady teachers were expected to leave if they married, the perceived wisdom being that a family and a class of pupils was just too much and a massive conflict of interest which would be good for neither group and too great a burden for the teacher. Only serious deviations by pupils were considered as matters requiring discussion with the headmaster — these were very few. This separation of worlds led the children to fight their own battles, which has nearly always been the best teacher for life. Intrusion by parents or others rarely leads to better results. I kept quiet at home about Miss Leamy and her grudge against the family name.

I had made my first communion the same year I entered Miss Leamy's class and now for the first time I joined the school ranks assembled for confession in the beautiful St Alexander's church, with its lovely gilded and decorated altar. The confession boxes were on either side of the nave and we sat in the side aisle benches leaving the broad middle aisle benches empty.

It was a big moment for me as it was my first confession under my own steam. We were on the right wing and in the group going into Father Coupe, who was the least popular of the priests. Quite young (around thirty), pale-faced, ascetic; unlike the others, little given to smiles or laughter. The waiting time was supposed to be spent in preparation for confession by examining the conscience and seeing where we'd offended and done bad things. Most seven-year-olds don't have a lot of bad things to confess and I was somewhat confused by the order of the Command-ments from one to ten, as well as my efforts at manufacturing sin and things to confess. I had no difficulty with understanding stealing, killing, keeping holy the Sabbath day and even calumny and detraction — my liking for words got me round that one, but things like adultery, I couldn't at this stage, get a handle on, though I was sure whatever it was I hadn't done it. I blundered into the dark of the confessional past the boy coming out and knelt down. "Bless me father for I have sinned" so far so good, but it was the fourth commandment that did me. I couldn't get the sin and the order right and I came to a halt. A gruff, impatient voice urged me to "get on with it", but I couldn't. The voice grew angrier but no response.

"Get out!" it said, and I did, and as I left, his own door opened and I was abused in a loud voice in front of all the waiting confessees all the way as I left the church, blessing myself from the holy water font on my way out. Undaunted, I then re-entered by the door on the left for the other side of the church, blessing myself yet again on re-entry. It was dark inside and no one noticed my arrival. I joined the back of the queue for Father Rigby, a jolly, red-faced priest, and eventually made my confession without any difficulty. I was late getting home but said nothing to anybody.

This experience gave me an unjustified status with my fellows who questioned me later. What great sin had I committed? My inability to tell them was regarded as a reluctance and unwillingness to reveal more, due to the immensity of my crime against God. I was certainly not big enough to have killed my father, but my sin must be great! I had been refused absolution. It was like a junior version of the *Playboy of the Western World*. My status was immense. Thinking about it at the time, I thought Father Coupe was not well, which he may not have been and hearing a couple of hundred schoolboy confessions in a single day could be said to be enough to unhinge anybody.

Whatever, it in no way affected how I thought about the priesthood or my religion. I was fighting my own battles early — Miss Leamy and Father Coupe within a short time of each other — it had to get better. And it did.

Miss Lee was slim, in her mid-forties, with grey hair and flashing eyes with a reputation as a martinette, which was probably justified. She was a disciplinarian and had a reputation for being tempestuous. She was also a good teacher. My entry into her class at the end of the year was assisted by her liking for my father. I don't know how or why they met, but in her class my name was a positive. Fran seems to have passed through her year without difficulty, which helped. With her I made rapid progress, particularly in arithmetic, which I discovered was my best subject. It was genetic — inherited from father who had an exceptional gift for numbers and using them. He would later delight me by showing me how to add up by starting at the left-hand column, not the right, which is how it is conventionally taught. It was a good year with Miss Lee and it was to be my only complete year of normal schooling for some years. England was now at war and preparations for evacuation were well in hand.

At school everyone was getting ready for travel — to Wales mostly — but also more locally to rural and non-strategic areas outside the city with schools and space. St Alexander's was to close except for a small skeleton staff which would continue using part of the school presbytery next door. This was for children who couldn't leave. The church was staying and preparing itself for the worst, being located right in the centre of the docks area.

The evacuation process was simple in its execution. All the children were collected at school and put on a train with supervising teachers and with an identifying card around their neck (for the youngest) and with a small case or bag containing spare clothes and despatched to a "safe" area. There they were taken from house to house, or assembled in a local hall for selection by local families and offered as paying guests at a rate set by the government. What is remarkable is how well it all worked. Both sides adapted, hosts and children, and the local schools changed character completely as they accepted the large influx of worldly-wise city children. There was adjustment on all sides, sometimes painful but all educational. Country meets city widened perceptions at a stroke.

Our group was sent to Ainsdale — up the coast near Southport about fifteen miles away and easily reached from Liverpool and Bootle by the train. It is a nice pleasant resort — not on the sea but about a mile inland. We were offered to a Mrs Bimpson, who had a confectionery and sweet shop on the parade, near to the station. She seemed quite happy to have us, and as the operation had been advertised in the area, nobody was surprised when the refugees appeared. The authorities had sensibly insisted that brothers and sisters be kept together, so Fran and I joined the Bimpson household and were given a pleasant room over the shop, facing the main road. We were not to be there long, however, for May considered that an ice cream cornet was inadequate for supper and we were repossessed and returned to the city after a few weeks. We had mixed feelings about this as Ainsdale offered pine woods, red squirrels and seashore, which were new to us and we found it attractive. Mrs Bimpson was OK, the food was not the greatest in either quality or quantity, but she was clean and pleasant and had no children of her own. We were quite happy there, not far from home and the school was fairly new with gardens, and beautifully located with nice teachers. But, it was not to be, and back we went.

Most of the others remained and Leonard Mudd, who was in my class, was particularly lucky in placement with a nice lady with a large house on the left-hand side of the road to the beach, just over the level crossing. She was very kind and allowed him to show me round. She had no children of her own and though young, I made an immediate comparison with no. 3 Rooney Street, where he lived. It was no contest.

The Marine was like the docks. People always coming and going like ships. No one seemed to stay long. They would arrive and go but would then reappear at odd moments when totally unexpected. I liked this as it brought all manner of interesting characters into the house. Father was always bringing people up from the bar without warning for May to feed, and there was always something for them. This resulted in many friendships — some short, alas, owing to the war at sea and the battle for the Atlantic. Most

153

were merchant seamen and foreign, cut off from their homes and families by the German conquest of Europe. Their delight and appreciation of a home and having a meal surrounded by children and pets was manifest, reminding them of what was out of reach in their own life — how long would it be so? For me there was the benefit that they would happily talk to small boys in their broken English with exciting tales of war at sea. Additionally coins were often received, which were always welcome. The giving of money to children was a common and popular practice in those years, which seems to have almost completely vanished, mostly it seems due to parental opposition, certainly the children were all in favour.

The visitors were sometimes able to return the hospitality and visits and tea on their ships would follow. The Royal Navy were the best for such trips with their guns, torpedoes and depth charges — a particular attraction and chance for me to expand and expound my cigarette-card knowledge. One visit to the cruiser *Sussex* in March 1940 (guests of Senior Chief Petty Officer Tunnicliffe), was particularly memorable for both the excitement of entering the 8-inch gun turrets and the splendid tea which followed. She was a lucky ship and would survive the war, though she was quite old and not fast.

A favourite visitor was "Jimmy the Greek" from Piraeus, a bosun in a small Greek freighter who lived close by with Phoebe and Charlie Randall when his ship was in port. Small, dark, flashing eyes and heavily jewelled — he became my friend and always took any opportunity to talk to me on his frequent visits.

"Look in there!" said May, indicating the sitting room to me in the autumn evening as I came in from play. I opened the door, switched on the light and on the table in the centre of the room was a model ship — Jimmy's ship with the paint not yet fully dry. I was transfixed — about 18 inches long on a stand — every bit made by Jimmy from bits of wood and metal while he was at sea.

"Is it for me?" I asked.

"Yes, it's from Jimmy, it's his ship."

It became my proudest possession.

Jimmy didn't have much luck. Leaving Liverpool next voyage, his ship (my ship) was torpedoed just into the Irish Sea and so he was back in Liverpool a couple of days later. His next ship, a week later, failed to get as far, hitting a mine in Liverpool Bay and sinking in minutes and so he was back again. He had for some time suffered from "a grumbling appendix" and had been told that it would need removal at some time in the future. Not wishing for it to flare up while he was at sea, for only the largest vessels carry doctors, Jimmy thought he'd have it done now, which would also allow his nerves to recover after his recent sinkings. So he entered Walton Hospital and had the appendix removed without complications. A shipmate visited him in hospital and brought him some fruit. He was not allowed food after the operation to allow healing, but for some reason couldn't resist an apple. The apple skin caught the surgical stitches and septicaemia set in. He died in a few days — there was nothing anybody could do. The irony of dying from an apple after surviving two explosive shipwrecks affected everybody. The ship he gave me was his memorial — I see the ship and I see Jimmy, with his heavily ringed fingers and infectious smile.

May had a lot of visitors, but rarely had the time to go out visiting herself — there was too much to do. Tom was different. Every Wednesday he took his half-day off and went to see his best friend Herbie Bolton. They were long-time friends and Herbie was also a pub manager — of the "Banjo" at the bottom of Wolsey Street. Before arriving at the Banjo, Tom always visited his mother and sister Winnie, never without gifts. He was the most generous of men, and children were particularly favoured. Winnie had married a French sailor in the Free French Navy, whose ship had made for Liverpool following De Gaulle's call to arms when France collapsed in the middle of 1940. I was much taken with Alex and his happy, brown, handsome face and flashing eyes. In his matelot's uniform and red pom-pom hat he was an attractive sight. He always seemed to be smiling. Winnie was the youngest in the family and a slim, pure white, natural blonde and a fine pianist. It was a case of strong mutual attraction and although Alex was away in the Battle of the Atlantic nearly all of the time, three daughters were produced in a short time. As Alex was away, Winnie and the children lived with her mother. Winnie and grandmother made up one of those relationships based on mutual devotion and love for each other, and the constant mutual expression of strong emotions affectionate or otherwise, "so all day long the noise of battle rolled" (Tennyson).

Jim, husband and father of the contestants, was a serene man, totally untouched by the turbulence around him. This serenity, grandmother regarded sometimes as a provocation itself. Jim, in from work, washed and waiting for tea, reading the *Liverpool Echo* by the fire while Mary Jane would be talking rapidly with a friend from up the street.

"Isn't that right Jim?"

"Yes Mary Jane, that's right."

(A pause!) "No it isn't!" she'd reply, and then subject him to abuse like, "you don't know what you're talking about", before carrying on where she'd left off with her crony. Jim carried on reading the paper totally unperturbed.

He was, in appearance, slim, medium to tall in height and extremely well-groomed, the result probably of his long-service as a regular soldier in the King's Regiment (as a sharpshooter). He had been in Egypt for many years with the army but he and Mary Jane had still managed to produce six children — three boys and three girls. Jim was a man of many parts. According to Mary Jane he couldn't read or write when she met him and his letters from Egypt, she said, were written for him by a Madame Serafini. I never knew if this was true, but he read the *Echo* every evening before his tea and he wrote with a fine hand, so I had doubts about this story. Madame Serafini's name often seemed to enter the conversation in the house and I nosily interrupted Mary Jane one day when she mentioned it as she talked to a crony as she buttered the bread.

"Who is Madame Serafini, Grandma?"

"She's a friend of your Grandfather in Egypt who wrote all his letters for him when he was there."

"Why didn't he write them himself?"

"He couldn't write then, and so he found this woman — now go and play," and she passed me a butty with the crony smiling archly beside her.

I liked the sound of Madame Serafini — it was an exotic name in an exotic land and I wanted to know more. Why did Grandma seem to not like her? I wanted to ask Grandfather, but was deterred by his natural authority as he quietly read his newspaper.

After the army, he went to work for Wilsons, a steel fabrication company, and produced for us many items including knives, fire irons, and a set of stainless steel cooking pans, still in family use. In the evenings he worked as the commissionnaire at the Metropole Theatre in Bootle, where he looked very grand in his dark-brown uniform overcoat and peaked hat with gold trim. His military bearing, added to his calm manner, gave him a natural authority which I recognised also in his son, my own father. It was a useful characteristic, particularly for Tom in controlling a lively public house. I also saw its value as bowler-hatted, umbrella-in-hand, he walked unchallenged past armed sentries on the landing stage for the Dublin boat on our trips to Ireland.

Depending on the season, Tom and Herbie usually spent the afternoon at the cinema with dinner to follow at the Turkey Shop in London Road or playing golf or bowls. At other times the managers' association "The Kitty Blues" would arrange an excursion and this was always a good opportunity to talk shop and meet other publican friends. Many managers were ex-footballers — like Dixie Dean, Norman Greenhalgh and Ted Sagar, the former Everton players. Ted was a footballer until he was over forty and much liked in the group. League football ceased when war began. All the players were conscripted and games were arranged as and when it was possible. Players turned out for whatever team was near their barracks or station. There were some wonderful wartime games with combinations of players that fans could only dream about. Some regimental sides were of international standard and the British Army team featured the best of the four nations players — not just the English. The only limitation was whether you could get to the game if you were picked — travel was difficult.

Shortly after arriving at the Marine, Tom met Bill McConnell. Bill was a caterer who ran his family company which operated a chain of canteens on the Mersey Docks Estate on both sides of the river. Feeding the docks was a massive task with perhaps around 100,000 working there every day: dockers, ships' crews, ship repair workers, suppliers, security staff, carters and drivers, etc. Bill was up to the job, handling supply chain, Ministry of Food regulations, licences, rationing, staffing, bomb damage, etc. and he always seemed cheerful. They got on very well together and Bill was soon suggesting that Tom would do much better if he came and worked for him. For whatever reason, Tom resisted these entreaties although they saw each other most days, for Bill's office was only a few doors away.

I was sorry Father didn't join Bill for many reasons. First we would have moved from the Marine, which though exciting was always in the thick of the action and very limited in what it could offer in terms of lifestyle and leisure. Even more important was the fact that Bill was a director, and later Chairman of Liverpool Football Club. When competition restarted after the war, Bill and Tom would go off to the match together and on one occasion (an FA Cup semi-final against Burnley in 1946), took Fran as well. I was too young, they said, even though I was going regularly to Liverpool at Anfield under my own steam. There was a "Boys' Pen" at one corner of the ground for lads like us, but we wanted to be with the big boys and the men. We considered the pen beneath us. It was 1s 3d to get into the Kop — roughly the price of a pint of beer — and that was where I went with Bernie O'Connor, a classmate from school. Queuing with the men to get in we'd listen to their talk about the team — our team.

"Nivvy's past it, he's blowing for tugs before half time."

"Priday's no better, they should both go back to South Africa."

"The only winger we've got is Liddell and the RAF won't let him go."

"Laurie Hughes will do for me, there's nothing gets past that lad and he's only nineteen."

Then we'd arrive at the turnstile, manned often by ex-players. When I'd learnt who they were I'd push my autograph book with the entrance money and a pen through the tiny window.

"Can I have your autograph, please?"

With a smile they'd sign and pass the book back as they released the gate, pleased to be recognised still, long after they'd last heard the adulation of the crowd. My first signing was Ephraim Longworth, then nearly sixty, captain of Liverpool and England in the early 1920s — a legend and at the club since 1910. Liverpool FC was like that — you could be there for life. Once inside we were entertained by a musical selection from the resident Edge Hill LMS Brass Band on the centre of the pitch and with the flag flying strongly from the mast of Brunel's "Great Eastern" at the corner of the Kop we waited.

Just before 3p.m. the band marched off to applause and the teams came on. Kemlyn Road side saw them first and triggered the roar which spread and reached a crescendo audible a long way off. Game on, and the tribe at play. This was why God made Saturday and we hoped he'd be on our side today.

We'd get down to the front behind the goal, for being small, we couldn't see the game from anywhere else on the Kop. Shouting and singing, abusing and praising along with the rest of the Kop's 28,000 we had a great time at every home game, even if we lost. Being a caterer, Bill McConnell the Chairman, knew the value of good nutrition and so took the team to America on a pre-season tour before league football resumed after the

161

war. This was away from the austerity of Britain where no one had seen a good steak for years. He also brought Albert Stubbins, the Newcastle United centre forward, to the club. He was the missing piece in the team jigsaw and Liverpool were triumphant as champions for the fourth time, in this first post-war season.

Travel was difficult at this time but the American tour logistics were easy as Cunard liners sailed for New York from the landing stage at the Pier Head. The departure point was roughly only a mile from the ground at Anfield.

During this period Bill was still trying to get Father to come and work for him and, eavesdropping as he and May talked, I knew all about it. It was a subject which persisted. I was naturally in favour of the combination, and maybe it could lead to Father working at Liverpool FC. Tom was an excellent manager and Bill knew it, but for whatever reason it never happened. Perhaps Tom felt it would damage their friendship or maybe he just lacked ambition and liked his pub. Being of a philosophical nature I reasoned that I preferred standing in the Kop anyway, to being with the great and the good in the stands where behaviour is more restrained and restrictive. I like being with the mob and shouting encouragement and abuse at the players. I blame the Commodore and our Saturday matinées.

Money, they say, has ruined the game but it was money which brought Liverpool the Championship in 1947. At that time, all clubs were limited by maximum wage legislation. No player could be paid more than £10 per week plus a bonus for winning. It didn't matter who he played for, the wage was the same. There was no financial motive to change club. This restricted the movement of players between clubs which also had the power to keep a player at the club, even if he wanted to leave. This would last until the 1960s when George Eastham, an Arsenal player, challenged the legality of the rule and had it revoked. From then, freedom of contract applied and players began moving between clubs in search of higher earnings and the glory of winning trophies. In 1946 it was different — there was no legal financial incentive for a player to move clubs though there were plenty of things against it, such as the disruption of family life and going to an area where the player and his family knew nobody. There wasn't the compensation of more money to ease the process.

Albert Stubbins came because Bill gave him another job as "Inspector of Canteens" with his company at an excellent salary — more than he was getting for playing football. His inspectorial duties were heavy and necessitated in total going with Bill to a different canteen roughly once a week for an hour or so after morning training. The visit involved "testing" the quality of the tea — served in one-pint enamel mugs and chatting informally with dockers, etc. many of whom were Liverpool supporters. It was good PR and mutually beneficial, but Albert would never have transferred without Bill's temptation of a second salary to make it all worthwhile. When Bill died suddenly a few years later, everything changed and soon after the club was relegated to the second division. It is unlikely that this would have occurred had he lived. Like most of the supporters, I still continued to turn up on Saturday to watch them in the second division — playing inferior opposition we thought, but the team found it hard to get back to the first division and despite a number of near misses it would not take place until a man named Shankly became manager in 1963.

Bill McConnell introduced us to another ancient sport — "Ratting". This was a popular sport in earlier times and the local Merchant Taylor's School Records chronicle one headmaster who would close the school for the day and take the boys ratting — so there was a tradition. There were rats everywhere — especially in the pubs, canteens and warehouses anywhere there was food. Father set six rat trap cages in the cellars every night and it was rare to find any one without a tenant the following morning. Cage and incumbent were then submerged in the large cellar water butt and that was that for the poor rats. The cages were then reset that night and so it continued, but we never noticed any reduction in their numbers around us in the cellars. Bill had the same problem with his canteens and he employed a full time rat-catcher who started to use "live-in" terriers in each canteen. They were very effective — much more so than cats and to settle an argument it was decided to hold a competition to see which dog was the best. This involved putting each dog and twelve rats in a steel tank with wire mesh top. The dog was timed from entry to the last rat. A small Lakeland Terrier was the clear winner (a bitch) and so we got Spike, one of her pups. Spike never took to the job, probably because he was too well fed. The rat problem was with us all the time and there were also problems with other species. There had been some pilfering in the bar — of cigarettes (Woodbines in packets of five at 2d a pack). Father one night emptied the cigarettes from the Woodbine box and put in two dead rats. He was summoned hastily from bed the next morning by one of the two cleaners. The other had fainted and still had the lid of the Woodbine box in her hand. She soon came to and nothing further was said other than, "Are you alright Maggie?" and a faint "Yes" in reply. The lid was replaced on the box but Father forgot to remove the rats and there was a repeat performance from the beautiful blonde Gwladys the barmaid when she opened the box for an early customer who wanted "Five Woodies".

The rats, like ourselves, were hungry and after food all the time. Food began appearing in strange guises as America started to feed us. Apples were apple rings — peeled, cored, dried and ready in wooden boxes. Eggs were powdered and butter, cheese, bacon and a host of other provisions were now in tins. Items supplied in bulk, like butter all tasted of their time in the refrigerators of ship and cold stores. Tinned meats replaced fresh in many areas, including restaurants, and were quite popular. I loved the large 6lb tins of corned and brisket beef with their tasty juices and jelly and couldn't understand why they came in rectangular tins and the ox tongue came in round ones. These were May's reserve when all the beef was gone and then Spam arrived from America. It was popular immediately and a factory was set up in Liverpool to manufacture it locally, such was the demand. I loved it — in sandwiches, fried, with salad — anywhere. Being in tins, the rats got none.

I was fascinated always by the butchers' slabs. There was not a lot on display in the war as the butchers were rationed too, but nevertheless they made attempts to put something in the window. Offal and unpopular cuts of meat were not rationed and as there was little else, people bought them. Bloodied sheep's heads, with skin removed and empty black eye sockets glaring menacingly at us, were a regular on the slab. These made a rich and good soup with barley and carrots and any leftovers. At 2*d* a head they'd always been an item for the poorest who'd developed great skills in producing tasty, warm fare for a winter's day. The butcher cleaved the head in two lengthwise and the customer then just dropped it into a big pan and boiled it — for hours. The smell was terrible, even when the windows and doors were open. The aroma of sheep's head soup became a subject of jokes and humour. The pig's head fared better, but not by much. It was on the fire or stove longer and the smell was as bad, but it produced brawn which was a local favourite. Pigs' feet, another favourite, sold out quickly after arriving pickled in barrels of dry salt. I liked all the pigs' produce but kept at distance from the sheep. The baleful sheep's head and the aromas as they boiled had put me off.

CHAPTER
TEN

Music, Miss Morrison and
the Cake

One afternoon we arrived home from school and there, in the sitting room, was a brand new Van Gruisen highly polished walnut piano from their shop in Bold Street. It was a complete surprise though May had long planned it, but not told us. She was going to learn the piano and play it properly — a considered decision — no spur-of-the-moment thing, but she never revealed the real reason until years later. I sang a lot in the house and May liked it and decided to develop it, so that was why we got the piano.

On our next trip to town we bought a piano tutor of the "learn to play in 10 easy lessons" variety, and the sheet music for one of the popular songs of the moment which I liked. Then May went to work. Teaching herself from the book, she applied herself and was able to play quite soon from the sheet music bought on our trips. She practised while we were at school and when she had mastered the piece she subtly inveigled me into the sitting room and taught me the songs we had chosen. I was a willing pupil and progressed and she then took the next step and persuaded me to sing for our guests for my first professional fee of a shilling at one of our parties. It brought with it applause and extra coins from the audience (both pleasing) and in the course of time she had produced a singer who, though only eight years old, was a regular public performer with a repertoire — all sung correctly in the right key both verse and chorus.

The chorus is the part that everyone knows and can sing but the verses are usually little known, yet therein lies the beauty and poetry in the composition, the story and feelings behind the affirmation of the chorus.

May understood this and stressed its importance. "The verse tells the story of the song," she would say, and I remembered.

Here is a mother's tale — the buying of a piano she can't play and her struggle to learn so she can teach her little son to sing properly.

"You are telling a story but with music — each will help the other, and don't rush."

I was unaware of what she was doing and the value of what she was teaching me at the time, and only realised later in life that she was "orchestrating" me, as mothers do. It changed me and my life and was a lasting benediction. "The law gives little power to women, since nature has given them so much." (Dr Johnson)

May's visitors were mostly relations — brothers, sisters, cousins and in-laws. These were quite numerous and then there were friends she had acquired along the way. Of these, Mrs Morrison was the most important. She was older than May by ten or fifteen years and very different — I found her interesting. Every week (on a Wednesday) she would appear at the same time in the afternoon and stay for about three hours. She was Irish, nicely softly spoken and the latest in a long line of Mrs Malaprops — her main felicitous misuse of the language consisted of an inability to distinguish between occupations and the tools of their trades. A friend of her daughter was "a typewriter", not a typist, and she was going out with "an aircraft carrier" not just a fleet air arm pilot. Another beau was a "confounded" bachelor (not a confirmed one). May never attempted to correct her — in some ways the story was improved by her choice of words, or so we thought, for immediately on her departure I would go to May and ask, "What did she say?" and smiling, she would tell me. Mrs Morrison had other qualities also. She had been born poor and had joined the household of a gentry family (Lord Winnington) where she had graduated over the years to the exalted state of ladies' maid. This was the summit in "service" for any lowborn female and it was akin to the position of companion in many places. This was something she was obviously well suited to and over the years she became gentrified, adopting the graces and manners of her mistress. Dressed like a lady in neat black suit and hat, cream blouse and cravat with single row of pearls and black shoes, with handbag and gloves to match, she was an exotic in the jungle as she stepped off the tram outside the Marine.

She was so different from most other women we met that I wanted to know more about her. Being in service

169

since the age of fourteen, she took the values and standards of her employer for her own. People who worked were "in trade, my dear". The gentry never worked — it was degrading, but she was without side and not a snob. Though in domestic service, her duties had never been on the culinary side and she couldn't cook. She didn't have any idea how food was prepared — and could just about manage afternoon tea with neatly cut cucumber sandwiches and a cake bought locally. Every Christmas she would arrive some weeks before the great day with a Christmas cake she had "baked". It varied little from year to year. The thing was about two inches thick and a little wider than a side plate. She brought it each time to May for her to put on marzipan and icing. "You do it so nicely, my dear". This task was beyond her competence and this day she had been and gone, and lying on the table was her cake as Father sat down with us to have his tea before opening the bar at 5.30. His eyes lighted on the cake.

"What's this?"

"Mrs Morrison's cake for icing," said May.

Father picked it up and felt it.

"It feels more like a cartwheel to me."

May smiled, "Yes just a bit."

I knew there was mischief afoot as he looked at me and said, "Shall we see if it is?"

"Yes!" I replied immediately, and with that he rolled the cake like the fine bowler he was along the kitchen floor at high speed. It went the length of the room and hit the skirting board at the end with a dull thump and fell over and lay face down. It was undamaged, not a crumb was lost in the travel and collision. We all burst out laughing.

"She does her best," said May, as she picked up the missile and put it on the draining board away from Father.

"See, I was right, it is a wheel," he said as he left the table grinning and went below.

I cannot remember a year in that period when the cake didn't arrive on schedule. Neither can I remember a year when Mrs Morrison got her own cake back, for May baked and iced a clandestine replacement — the same size — for her every time. The only occasion when May might have been found out was the first, when her cake led Mr Morrison to compliment his wife on the quality of her baking that year. "Himself said that's the nicest cake I've made," she said to May smiling with pleasure. Thereafter the cake came from the same source every year and suspicion was allayed. Her own baking never improved and each year she brought us a new wheel or piece of rolling stock for our amusement.

Then there was the fortune-telling. After the tea was finished Mrs Morrison would turn her cup upside down on her saucer and drain the cup of any tea left. But the tea leaves remained, adhering to the sides in patterns which could foresee the future, or so she believed. I don't know how it started but she really believed both the practice and May's ability to read the leaves. May was most convincing and with my ear pressed to the closed door, I heard the following exchange:

"What do you see, my dear."

"It's not too clear, it could be a visitor."

"That would be 'the Fine Woman' (a friend in London). I had a letter from her on Monday and she's coming to her sister's in Liverpool and then to see us."

Then a pause, "and what else?"

"Let me turn the cup," said May. "Looks like money, but it's hard to see any more about it." This was a safe prediction, for Mrs Morrison was in line for a small legacy when her aunt died and May knew this and so it went on. I wanted to know how she did it.

"How do you know what to say?"

"Just look at the pattern and shape of the leaves and think what they remind you of."

"You don't believe it?" I said, a little concerned and thinking of what Father Coupe would say if he heard about it. May smiled. "Of course not, but it's harmless and Mrs Morrison looks forward to it every week. You try it."

And I did. Picking up her teacup I turned it upside-down on the saucer like Mrs Morrison did, to let it drain and show the leaves which would reveal the future. May looked at me, all attention as I lifted the cup and looked into the bowl. There was a good leaf dispersion but what did it suggest? The sky at night with all the stars, bed, sleep and dream perhaps. Yes that would do. "You're going to have a dream," I said.

"What about?" I was now on my way and saw a pattern which suggested a shamrock. "It's about Ireland." "Anything more?" said May, but there wasn't anything more because I burst out laughing. She was amused.

"Well you've got an imagination, anyway. Maybe you should do it for her next week?" and we laughed.

Perhaps Mrs Morrison's finest hour was when she discovered racing and betting.

She arrived one afternoon when the *Echo* was being examined on the kitchen table. All the runners for the Grand National were listed with weights, owners, jockeys and prices. Father and May were discussing form and odds as Mrs Morrison arrived.

"I still fancy Battleship," said Father "and at 10-1 it's the favourite." May was good at this and had been studying form for the great local race for some weeks. We got four newspapers every day for the news rack in the bar and May, who got up first to let the cleaners in and make the sandwiches, had studied the racing pages before placing them on the rack for the customers when the bar opened. She was well informed.

"I'm going for an outsider — Morning Glory. A shilling each way — at 50-1 it's a good each-way bet."

This was an unfamiliar world to the listening Mrs Morrison. Horseracing and gambling — not allowed at home where the Dad's strict regime applied.

When Father went below and they were talking as usual over tea, Mrs Morrison suddenly said.

"The race sounds exciting, could you put a bet on for me"

"Yes, if you wish," said May, and so after scanning the runners for a name she liked she said, "Leprechaun," and copying May said, "A shilling each way." She then opened her purse and passed a florin across the table.

Leprechaun came nowhere and the following Wednesday at a break in the conversation she said,

"And have you got my winnings, dear?"

"But you didn't win."

"I know but my bet was a shilling each-way, a shilling for winning and a shilling for losing."

"Each way means only the first four places, not the whole field," said May who then had to explain how it all worked. Though saddened, she took it well. Her naïvety surprised even May, for she imagined the Irish to be horse people and to love and understand a bet and all that goes with it.

Being a nosy child, I always wanted to listen to her conversation with Mother and this was allowed but only up to a point where our visitor would consider she had something to tell May which was not suitable for the ears of the young. At this point she would smile at me and say, "Now Jack I've something to tell your mother and you must leave us," at the same time she opened a lovely small black purse and took out a silver threepenny piece which she pressed into my hand. This always softened the blow of rejection, and I would immediately leave the house and spend my newly acquired wealth. On one occasion I remember walking all the way to the fairground at Seaforth and back to spend it on the roundabouts. The tram would have cost a halfpenny each way but that would have meant one ride less. I was always impressed by her style which was apparent in everything — even the silver threepenny piece. At that time they were being replaced by the larger, heavier ugly brass version but they were to have no place in her purse and I remember thinking how well silver and slim black leather purse matched. She smoked de Rezke cigarettes from their distinctive orange-lidded box. A ladies' cigarette — smaller than full-size and named after the famous operatic tenor idolised by women worldwide. "It's a nice cigarette, my dear."

She was married to "the Dad" and this was a matching of opposites — the beauty and the beast. He was large and powerful with an organ voice which was audible even in the noisiest of gatherings at Christmas. He was as rough as she was refined, and basically a bully, but he was also entertaining in a totally different way. They had two daughters — Blanche, the elder, feminine, like the mother, and Muriel — a female version of "the Dad". Their family story was interesting.

They came from Cork where the inhabitants have a reputation for being keen on a penny. During "the Troubles" and the civil war in Ireland, terrible things occurred. Many of them, pitting family and friends against each other. The effects linger still.

The Dad was in the RIC (Royal Irish Constabulary), for Ireland was under British rule and there was very little work available, so the biggest employer was the British Crown with the army and the RIC to keep law and order. The Nationalist movement was growing in strength all the time and though the principle of self-government had been agreed and given status by

Parliament in 1914, the House of Lords and Ulster were holding things up. As a way of increasing the pressure on the British Government, a group of teachers decided to embargo the teaching of children of servants of the crown. This led to the children of soldiers and policemen being sent home from school. The leader in this seems to have been a virago named Miss McSwiney, a teacher in Cork. She was very active politically and was the sister of the Mayor of Cork, Terence McSwiney. At this point things got out of hand and accidentally beyond local control. The dispute became major when the RIC decided a little local pressure could restore the "status quo" and get their children out of the house and back to school so they arrested the mayor and sent him to England. There he began a fast which ended in his death and martyrdom. All the participants knew each other and the arresting party (the Dad and three others) became marked men under sentence of death. The authorities shipped them and their families out of the area to secret locations in England and after the anonymity of London, the Morrisons came to Liverpool, where they had friends. The Dad kept a low profile. His three companions at the arrest were all found and "dealt with" in the years following but the Dad survived, though he feared a knock on the door until he died nearly fifty years later. During all that time his family lived quietly on his pension, which must have been generous for they lived in their own house in Waterloo, and seemed to have most things. The only time he worked was during the war when he served as Master at Arms on troopships.

This position involved the maintenance of law and order among the troops on ship and command of the brig, the ship's gaol. He enjoyed those years and was well suited to his duties.

Afterwards, he settled into a daily regime of long walks along the coast of Liverpool Bay with a bottle of water in his pocket and when there was a game on, a visit to Waterloo Rugby Club. Visiting with mother, I joined him one day on one of these walks and he entertained me mightily talking of all sorts of subjects — but never of himself. Rugby in those days was an amateur game and entry to the matches was free. A collection for expenses and maintenance would be held after the match at the gate on the way out and the Dad instructed his wife to obtain a shilling's worth of farthings for him from Mr Maddox (the pubs had change). Even then the farthing was almost redundant and little used though it would still buy a box of matches. Forty-eight farthings was enough for a lot of matches and nobody could see his offering in the dim light of the winter afternoons. Very keen on the pennies they are in Cork.

The daughters, Blanche and Muriel, I remember well. Blanche was slim and in bad health with TB — that scourge of the time. She had spent time in sanitoria in Arizona and locally at Rufford Hall but she died young — a soft gentle girl. One evening the Dad found that she had by mistake used his knife and fork. He raged and bent the cutlery shapeless and threw it into the fire in front of poor Blanche. She was dead less than a year later. Little did he think he would be similarly afflicted in the future but his iron constitution carried him through, helped by the advances made in drug treatment since Blanche's death.

Muriel had the heaviest legs I've ever seen on a woman. I think they were bigger than the Dad's. I first became aware of her when she was about fifteen when we made a rare visit to the Morrison household. Muriel arrived home on a massive three-wheeler bike. I had never seen such a contraption and with her mounted and the enormous legs pedalling strongly and without any embarrassment it was a most unusual sight. Evidently she couldn't ride a two-wheeler so this was her regular transport to and from school and everywhere else. She later became a teacher and had an unfortunate marriage to a Mr Pietersen a policeman from South Africa whom she met on holiday in Switzerland. He had plans to be a hotelier when he retired and was planning an emigration to the USA. He was spending his leave at a hotel school in Switzerland and his plans were well advanced. They included two young mute black men whom he wanted to take as (probably unpaid) cheap labour. Would Muriel like to join him and his great venture in the future?

Poor Muriel, nearly forty and feeling comfortable with his police background and behaviour, said yes. Another case of the girl marrying her father syndrome. The two policemen met and got on extremely well and so she emigrated and married. The Dad was glad it was in South Africa as he escaped having to pay for the wedding. What luck, he thought. In a short time Muriel's passport was in the police station safe and everything fell apart. With clandestine assistance from the embassy she was secreted across the border into British jurisdiction in Rhodesia, issued with a new passport and returned to the Dad. She lived to a good age and took to visiting us in her advanced years. These visits brought to us the didactic and instructive dispensation of advice on many things and invitations to tea. The latter were to be avoided at all cost. May had succumbed to her invitation on one occasion and gave a description of the ham sliced thickly and bread cut with a chain saw — truly her father's daughter and the extreme opposite of her dainty, refined mother.

Downstairs in the bar there were always some unwelcome visitors intent on trouble, but a public house is open to all and for the benefit and welcome of everybody, unless they transgress and interfere with other customers' enjoyment of the premises. Trouble-makers were asked to leave and if unwilling, would be thrown out. It was as simple as that. Normally this would not be necessary but when it happened, it could be spectacular. I was playing in the bright, sunny evening in the street outside. We had moved in a few weeks earlier and we stopped our game as voices were raised in the pub.

"I'm staying here till you serve me."

Then I recognised Father's voice. "You're banned, now go home."

"No, I want a pint."

"Well get it somewhere else."

The next thing that happened was the main door opening and Father emerging at pace dragging by the

179

collar a man I didn't recognise. Father halted suddenly and released his hold and the offender was propelled from the door to the far set of tramlines. He usually delegated this duty to the head barman but on this occasion he was having a break and a smoke in the cellar, and so father gave a demonstration of how it should be done. Fortunately there were no trams or traffic passing at the time.

"Gosh your dad's tough!" said Stevie Porter. I didn't reply, totally occupied with the action and thinking that it was a bit like the saloon scenes in the cowboy films where all the fighting takes place. I think it was the first time I'd seen him expel somebody. He was not an aggressive man and never hit Fran or me in the whole of our lives. He didn't even shout at us, so seeing him in the rôle of sheriff — and preserving law and order and driving the "baddies" out of town, starting with the saloon, surprised me. I felt proud to have a father like that and even Stevie, my friend from the notoriously wild and tough Porter family, had been impressed — and they knew about these things.

After ejection, offenders very rarely tried to re-enter and on this occasion the poor ejectee just picked himself up got back on the pavement, picking up a small child who'd fallen over who was in his way and walked off back to where he'd come from.

I saw many of these ejections and contests which provided a constant sporting bill over the whole period. Many years later I was talking to a man named Joe Macken who was an adult witness of many of these events. He worked at Blackledges the bakers and on

180

summer nights he would spend his breaks sitting on the pavement outside to escape the heat of the bakehouse and to cool down. He was reminiscing and said with a laugh, "Yes it was as good as the stadium, we'd come up and watch the manager in the pub opposite put his title on the line every night — I think he was unbeaten."

I told him that he was talking about our pub and my father. Joe was there most of the war and particularly remembered the hectic times of the Atlantic Convoys and the Battle of the Atlantic. Our recollection of events tallied closely which gave us both a lot of satisfaction.

One visitor who didn't accept "no" to being served more beer was Wah Hoo. Wah Hoo was an Indian, or a Native American as they are now called. Wah had come into the Marine with some shipmates from a Lykes Line boat — America was not yet in the war. The Yanks had been elsewhere, and already they were showing signs of intoxication or "drawing a lot of water" as they say in Liverpool. They were served a drink as they didn't look troublesome, but soon Wah began abusing his two shipmates who were white. "You not American. Me only real American on ship. You no good." His friends left, obviously well used to his behaviour, which left Wah without both friends and without a drink as he was told he would be given no more. This infuriated him and ranting and raving he was ejected into Raleigh Street, one barman holding the door open as the other threw him out.

181

It had been snowing outside and his fall was softened by the deep snow. He raised himself and removed his heavy oilskin jacket which he placed on the snow. Feeling in his pockets he was unable to find what he wanted and called a watching urchin over, gave him sixpence and sent him for a box of matches. The urchin soon returned with matches and was given the change to keep. He was well pleased. We all watched.

Wah now attempted to set fire to his coat, preparatory to throwing it in the Marine to burn the place down. The coat just wouldn't light, he used the whole box attempting it and tried to assist matters with incantations and a high-step short dance as part of the action. It was no good, he picked up his coat and put it back on — clearly cold by now. Off he went back to his ship.

This was my first sight and experience of a genuine "Red Indian" and having the benefit of Johnny Mack Brown behind me I decided that he must be an Apache because they were the fiercest. It also convinced me completely that John Wayne and the US Cavalry were right in forbidding the traders to supply "firewater" to the Indians.

Then there was "Popeye". It was a quiet afternoon in the summer holidays — with few in the pub as everyone was back at work. A voice from below broke the silence — I knew this voice from my Saturday afternoon matinees. "Popeye!" I said as May and I looked at each other. The voice was so close to the cartoon hero's I felt he'd sailed into Liverpool and into the pub. But this Popeye was looking for trouble — he was more like Popeye's adversary Bluto.

I went to look, to see if it was really Popeye — peeking around the corner of the bar door. He stood at the angle of the counter staring at Father — a small, stocky man wearing a cap. "I'm the great Mickey Syers."

A pause — Father silent as he viewed him.

"Never heard of you — what do you want?"

"I've come about you not serving our Dick."

"If people can't behave properly they won't be served in this establishment while my name is over the door — and that goes for you too."

"You serve him or you'll know about it."

With that, Arthur the barman ran around the bar and held open wide the side door, and Father didn't walk, he vaulted over the counter, grabbed the collar of "the Great Micky Syers" and gave him the bum's rush into the middle of Raleigh Street. Arthur closed the door and returned to the bar. Father remained standing in the middle of the floor and waited for re-entry but there was none. May said it was because he hadn't eaten his spinach.

Pubs were places where the bliss of a quiet pint could be enjoyed. The customers' homes were usually a couple of crowded rooms with not enough space for a large family to eat, sleep or even sit down and all families were large in Liverpool. In winter it was cold — the pubs were always warm. They fulfilled an important rôle as the place of relaxation — the sitting rooms of the working class where a man could have a

183

little rest away from the noise of the children and the cacophony of the docks. Harmony was the key quality — everyone in the pub was at ease and that was a big attraction. The rest of life was noise and strife. Pub managers and the brewers set great store on running a happy house and dissent or disagreement was tolerated only if it was taciturn and didn't interfere with the pleasure of others. Fighting and shouting always led to instant ejection. But there were other threats to tranquillity — from outside, like Mrs "Kill the Cat" (Malone). This woman was a small, vital, dark-haired attractive creature with a husband and four children. I don't know why she was called "Kill the Cat" but all the children knew her only by that name and would sometimes call after her when she was on the street. She had a hot temper but took no notice of the shouts which were always delivered from a safe distance. Her husband was a quiet, hard-working docker who went to the Blue House at the bottom of William Henry Street, just once a week on a Friday night after he'd been paid and had his tea. The time of attack on the pub and Mr Malone varied, but was usually around half an hour after Mr Malone had arrived. That crucial time when the second pint is approaching. This feisty women would step briskly out of the house leaving the front door open behind her and go to the door of the bar. Prising it open to see he was in the usual place she would begin, "There ye are, drinkin' again and the childers without a crust in their mouth."

"You with your fine friends and me left in the house with neither food nor fire."

184

"Is it all ye think about — drinkin and the childers without a shift to their back."

"And where do you think I'll be gettin' the food to put on the table — is it the 'Parish' you want for us?"

"And there's you playing the fine man with your cronies and your big black pints and us without a sup o' tay in the house."

The incessant abuse in a high-pitched shriek would go on for some minutes. The prospect of a second pint vanished and eventually, sighing Malone would drink up and leave — the subject of universal in-house sympathy. Now the action commenced and we'd be waiting outside with a ringside view. He said nothing as he came out of the door and just grabbed her by her long, black hair and dragged her screeching and abusing him (but no bad language) back up the street to no. 14 — in the door, door closed and battle commenced. It was always a short engagement and every time ended the same way. She was dragged upstairs to bed and the hostilities ended abruptly. It was an entertainment we enjoyed regularly and we'd press our ears to the closed door trying to hear what was going on. Sometimes we forgot it was Friday night and then one of the gang would come running, "She's at it again!" and we would hurry to the scene of combat. "Mrs Kill the Cat" would not be overlooked and she knew "himself" was at his weakest in the pub. An audience was essential. At home their life was peaceful and happy.

Most of the customers, of course, were regulars and normal in their behaviour — but they're not usually the ones remembered. One group of customers was very different, mainly because they were female. They were a group of five who arrived every Friday evening in the football season at around six when the pub was still quiet, resting before the evening stampede. They were all young — between eighteen and twenty-five — and they came from the Littlewoods Football Pools HQ at the bottom of Strand Road. Pools coupons sent in by punters were all examined and checked on the Sunday following the Saturday games, and the big winners were notified immediately, usually by telegram. The popular newspapers were also given the names of big winners in most cases for this was excellent publicity and attracted new business without fail.

The girls who checked the coupons were the elite of the Littlewoods workforce and they were extremely well paid. It was pressurised and demanding work and required exceptional skills as well as having to work every Sunday in the football season. They worked hard and played hard and they had a standing order with Father for champagne every Friday evening. After finishing work they made themselves up for the night in the Littlewoods toilets and changed into some "fancy gear" they'd brought with them that day before leaving. Then, ready for the night, they arrived in the Marine and the Ladies' Parlour where the champagne awaited them in silver ice buckets. They always greeted Father as they entered.

"Hello Tom, here we are again."

"So I see," and he'd smile and make his way to the parlour and as they hung their coats he'd start pouring the champagne into the highly-polished glasses standing on new drip mats on the shining mahogany table. Service from the boss himself. He was very popular with the girls and he looked forward to their arrival. "They make a nice change from the sailors and dockers," he said to May one day.

"It's the admiration you like and the style — there's not too much of either around this place," replied May — she understood him well.

The girls stayed until eight doing some serious damage to the champagne and then their car would arrive — a hackney.

They left the parlour via the lower entrance in Raleigh Street, always to amusing banter and shouts from the bar and they gave as good as they got in return. Squeezing into the car they left for town and the continuation of their night at Reeces or the Grafton ballrooms. They all earned lots more than their fathers — and spent it. They believed in putting money "on your back and in your belly" and shared with Father and the rest of the city the maxim that, "There are no pockets in shrouds". When hostilities commenced they were all redirected to other work soon after when the pools companies closed down for the war along with the football, and switched to making barrage balloons and other war equipment. Like the champagne, when France fell, they ceased coming in. Each Friday was ladies' day. On the pavement outside, the women assembled around 5 o'clock. The men had been paid — the Marine was the next stop. Ambushed at the door, they were relieved of "the housekeeping" before entry

— later would be too late. The business was brisk and soon the crowd cleared, none quicker than the kids who had joined the crush and got a penny from "the da".

Soon after we moved to the Marine, May's elder brother Jack returned from Australia where he'd been working for a couple of years. He was unmarried and had saved a comfortable amount, being temperate in character. He came to live with us, and Father gave him a job in the bar where he was excellent. His zeal at work led to him sweeping not only the pub floor but the pavement outside. He was noticed doing this one morning by the Outside Manager who was passing and on his next visit Jack's wages were increased by 10s a week — that was a big raise.

Jack was quiet by nature and very similar in many ways to his sister with whom he was very close. Having no mother, he had always relied on May for female guidance. Grandmother, who'd brought them up from when he was nine, was not the sort of woman who would invite confidence from the young, so May, a year younger, had filled that rôle. He took a great interest in me, which I reciprocated from our first meeting and we became very close. On his half-day off if I was not at school, he would take me out — to Liverpool or New Brighton or somewhere of interest where there were things to be seen. On our way home, instead of getting off the overhead railway train at Canada Dock, we'd stay on until it reached the terminus in Seaforth. From there it was nearly two miles back on the no. 17 tram. After alighting from the train the same conversation always followed.

"Well, Mate — we can get the tram or you can have a penny for an ice cream instead — which is it to be?"

"The penny." We never took the tram even once.

He had a great effect on my development and was always telling me about the sort of things boys like to hear. We'd take the overhead railway to the Pier Head for the ferries and he'd point out the different shipping lines marked by their individual funnel colours and designs.

"Blue Funnel — they go to China and the East, and all the Lascars you see walking along the road behind one another, never together, on the way to Paddy's Market — they're off those ships. Lamport & Holt are on the South American run, Buenos Aires and Rio. Your uncle Jim sails for them. Ellermans are in the Mediterranean and the food on their ships is terrible. T&J, with the striped funnel, handle the West Indian trade and bring all the sugar for Tate & Lyle and of course the rum your dad sells in the pub."

Grandest of all, Cunard White Star in their home port at the Pier Head, took on passengers from the London Express at Riverside station to the landing stage only a few yards away from the ship's gangways and disembarking onto the train those they'd carried across the Atlantic from New York and Baltimore. It was all magic and he'd tell me the places they sailed to and point out what they brought back which was there lying on the quays waiting for the horses and carts and trucks to carry it away to goods yards and warehouses. He was a mine of information. He had travelled widely and loved to talk. I couldn't get enough of it. He kept all his cigarette cards for me and would quiz me on them to see if I'd remembered what they told. I had. This delighted him and one day out of my earshot he was telling May how clever I was. His sister put everything in its true perspective by replying that "he's a little boy who's bright, but we don't want any of that sort of talk in front of him — it's not good for him."

She was, of course, right, so Jack was careful not to praise too easily in the future. Having no children of his own he was unaware of the effect of an excess of either praise or correction on the young. He was closer to me than my father, of whom I was also fond, but unlike Jack he spent little time with me because of his working hours. With the war came direction of labour and Jack went to work for our close neighbour — Harland & Wolff the ship repairers and builders of the *Titanic*. I continued to see much of him until he died early of leukaemia just after I left university. After the war he would marry Phoebe, the widow of Charlie Randall, and also paramour of Jimmy the Greek. May disapproved totally and told him so, but having fallen under the allure of the dark Phoebe he was helpless. "It's the line of least resistance," he explained to May. Phoebe's charm was obvious and she had successfully kept three men happy in the same house — quite an achievement I realised later in life when I knew more about such things. Perhaps her real vocation should have been in the diplomatic service. She got through Jack's savings and there was little left by the time he died. She gave him both pain and pleasure but he was happy most of the time.

190

He was quite inexperienced in adventures with the female sex and naïve in the true sense of the word. Things around him sometimes seemed to make no impression — there was something of the innocent about him. Having suffered the hardship and poverty of the Depression, he still maintained a faith in authority and government to make things right. How could this be when he'd had to get out of the country to find work and illegally jump ship in New Zealand to make a little money? It was a puzzle.

CHAPTER ELEVEN

The Captain, his Gun and the Swing

When we returned from evacuation to Ainsdale at Mrs Bimpson's, St Alexander's was closed and evacuated to Wales and lessons for the few remaining children were now provided at Iona House on Merton Road, premises of the Knights of St Columba — a Catholic men's organisation for social and good works. It was a bit like the early nineteenth-century schools before the government took matters in hand. There were about twenty of us in two or three classes covering ages from five to fifteen and the teachers were the old or the lame left behind when the main school evacuated and all the able-bodied male teachers were called up for the services. I suppose we must have learnt something there, but despite the teachers' best efforts, it was not really possible to pursue any meaningful programme or syllabus.

Most of our street pals for some reason also seemed to have escaped evacuation. This was nice for us but in some ways regrettable for them as it would have provided an escape to a better life for most of them who were from the poorest families. Some of the evacuees were away for three years and more and it had a significant effect — mostly beneficial — on their lives. While away they learnt different things from different people holding different opinions. The greatest benefit though, was the uninterrupted schooling in a quiet area which they received. I missed all this and when I got to grammar school later I would struggle, for I'd missed over three years regular school and had yet to make the acquaintance of subjects such as French, Geometry and Algebra. All this was to come later and meanwhile, the excitement on the streets continued. Soldiers were appearing everywhere, most of them waiting in nearby barracks and warehouses for troopships to take them to Egypt and the East and other places and others doing fire watching duty in warehouses and elsewhere.

The pubs were crowded all the time as this massive, ever-changing population of seamen and armed services personnel, all in transit, stood elbow-to-elbow drinking in the smoke-filled bars with the natives — the indigenous dockers, sailors and families from the surrounding streets. In the holidays Fran and I always stayed up late and when the pub closed sometime after 10p.m. we would go down and help to tidy up. We liked to do this as we often found coins on the floor and empty cigarette packets containing cigarette cards. Sometimes we came across something more substantial like a Sam Browne belt with holster and Webley service pistol (the biggest pistol in the world). We handed this with excitement to Father who said, "Ah, another one."

He allowed us to examine it closely, made sure it was not loaded and then we followed him down the stairs as

193

he took it to the spirit cellar for safe keeping and locked it in. There were other firearms already there awaiting reclamation and they were joined later by a Thompson sub-machine gun which was never to be returned or asked for. After a week or two Father handed them over to the police. Gwladys the barmaid remembered who'd been sitting there — a young army captain — much taken with one of the local girls. It had been a hot evening — particularly in the ladies' parlour and he'd removed his belt and holster and opened his tunic soon after arriving. He'd remembered to button his tunic as he left with the beauty but had forgotten his belt and gun under the seat in his euphoric contemplation of pleasures to come. Their festive drinking was clearly a contributing factor Gwladys thought, as she'd served them at table all evening. They had drunk copiously and she had been tipped often and heavily — always a sign that things are going well.

Somewhere between 2 and 3a.m., the house was alerted by heavy banging on the main door. Rising, Father descended the stairs, opened the door and there was the captain. He was in some distress as he apologised for waking everybody at such an ungodly hour and asking had he left his belt and gun in the parlour. Father said his face changed immediately he heard the word "yes". He was taken down to the spirit cellar and reclaimed his property, explaining that to lose one's weapon was a court martial offence and he would have been in serious trouble. He was due to leave that same day on the evening tide with his regiment.

194

He wanted to reward Father in his gratitude and relief but this was politely not accepted. In its place were poured two halves of mild beer. "Have a good trip and you can buy the next one, when you get back," said Father. I still wonder what happened to the captain. Perhaps he had a good war and still remembers the beauty and his lucky escape.

Around this time I met my cousin Eddie Farrell and his brother. Eddie was three years older than me. His father was my grandmother's brother on my father's side, so he was my first cousin once removed. He'd had a hard childhood, for his mother had left his father who'd had a tough time in France in the First World War. He'd been commissioned and had survived but it left its mark.

Eddie was a handsome, happy boy and full of life and we decided one day to go to the small recreation ground at the bottom of Miller's Bridge, just down the road. This was a popular amenity with swings, see-saws and roundabouts laid out on a fine, yellow, sandy gravel surface. We got on a swing, him standing to push it, and me sitting. He had great energy and soon we were flying high — and then I fell off. I landed on the gravel on my head and sustained a fractured skull. The first I remember was waking up in Bootle Hospital which was fortunately only 100 yards away — carried there by Tom, the playground keeper. They kept me in for a week and I had head bandages for months as the small pieces of stone and sand came out from the wound. Fran told me it was my own fault as I'd refused to go home with him for tea.

195

"You should have come home with me when I told you it was tea time."

"I know, but I wanted one last go with Eddie."

He was right and I knew it. I was chastened.

While I was in the hospital I was surprised at how much quieter it was than the Marine, though they were both close by and on the same road. The main road in front of the hospital was laid in wood blocks which deadened the noise of the horseshoes and cartwheels as they passed. This was to allow patients better rest and less disturbance from the noise of the constant passing traffic. It was remarkably effective.

Poor Eddie, feeling responsible, kept a low family profile for some time. He felt responsible, though it was just a childhood accident. Later he became a physical training instructor in the King's Regiment and afterwards a policeman rising to the rank of deputy chief constable in Liverpool. I think he also did his bit for the peace process by marrying a German girl when he was stationed with the army of occupation.

Towards the end of 1940, after the fall of France, the air raids started. They were always at night and followed no regular pattern when they began. We really started to become the centre of attention for the Luftwaffe that Christmas. The raids then became heavy and continuous and there was extensive damage, most of it along the waterfront on both sides of the city. It was obvious that the bombing was well-directed and there were many casualties.

In terms of defence there didn't seem to be very much and I cannot remember seeing or reading of a single enemy plane being shot down over the area in the period. I do remember a 3.7-inch mobile anti-aircraft gun parking one evening outside the Marine. When the raid began it went into action and when it fired its first shot it blew in the side windows of the pub in Raleigh Street, miraculously injuring no one. It moved on to somewhere else almost immediately assisted by lots of advice from the customers. Father was cross. He and the Führer shared the same birthday — 20 April — and he would joke that this gave him and the pub protection from the bombs. Perhaps it did, but not from our own. "I thought they were on our side!" said Father.

Fran and Ray Lee from the pub on the other side of the road would go off to school together, and return at around 4.30 p.m. There was, during this period and the whole of the war, an advertising campaign telling people that "Walls have ears" and generally telling people to be on their guard with passing information generally. There were spies everywhere we were told and "Careless talk costs lives" — be watchful of those around you. This led to our grocer George being arrested, questioned for some days and then released. Anybody stating non-partisan feelings was suspect and Fran mentioned quite innocently to Father who was having his tea some remarks of a teacher who was sympathetic to Hitler's efforts in reviving Germany. This was conveyed to the police who made poor Fran meet them a little way off from the school at 4 p.m. and point out, from the recesses of the car, the suspect. He was taken in and questioned and then released totally unaware of why he'd been interrogated. There was a panic loose at the time because of the advertising and a similar phase of madness would occur in America a decade later with Joe McCarthy and the Reds. May didn't like any of it, comparing it to Judas fingering Christ, and Tom was told so. He agreed, but said that you can't be too careful. Whoever said advertising doesn't work?

St Martin's decided after the Christmas Blitz that it too, should evacuate, and it did. The school moved to the peace of Southport, just the other side of Ainsdale, and it never came back. Fran was now schoolless also and it was decided to send us to Ireland to our aunts and cousins. May wrote off to Aunt Mary to make arrangements. I do not know why we couldn't all have gone to Southport to live and go to school because lots did, working in the city in the day and going home to safety at night. It would not have been possible though for Father, because he was on duty all night and his employment contract demanded his presence overnight, and May probably felt she should stay and support him. Aunt Lily who was married to Albert in the fire brigade went with Muriel their daughter. She got a job in Broadbents, the department store, and in the meantime Albert received the comforts of a lady friend in his empty house. Lily only discovered this years later whereupon she threw Albert out, refusing to see her part in what had happened. This was an unusual response as most considered life and death more important than infractions of the marital code at this period.

CHAPTER
TWELVE

Ireland and The Ogre

The first nine months of the war, from September 1939 to the fall of France in May 1940 has been called the Phoney War because in the period not an awful lot happened at the front in Western Europe. Ships, however, were being sunk and most things were happening on the water. My first realisation of how serious things would become was when HMS *Royal Oak* was sunk in Scapa Flow by a U-boat. The *Royal Oak* had become a familiar sight as she lay in Gladstone graving dock getting a massive overhaul over a six-month period in 1939. She was a great battleship from the First World War — 35,000 tons and eight 15-inch guns. All the work and expense was in vain as she never saw any action after having left Liverpool to join the rest of the fleet in the Orkneys. Having looked at and admired her so often, for she was a handsome ship, it came as a shock when her loss was reported on the radio. Fran and I were playing soldiers at the time and we found it hard to believe that the great ship was no more. She had impressed us as being indestructible. How could a small submarine sink such a giant which had 18in of armour plate to protect against torpedoes? We couldn't understand.

I don't know why it was we were there when enemy bombs dropped on the city because we knew what was going to happen and were twice evacuated but came back. We missed none of the action but weren't there when everything was quiet, so early in 1940 it was decided that although nothing was happening, maybe evacuation was a good idea — the Ainsdale experience notwithstanding — and so off we went to Ireland. Parental timing was abysmal.

Dear old dirty Dublin — Liverpool's Siamese twin — linked by the blood of ages and even poorer. Liverpool had had many years of prosperity interspersed with poverty, but Dublin could not say the same and it had not benefited from rearmament and preparations for war. We arrived on the *Louth* of the B&I Line from Liverpool at around 7p.m. in the calm of a still sea and a watery sun. The Irish crossings were the worst of all the ferries operating from UK ports. Steerage accommodation was primitive and that was all we could get, despite connections with crews and the B&I offices but it was difficult anyway owing to the large number of servicemen coming and going between the two countries. The Republic provided over half a million servicemen and women during the war — all volunteers. It was a higher per head percentage of the population than England, Scotland or Wales where conscription applied, and Ireland (or the southern part) was neutral, with a very busy German Embassy in Dublin.

The ship docked at the North Wall very close to the brightly lit city centre and as we disembarked into

200

the smoky winter evening, struggling under two heavy suitcases, we were met by a crowd of runners shouting the merits of different hotels and lodgings of every sort. A spare woman of about fifty engaged mother's attention and after a question and answer session we all got into a horse-drawn carriage in a long rank by the boat. The spare woman gave the address in a no-nonsense voice and "your man" touched his forelock and off we went. It was too late for our train to Wexford, as it had left and we would get one in the morning. The Jarvy looked about eighty, but like the woman, moved quickly and when we arrived after about half a mile he was quickly down and had the cases at the door in a moment. The woman was engaged in opening the door to a large Regency terraced house which was in an area that had seen better days, like the rest of the city, but we were there. May opened her bag to pay the Jarvy and as she did so he said, "have you something for a poor orphan, ma'am?" May looked back at the carriage thinking she had missed seeing some diminutive child next to him but no, only the horse and an empty carriage. "Where's the orphan?" said May. "'Tis meself, Ma'am and neither mother nor father have I since that high," lowering his hand to his knee. May was giving him a good tip anyway and she was as amused as he was delighted. It was a fair exchange she thought and worth it for the humour.

Inside, the woman was already in action. "You'll be wanting something for your supper and I'll take you up now to your room and it'll be on the table in two shakes of a lamb's tail." She took us up to the second floor and showed us into a large room with two double beds, a washstand, a chamber pot under each bed and holy pictures on the wall. It was sparse but very clean and after a quick wash using the jug of hot water she brought, down we went and got fed.

The food was good, for there was no rationing in Ireland, though the bread was a strange grey/brown colour as it became later in England. White bread did not reappear in either place until well after the war. It was something to do with higher nutrition and the lack of availability of the flour needed for white bread. The only other food which was scarce at the time in Ireland was tea, the bulk of which came from England. The woman was chatty and wanted to know about the bombing. I received great sympathy from her, for I was still wearing the head bandages from my encounter with the playground and she decided that the Germans were responsible. May felt she could not disillusion her. On our way to bed after the meal she pressed a coin tightly into my hand. "There, that'll get you a bar of chocolate." I felt an imposter but just murmured, "thank you".

She told us she would call us at 7.30 and that would leave us plenty of time to get to Westland Row station, which was "just down the road — you'll be there in no time at all." We were soon asleep.

The morning was bright and clear and rushed and the strongly distinctive and evocative smell of burning turf fires filled the air. Though everything was ready, we were not "just down the road" from the station. Slowed down by our heavy cases we moved tardily and no carriages were in sight. Everybody seemed to be still in bed, for unlike Liverpool, the streets were empty at this hour. The woman was encouraging us all the time with "it's just a little further now," but she had miscalculated how long it would take to travel the mile or so and she said, "I'll go ahead and get them to hold the train for you," which she did. When we got there, there she was chatting amiably with the guard who was quite happy to hold the train and wait for us and see us all ensconced before he blew his whistle and climbed aboard himself. I had first come to Ireland when just a couple of weeks old and had been a regular visitor from that time. Then and since, it has always been for me a magical experience, particularly in these early years and we were all excited and happy as the train proceeded slowly down to Wexford 90 miles south. Progress was slow, for there were many stops — Bray, Arklow, Wicklow, Enniscorthy and smaller halts at places like Inch to drop off parcels and mail. Inch was not really a station — more a halt for loading cattle. "Which are the two closest stations in Ireland?" would say Uncle Fran. "Arklow and Gorey," was the answer, "because there's only an Inch between them." I liked Inch and always looked forward to the stop there to see if anyone got on or off. This time was another blank. The locomotives were all old and had all been built in Inchicore in Dublin in the 1880s and each had a plate recording those details. I always wondered whether they had built any after that date. Perhaps the works closed. They were very reliable and never broke down but had difficulty getting up enough steam and power due to a shortage of coal and they burned mostly the native turf which was very inferior for steam production. The journey however, was very pleasant with the line running beside the sea for most of the way and beautiful country on the other side totally unintruded by the sights, sounds and smells of industry — just fields, farms and woodland.

Aunt Mary met us at the station in Wexford which was only around 100 yards from where she lived. The house was in Monck or McDonough Street, depending on your political persuasion and it was very old, stone with thick walls on the corner of the terraced street, with the ground floor front divided into an entrance and hallway, a sweet and ice cream shop and a little utility/sitting room. Behind the shop was the parlour and the main hall which led to a kitchen and yard with pigsty, and stable and toilet. My overwhelming impression of Monck Street was its tranquillity. No noise other than the sounds of horse and donkey hooves and their little carts and the occasional car or wagon. This was such a strong contrast to Liverpool which seemed always to be in perpetual motion and going somewhere, like a great symphony orchestrated for tramcars, workshops, wagons, horses and carts, ships' sirens, fog horns, voices and a choir of thousands overlaid like solos on the ensemble of the thematic low hum of the flour mills and edible oil refineries. When we came to Monck Street it was like the concert interval. There were no toilets in the house and the po was in service in every bedroom (five). The house had

been in the family since about 1830 and it was to this
that Mary and Annie had decamped when they left
May in Liverpool fourteen years before. And then there
was Johnny. Johnny was Mary's husband. Short, fat,
red-faced and usually cross and bad-tempered. He had
once been a seaman but contracted malaria on a run to
the West African coast and he'd never worked since. His
duties were the running of the sweetshop. A bell
sounded in the parlour where he sat when anyone
entered the shop and rising unwillingly he would
mutter softly curses upon them as he went and served.
Mary spoiled him. He did not provide for either of
them but liked and indulged his love of good food to
the full. Most days he would have a large steak as his
main course — nobody else got steak. He had a great
fondness for HP Sauce, which was unavailable locally
and all visitors had to bring a bottle with them to please
the great man. Mary would be constant in her letters to
remind them before they left England not to forget. He
was a tyrant, though Mary never complained about
him. She was very tolerant but over-indulgent. He was,
for his part, totally over-benefited. Every day he would
take an afternoon nap and I quickly fell into disfavour
because of my singing. I liked to sing from very early
on, and May had encouraged it. I particularly liked the
acoustics in the high roof barn where the toilet was
located. So it was there I usually gave full voice to my
repertoire. Some people read when at the toilet, I sang.
Unaware of my great offence, I was confronted by a
wild-eyed, angry Johnny who abused me at length
telling me I was nothing but a "Bootle Buck". My

singing from then on was outside the confines of 12 Monck Street, though I sometimes found myself starting a refrain before the embargo was remembered.

May overheard the attack and told Johnny later, in private in her quiet but firm way, that he was "out of order". This upset him, for he liked May and he immediately raided the cash drawer in the shop, put on his coat and cap and went next door to McGuinness's Select Bar. This practice continued for some days until Mary asked May to speak to him as he was drinking all the profits. Instead of him apologising and revising his view of his conduct, his woes were blamed on me and his dislike became even more intense. This became permanent but he did some good things for me. I had a large wart on my left hand and one day he said, "let's get rid of it." He then put a little water in an egg cup and opened a box of red phosphorus matches. Dipping the head of the match in the water he rubbed it on the wart. He did this for a couple of minutes every day and in just over a week it was burnt away and never returned.

Mary's younger sister Annie, had by this time seven children (two more were to come later), and all of them were with us in Monck Street. Annie and Fran had taken the lease on Clarence House which was a crown property built against the old town walls and entered via a large archway carriage entrance in the middle of the row of terraced houses. On entry through the arch it opened out to a large house on the right with stables and yard further ahead to the right abutting the old town ivy-covered walls. In front of the house was a broad carriageway and parking area meeting a neat quarter-acre garden containing all manner of things, some quite unknown to us. To the right there was a giant mulberry tree, whose berries stained the courtyard with purple patches and provided us with an ink supply for our writing. The house had been empty a for long time and was completely hidden from the street. It was now in the course of renovation and decoration. Everybody was excited about it and in the meantime we were all together in Monck Street under the watchful eye of the ogre Johnny. My cousins in order of birth were Madge (1927), Pat, Lar, Marie, Angela, Veronica and Bernie, and despite the crowding we were the happiest of gangs. Mary had Kathleen, a domestic, who did most of the cooking for us and we were fed simple diets suitable for production in quantity. Potatoes, cabbage, ham, cheese, bread, butter and jam and lots of tea were the mainstays and we never left the table hungry, though we were always ravenous from playing outdoors or at school all the time. The house we used only for sleeping and eating if we could manage it, out of sight of adults and in particular Johnny, who had now placed Lar on his list as enemy number two. He had been singing rebel songs in the bedroom at the top of the house and he was given a serious warning to desist. Pat and Lar were great fun. Pat was around the same age as Fran and Lar was a year younger. The girls were utterly delightful. Madge — the kind but serious eldest daughter and surrogate mother; Marie — a bonny beauty with her mother's great shape; Angela — a pre-Raphaelite blonde vision; Veronica — the sensible red-haired one and my particular favourite and Bernie — a pretty golliwog. In the fashion of the time Mary, having no children of her own, was given Bernie by Annie who had plenty, so Bernie always lived in Monck Street and had the life of an only child. She was allowed to eat with Johnny and Mary in the parlour and received the best of everything. Johnny doted upon her. She could do no wrong and it was surprising that this different treatment didn't spoil her or seem to affect the relationship with the rest of us, even when the discrimination was obvious. I think we all felt that our lot was better — all together at table in the kitchen laughing and baiting each other noisily all the time. The alternative of eating in the parlour with Johnny would have been a poorer and unhappier substitute, even with the additional table luxuries so in the end both sides were happy.

Before coming to Ireland to marry Fran, Annie had decided and planned to open an ice cream and confectionery shop in Wexford as it would be unlikely that Fran would be able to find well-paid work, as there was little in Ireland. By 1940 she had been in business for over ten years and they had a well-established shop at the south end of the main street near the Capitol — the better of the two cinemas in the town. She had also opened a second shop half way down the Main Street at the corner of Anne Street and this had a small bakehouse which was producing cakes for sale in the shop in addition to the regular ice cream and sweets. Neither of the shops had much in the way of living accommodation, hence our crowding together in Monck Street.

Annie and Fran were an interesting combination with Annie very much in charge and the commercial brain behind all of the activity. She was a fine figure of a woman — tall, harmoniously proportioned and rather on the generous side. She had the family characteristic of stability and never got excited or over-responded to any of the daily emergencies and crises which accompany large families. She was totally in charge and always referred to for judgement and settling of conflicts of her offspring. A very kind woman with a deep love of humanity and the little ones in particular. Whenever I recall her I see her in her favourite dark navy coat and hat and her large handbag. Ah, yes her handbag. To me that bag was a continual source of wonder and imagination for it seemed to contain solutions to all the world's problems. It was like a good version of Pandora's Box and in it there was something for every eventuality. If she had ever revealed the full contents, I'm sure things would have appeared which would have surprised everybody. Being nosy, I was always anxious when she opened the bag to see what emerged. A selection in response to different situations or demands included: cigarettes (always three packets of Afton Major as basic stock); money — large thick roll of banknotes with rubber band; cigarette lighter and matches (never caught without a light); plasters and bandages and small scissors; antiseptic cream; smelling salts; violet cachous; extra handkerchiefs; passport and birth certificates; chocolate and big bag of boiled sweets; purse with coins for public toilets, etc.; a holy picture; a small crucifix; rosary beads; a penknife; string, and wrapped in anonymous brown paper, some sanitary towels. I felt that if we'd been shipwrecked she would have produced lifejackets for each of us out of the bag.

Fran was the exact opposite, which was perhaps why they were so strongly mutually attracted. He was of medium height and sparse in figure. He possessed a fine head of hair and a wild eye and was quick in movement. Excitable, enthusiastic and engaged with everything around him, he was a great lover of his country. During "the Troubles" he'd been very active with the Republican forces and he seemed to know everybody. Everywhere we went he was greeted by people whom he'd known a long time. In Dublin, which was far distant, he seemed to be stopped every ten minutes by someone he'd not seen for a long time whenever we went there. This held our travels up constantly and often required Annie to intervene to get free. Without Annie there were problems. Fran and crony would slide into the nearest select bar (all bars in Ireland had "Select Bar" inscribed on their window) and no good would come of it, for Fran and drink should never have been allowed to meet. Part of the difficulty was that he never drank at all for most of the time but he possessed the inability to drink in moderation or just have the odd one. It was feast or famine, all or nothing. Most of the time it was nothing, for Annie saw to that, and with good reason. Like Wah Hoo in the Marine in Liverpool, he became fiery in drink and very argumentative. At such times he would not let you agree with him, he was contrary and he wanted an argument and he would have one. When he fell from grace on such occasions, penance and submission would follow and he would become a subdued and different person until the next breakout.

He was a good man and I was very attached to him. I always tried to sit next to him in the car and get him to tell me about cars or his adventures in "the Troubles". He was a great patriot and did much to foster my love of Ireland with his tales, and then there was the singing. If my singing got me the enmity of Johnny, it also got me the love of Fran. He loved a song and taught me his own favourites with "Slievenamon" the one I remember best. He had a good voice and we'd all sing in turns in the car and anywhere else where the opportunity arose. Knowing that I would sing with little persuasion, he put me through my whole repertoire time after time. There were few cars in Wexford at the time and Fran had acquired a Ford V8 1936 model. This was the biggest and most powerful of the Fords available and we were all exceedingly proud of it. It was big enough to take all of us and it was a great workhorse. It delivered ice cream, went to Dublin for spare parts and delivered and collected people at the Liverpool boat as well as taking us all on days out to see the country and the seaside. Very little was spent on our excursions, because we always ate well before we left and even better when we returned and we always had a wonderful time. It was through these excursions and passing through villages mentioned in histories that

211

I heard for the first time from Fran stories of the Wexford Rebellion of 1798 and Father Murphy, the leader executed for his part in the action.

Look out for hirelings King George of England
For every nation that breeds a slave
For Father Murphy of the County Wexford
Sweeps o'er the earth like a mighty wave

What small boy could fail to be excited by words like those? All this had happened here in Wexford and in Ireland time had stood still. It was as if the action had ended only yesterday. I almost expected to see the rebellious father coming down the road.

I liked the sound of him — a very different sort of priest from Father Coupe who'd thrown me out of the confessional, though they both shared a lot of ferocity, I thought. I mused on the matter and concluded Father Murphy wouldn't have thrown me out, but would have saved his passion for the invader. Father Coupe, for his part, was keeping a diary in which he would record the happenings and events of the forthcoming Blitzkrieg. This diary would later become part of the local records and be published. He would not live to see it. He died at forty-five and was probably already ill when we met at confession. Fran and I were taken to different schools soon after we arrived. I was put in the junior school with a jolly avuncular master named Tommy Roche. All the children loved Tommy and as a result he got good results from most of his charges for he was also a good teacher. I looked forward to going to school

212

each day and I was also taken regularly to see the family physician — Dr McCabe to check the progress of the gravel removal from my forehead. I still had the bandages on and was the recipient of sympathy (and the odd coin) from people who always added some words damning those terrible Germans. I felt I was doing my bit for the war effort by not telling them the truth. This deception made me a little uncomfortable, seeming to be close to the "bearing false witness" as well as the calumny and detraction in the Commandments. Father Coupe would definitely not like it, I thought, and it would probably merit another eviction from the confessional. In adult life it left me with doubts about evidence offered generally and when the war crime tribunals and trials began a few years later I was reminded of my earlier thoughts as I read the accounts of the defence and prosecution in the papers.

CHAPTER
THIRTEEN

Wexford

Fran was always interested in the sea, right from the beginning. It may have been the influence of all the uncles and seafarers in the family, but though the same references were present for me I never felt its pull as strongly as he did. In our games he would assume the rôle of a sailor and even in bed one night he decided that we were afloat and would have some diving practice. This can be difficult in a bedroom, but by standing on the doorknob and holding the top of the opened door he commenced diving onto the bed. I then had to follow suit naturally and then the bed collapsed with the spring and mattress resting on the floor at the bed head. The noise brought May and seeing our new sleeping position with head down and feet in the air she left us there without a word. We didn't know how to get things together again. (Fran was about nine) so we just went to sleep in that position. I woke in the morning with a headache but Fran was OK.

As soon as we got to Wexford we were even closer to the water and he started making little boats out of scrap wood and we all joined in. It was easy enough as we all had penknives and the materials cost nothing. Scrap wood for the hull, paper or card for the sails and a piece of broken slate for the keel to keep the boat upright. We had endless hours of pleasure launching them on the harbour waters and if the breeze was off the land, we watched them sail away until they were out of sight. Each September we were always plagued by shoals of jellyfish. Many of them were big — 2ft or more across — and we didn't like them at all. They could give a painful sting if encountered while swimming and when they arrived en masse in the river, it was sometimes difficult to launch our boats. At such times we amused ourselves by throwing stones at them instead until they vanished as mysteriously as they'd come. Then out came the boats again and sailings recommenced.

Fran went to the Boca, the senior school run by the Christian Brothers. Pat and Lar, our cousins, also went there, so his entry was eased as he was not alone and he was really Irish — he just spoke differently from living in Liverpool. The girls all went to the Loretto Convent and the nuns. It was very easy to make friends in Wexford for most families were large and once you know one you know them all. In Monck Street alone I had Barney McGuinness, my best friend from the select bar next door, Stikey Connors from lower down the street and then there were the Kellys three doors beyond Connors. The Kellys were also cousins but they did not mix with the rest of us very much. The father, Paddy Kelly, ran a successful drapery business in the Cornmarket. He had married a Welsh lady and they had five children. Toddy and Seamus were nice lads and Oona, the sister, was shy. The others were very small. We never went into each others' houses and I was to learn later that Annie owned their house as well and this was I think where the distancing began. It all started, as is usual, with money. When May's great uncle Jem died, he was a rich man. He was unmarried and left the residue of his estate to his sister after giving each of three nephews a farm. These were singled out for special treatment because they shared his name Kelly and Jem had been possessed of that particularly male desire to ensure the name Kelly successfully projected into the future. So Paddy Kelly and his two brothers, in true Irish fashion, proceeded to celebrate their fortune and the festivities only ceased when the last of the money and the three farms had gone. When Jem's sister, the aunt, died, the residue was then distributed quite widely as he had wished. This distribution included a legacy that May never got which went to Aunt Mary. Mary claimed that the beneficiary named in the will was herself (same maiden name) and she appropriated May's legacy, which both parties were aware of before the aunt's demise. May's plans to go to London were ruined but she never complained or held it against Mary. Mary expressed remorse some years later, but it was too late for restitution. The female line, having all married and lost the Kelly name, got lesser amounts and Annie's share was mostly property in the form of houses in the town. This had provided the capital for the start of her ice cream and confectionery business. The houses produced little income, for Annie would not charge economic rents for the houses in most cases because of the circumstances of nearly everybody living in them at the time. The property however was capital and banks would always lend against secured assets.

Paddy finally saw the light, and possessing some of the family gene for commerce he'd started a second-hand clothing business — travelling to South Wales by the nearby Rosslare Ferry buying stock and returning to Wexford to sell it. This provided the basis for opening the shop in the Cornmarket but he was only able to do so when Mr Kirk, Aunt Mary's lodger, lent him the money. Paddy and Uncle Jack had been great boyhood friends and were remarkably physically alike. Besides acquiring his stock in Wales, Paddy also acquired a wife, a Miss Power. She did not appear to socialise at all with the other side of the family, which was as much our fault as hers. The reason was never clear.

In Monck Street the houses were terraced on both sides, and houses which open onto the street bring people together — whether they wish it or not. If a front door is separated from the street by even a small garden it is a barrier to social intercourse. All the houses in Monck Street opened directly onto the street, as did the windows. Everybody knew a lot about everybody else. Next door we had the select bar of Mrs McGuinness and my friend Barney and next to them was Maggie Doyle. Maggie was the self-appointed moral guardian of the street. Everything was observed from the front window and reported and commented upon with whoever could be captured and made to listen. All the customers, in and out of Thorntons —

another select bar on the opposite corner — were noted and logged and their attendances timed, for was not drink the curse of the country? She lived with her sister — two spinsters with few interests other than the street. She was not malicious and really quite friendly and good-humoured, but very nosy. She observed everything and missed little from her observation post behind the curtain in the downstairs front room. Callers were viewed prior to entry, unaware they were under surveillance. If she could not get a full view of her caller, this caused little difficulty. She would move to the hall and put on her hat and answer the door. If the caller was welcome she'd say, "I've just come in," and take off the hat, put it back on the hook and put the kettle on. If unwelcome, she'd say, "I'm just on my way out," and reach for her coat and bag. With her hat on already it was a very convincing performance and the caller was sent away. On the same side, but at the bottom of the street on the corner with Main Street, which despite its name, was narrower than Monck Street, was Gaynors. This was a licensed grocer and long-established. Mr Gaynor, a man in his forties, was pro-German, believing that the English (always English rarely British) hold on Ireland would only be broken by a decline in England's powers. It was a not uncommon Irish feeling at the time and was borne out of the long struggle for independence. The Irish Free State, or Eire as it was then known, was only six years old and under the astute guidance of Eamon de Valera. He, like Franco in Spain, was anxious to keep his country out of the war. Both of them for similar reasons. Involvement would involve much suffering for no certain gains. Each country had recently been torn apart in a long bitter civil war where brother killed brother and friend killed friend, dividing the nation and bleeding it dry. Peace was needed to heal the wounds and rebuild the nation and Mr Gaynor was not so much anti-England as pro-Ireland. He believed in the old slogan of "England's weakness is Ireland's opportunity", and just believed that for Ireland the war could make England more generous in dealing with Ireland's difficulties — particularly in the North which was still under the English Crown. Across the street and halfway down was Aidan Kelly's Bar (also select!). Aidan was an early beau of Alice's who'd spent most of her life in Monck Street. He was a very pleasant man with a slight cast in his eye and Alice could (and did) do less well, certainly financially, when she later married, but attraction defies logic. Alice was unmoved. Mr Kirk was another admirer of Alice. I liked Mr Kirk a lot — he would talk to me and was the clerk at the railway station. Rather shy with adults, but as trains are interesting to all boys, I would seek him out and chat happily with him in the evenings after he'd had his dinner alone in the small front room. He was very quiet in nature and withdrawn but he seemed to enjoy our talk as much as I did. He always struck me as a good man in the full sense of the word. He had no relatives and died alone and financially very comfortable. Quite handsome, but careless in his personal appearance. A good woman would have been a great blessing and changed his life for the better. Next door to Aidan lived Lar Duggan.

Lar was a wildfowler and early each morning with his two water spaniels, shotgun under arm, bag of cartridges over shoulder and clad in waist-high waders, he passed the house. The cot safe or enclosed little harbour was opposite and stepping over the rail tracks running alongside he pulled in his boat. The dogs jumped in and he was off. He would return at sunset with the day's bag: wild duck and other varieties of wildfowl and do the same the next day and every day. To a boy's mind this seemed better than working and quite an idyllic existence. I wondered who ate all he shot and where he got the money to go and buy his cartridges, which were not cheap. I never realised that the day's "bag" went that same evening on the Rosslare-Fishguard ferry and was in London on the tables of St James's at lunchtime the following day. Lizzie Meyler took everything Lar got and had it expressed, the minute he delivered it from the boat. She was a fishmonger who financed people like Lar, and George Murphy, a fisherman who we befriended. She was not the most generous of sponsors but probably made little out of the business herself and without her, there would have been even greater unemployment. Neither Lar nor George had the contacts to sell what their labours produced. Lar spent most of his time a couple of miles up the River Slaney among the reeds. He was able to work most days, whatever the weather. George fished the grounds off Tuskar Rock in the Irish Sea. His boat — an old two-masted sailing ship — had no engine. If the wind was in the wrong direction it could take hours to get back to his mooring in mid

220

river. It was a harder life than Lar's, but he knew no other all his years. Lizzie sometimes sold his and other catches direct from handcarts on the quay if they arrived back early enough. "A penny a herring!" was a common cry, and even then I was aware that this was no great financial enterprise and that the total takings would not be substantial. Yet they supported George and his crew of two, Lizzie, and the women selling on the quay, plus the cost of carts, stabling, delivery and administration. Many days in winter there was no fishing when the weather was bad, but everyone still had to eat. George was a quiet man, softly spoken, with an uncanny ability to read and predict the weather. Medium height, average build — always in his old navy blue serge suit and sweater and tweed cap, smoking his pipe and cutting his black plug tobacco with his pocket knife which he kept sharpening with a small stone he carried. He was the first pipe-smoker I saw with a lanthorn cover for the pipe to prevent it being extinguished by rain. It looked like the top of a salt cellar — silver metal and a lot of small holes to keep the tobacco burning.

Unusually it was Fran who found him and then brought me along. Fran actually went deep sea fishing with George, for he always liked a boy aboard to climb the mast and free the shroud if it stuck — men were too heavy and could make the boat unstable. His boat was old and had no sleeping or resting places and didn't even have a proper cabin. When it rained, a tarpaulin was rigged aft to keep off the worst of the weather. For sleep, you dozed where you sat and for food there was the bread (now stale) you'd brought with you, and a bottle of water. Fran thought it was wonderful, despite the harsh conditions. He'd always liked extreme living conditions, as he'd earlier liked the Wharton's jam jar cups and sleeping on the floor, a real ascetic who should have been a Cistercian. I was considered too young to go but if the fish weren't putting in an appearance, George would take us out in a 14ft sailing dinghy called *Intruder*. We'd go as far as Curracloe and then land and take a walk in the sand dunes and get a nature lesson from George on birds and wildlife. He was very knowledgeable and showed us things we'd never noticed, such as the nests of the sand martins along the shoreline. George liked children and they adored him. *Intruder* would usually take George and three or four boys and we'd all be instructed in how to sail and how not to sail. I don't remember any mishaps on these days out. We all had our turn on the tiller and raising and lowering the sails and we had it drummed into us how to sail whatever the direction of the wind. At his command of "tack" we'd all lower our heads and move to the opposite side of the boat as the boom came over and the boat came around and started on the reverse course. If one was late hitting the street in the school holidays there was often an absence of playmates who'd already gone sailing or walking.

Walks were often pre-arranged and covered great distances. There were no "Keep Out" notices anywhere in the country and plenty of historical ruins and castles locally for our expeditions. Each with stick in hand we'd set out early. We could drink from the streams and if we were hungry a turnip from a farmer's field filled the gap. Like invading armies, we lived off the land. Walking was a great and popular activity partly because there was no money for any alternatives. The cemetery for Wexford is at Crosstown — across the river and a few miles from the town. The only cars or carriages in a funeral procession in those days would be one for the deceased and one for his/her immediate family. Everybody else walked behind the cortège and "everybody" seemed to be the operative word. All funeral processions were long and appeared to go on forever. I cannot recall a short or poorly attended one. A tribute to the deep Christian beliefs of the people aided and abetted by their freedom to attend due to a lack of employment. Everybody got a good send-off.

The biggest funeral was that of a German air crew who, mistaking Ireland for England, bombed a creamery nearby in Campile. Perhaps the bombs were released as a safety measure before trying to land. The plane was in difficulty and crashed, killing the crew. They were interred at Crosstown after a full military funeral with the German Ambassador and Military Attaché coming down from Dublin to attend. I watched with great interest as goose-stepping soldiers followed the coffins on open carriages all along the quay out of the town and over the "New Bridge" to the cemetery. The bridge was a difficulty. It had been deemed to be unsafe above certain loads for many years and accordingly it had been reduced to a single-lane zig-zag carriageway by the positioning of 60-gallon steel drums filled with sand. Two drums with a board in between were placed on alternate sides of the bridge every ten yards or so. It was an arrangement which did not make for an orderly, dignified procession.

I couldn't understand how all this extra weight would make the bridge safer and I can't remember ever seeing more than one car on the bridge at any time so I questioned Uncle Fran, Mr Kirk and anyone else who might know. No tenable explanation was offered. Two of the filled drums alone would weigh more than most cars of the period.

Fran and I joined the Scouts. The hall and HQ was very close to Monck Street and it was a very active troop. Our uniforms were attractive, navy blue linen and very hard-wearing. All insignia was in Gaelic but closely translated from the English of Baden Powell.

The motto of "be prepared" on the buckle of our belts became "bi uim" — neater and more exotic. Fran went off for a few days camping at Curracloe. Again, I was too young to go, but I was told I could visit, and I did.

It was only a small camp — eight boys and Kevin Kehoe — one of the assistant Scoutmasters. They were all quartered in an old British Army bell tent. The occupants slept feet at the centre, head at the tent wall. Travel was by bike, and a couple of bicycle carts carrying the tent and heavier equipment like the big "dixie", or cooking pot. Everything was well organised — two boys out collecting wood for the fire, two sent off to the nearest roadside pump for water and the rest on assorted duties — tying up the tent sides in the day to allow free passage of air, digging a latrine, shopping for milk and bread, etc. Kevin was an excellent organiser, a very happy young man of about twenty-four and we were all sorry when he left a few months later for England and the army.

Curracloe was about 5 miles from town and the roads were very quiet. I set off early and got there in no time on my bike and soon found them from the directions they'd given me. We had a wonderful day mostly in the water and playing on the deserted strand. If there is a more lovely beach in Ireland I have yet to find it. The surrounding area is very sparsely populated and in those pre-car days the only way to get there for most was to walk or cycle. There was one small hotel which in summer provided the sole social entertain-ment of the area – a weekly dance. Again, if you wanted to go you had to walk or cycle. Late-night road traffic after the dance often featured a boy riding a bike without lights taking another boy or girl home on the crossbar.

Most bikes were heavy roadster models and many of them made locally at Pierces' foundry — the town's main employers at the back of the school. Each rider took turns at doing the pedalling. Hurling matches with Carlow, thirty miles away, were well within reach for two lads and one bike. Somebody in the town owned a specially built bike for six riders, though it still only had two wheels. This was rumoured to be able to reach Dublin and back the same day. It took ages to stop and being a "fixed-wheel" with no neutral gear or brakes, would circle the monument outside the station four or five times before it could halt.

At camp there was a problem this day that led to my departure sooner than I had planned. The problem was dinner. The difficulty of storing food at camp makes daily procurement the best option. Anything stored is likely to be quickly found and welcomed by wildlife, and food which is fresh deteriorates rapidly in the warm summer air. This day's procurement had produced 4lb of sausages from the village butcher, which had been irresistible. On returning to camp the procurists were reminded that "today is Friday and a day of abstinence" — no meat or sausages for good Catholic boys on this or any Friday. Kevin thought about it and decided that tea would consist solely of tea and bread and jam. The sausages would wait for the midnight hour which would bring them into Saturday and make their consumption legitimate. Lacking preservative they would not keep until dinner the next day, and so it was. At 11.30 that night, the fire was relit and the cooking started and at midnight (or a couple of minutes past, to make quite sure) feasting commenced and soon all was gone. When the decision about delaying the sausages was made, my interest in staying until tea time waned and later in the afternoon I mounted my bike and rode back to Monck Street and a better tea than they were having in camp. I regretted missing the sausages and in bed that night my thoughts kept returning to them — "they'll be eating them now" I thought, as the church clock in Roe Street struck twelve. I had difficulty settling down to sleep. Fran's side of the bed was empty and he was pigging it on sausages in Curracloe while I was back here hungry in bed. Ah, the unfairness of life for the younger brother.

We loved living in Wexford. Aunt Mary took good care of us when mother went back to Liverpool where she was badly missed. Mary and May were in some ways similar — probably Cooney family traits. Calm, unfussy and good with people. Good with housecrafts. Every bed in the house carried a beautiful white crochet cover — all the work of Mary's hands. She had had a kidney removed when young and always took to bed a carafe of water to drink in the night. She was as pleasant as Johnny was unpleasant and kept a good house on little money. Mary was rounded in shape but fit and I remember my surprise when on a trip to Dublin she insisted on coming with us to climb Nelson's Pillar in O'Connell Street. The internal stairway was narrow and steep, but she managed it. From the top the view was magnificent and she was delighted with both the view and her achievement. Nelson's Pillar was blown up as a sign of English oppression by the IRA in the 1950s and everyone was sad. Why couldn't they just have removed Nelson and left the pillar? some asked. It was the main meeting point for the city and the terminal for the trams which all featured the word Pillar on their destination board. Trips to Dublin were always by car. Mostly they revolved around business — visits to suppliers, particularly refrigeration and ice cream manufacturers' agents. Aunt Annie, being the business brain, always made the decision but Uncle Fran did most of the talking — it worked well. Annie would also get in some shopping and always a visit to Hafner's in Mary Street for sausages and Clery's the department store nearly opposite on O'Connell Street by the Pillar.

The embarcation point for the Liverpool boat was very close by at the North Wall on the north bank of the Liffey a couple of hundred yards away. Clery's offered breakfast for early arrivals before the rest of the store was opened. It was a good service and attractively priced and later in the war, when rationing was severe in Britain, it was the first taste of plenty for travellers from there. Thick Irish rashers, sausage, black and white pudding and eggs — bliss!

We were often met at the boat by family who'd come up by car to collect us and the usual shopping and business calls and eating would take place before we started the journey back to Wexford — never without a large brown paper parcel of Hafner's sausages.

I still had bandages on my head and Dr McCabe was still removing bits of gravel, and at school I was enjoying things. I don't know if it was the bandages or the fact I'd come from England but I didn't get much attention from the teachers, except in the infant school from Tommy Roche. He was very kind to me and saw me as an injured temporary orphan. I was being introduced to Gaelic and seemed to like it better than most of my classmates. I was Seán (John) in the class register, and answered to it morning and afternoon and I liked it. I would grow up and remain Seán in Wexford to all who knew me at school in those days.

Miss Codd taught us music, or more correctly, singing. She presented us with an array of catchy songs and tunes with words in Gaelic and English and she accompanied herself on a melodeon. We weren't always sure what the songs were about but most children love singing and we enjoyed Miss Codd and all the lessons immensely. There was one song featuring somebody called "the dilsy dancy daro". Nobody except Miss Codd (or maybe not) knew who he was, but he seemed a fine fellow.

CHAPTER
FOURTEEN

The Bombing Begins

It was well into 1940 and the phoney war continued with little activity at the front and then suddenly everything changed. The German Panzer divisions broke out and through the Allies' lines. Holland and Belgium fell immediately and France capitulated soon after in May, with the bulk of the British troops managing to escape before the Germans reached the channel ports. All of Europe was now suddenly enemy occupied and in addition, despite General de Gaulle's call to arms, the vast bulk of France's army was now out of action and prisoners of the enemy. The French Navy was locked up in Toulon, Dakar and La Rochelle under the orders of the new pro-German Vichy French Government. It would not be used against Germany but it could, if things changed, be used against Britain. The strategic equation was now totally different. Some French troops escaped to Britain and so did a number of ships which decided to continue the fight following de Gaulle's call. The commanders of these ships were brave men as by defying the de facto French Government they became rebels and liable to execution. But they did, and that was how Alex arrived in Liverpool and became my uncle.

If the Germans were not now at England's gate they weren't far away — a mere twenty miles across the Channel — and things began to change rapidly. Britain was by herself and knew it. America was still isolationist and would not enter the conflict for another eighteen months, so it was "prepare for invasion" time. Entry to beaches all round the land was closed off with concrete pyramids to prevent tank and vehicle movement blocking all access points, and barbed wire and wooden posts planted on all wide beaches, which could possibly provide landing strips for planes or gliders. Blockhouses of concrete were built at vantage points everywhere. Though never used in fighting, they were much appreciated later by the GI's stationed locally in the build-up to the invasion. They had no doors and provided cover and shelter for assignations with the local beauties. The construction costs should really have been billed to the USA because the GI's were the only users. This was a period of rumour and some madness. The "spy" danger was being heavily advertised and real news of what was actually happening was scarce. The Ministry of Information as a title is a misnomer, as its main task was the suppression of information: then, as now, it believed that no news is good news and released little to the news agencies and media. HMS *Barham* was a battleship of the same vintage as the *Royal Oak*. She had also had an extensive refit in Liverpool over a long period early in the war. In November 1941 she was sunk by a U-boat in the Mediterranean with the loss of 868 lives. The information was only released two months later at the

231

end of January 1942. The secrecy was excused in official records by the statement that the Germans were unaware of their success! The ministry also maintained a tight censorship on all correspondence, particularly from and to the forces, and in such circumstances rumour and imagination run riot — it becomes difficult to be certain about anything. Later, following the heavy bombing of Liverpool, the government in London would itself come to believe that an insurrection had taken place in Liverpool and that the people were demanding that the government seek peace with Germany. It was totally untrue and London was only 200 miles distant — how could it be believed? It was, and the Queen's Messenger Convoy was despatched immediately to the city to help in feeding the stricken populace. This was a highly mobile soup kitchen. The blackout of course helped — everybody really was "in the dark". Signs of hysteria were visible. Reports appeared of an attacker who preyed on women in the dark of the night and an increasing number of incidents involving attacks by "the Slasher" were reported. The victims were all cut, though not severely and then he vanished into the night. The weapon was alleged to be a razor but no one could be sure. Nothing was taken and there was no other bodily or sexual harm — just the cuts. Police suspicions about the incidents were aroused when similar incidents took place at some distance from each other at similar times. There was either more than one "Slasher" or more than one hysteric. Closer re-questioning of "the victims" then took place and it became obvious that it was all down to personality disorders and attention-seeking. Today's equivalent would be those seeking media appearances on television or in the press at any cost or degradation whatsoever. The eternal "look at me" syndrome. When the word got out that the "Slasher" was imaginary the "attacks" ceased immediately. It was all part of the rumour and hysteria natural to a nation in a state of siege. Nobody knew when or how the enemy would arrive but we knew he was coming. It was also felt that Ireland would also be invaded despite its neutrality. Its ports could enable the U-boat fleets to cut completely the supply lines from America.

Maybe Ireland was not so safe after all, thought May and Tom, and so back we came to Liverpool where we were all united again. No matter what happened we'd all be together. We were pulling the drawbridge up and arriving in time for the start of the action and the main event though we were unsure of what was coming. We would soon find out.

The first round of the war ended with the fall of France and the second with the Battle of Britain. Having failed to obtain aerial supremacy, Germany changed tactics. The real reasons why an invasion of Britain was never attempted remain a mystery, but the inability to command the skies, which was a prerequisite for invasion, was probably a major factor. The build-up for the German invasion continued along the French coast and the main hostilities now became bombing raids on carefully selected targets — such as Liverpool. Liverpool was the key where most of the war supplies from America arrived. It was also the HQ for

Western Approaches directing the battle against the U-boat fleets, now sinking the merchant fleets in rapidly increasing numbers. Sink the supply ships and destroy the port — the German strategy was sound and now they began its execution.

It started quite slowly in the summer of 1940. The air raid sirens would sound, usually in the late afternoon and everybody would look up into the sky instead of going to the air raid shelters. Sometimes planes could be seen but mostly very little happened. These were probably Luftwaffe reconnaissance flights or even some of our own — everything was very casual and then the bombs started to drop and things became more serious. Fran and I were quite excited by the increased activity together with all the other boys, and the bombsites became a big attraction and were much visited. The Germans had surveyed the area closely over some years and they knew exactly what their targets were and they had a fair amount of success right from the beginning. Housing and industry in Bootle and Liverpool dockland were side by side and it was inevitable that there would be heavy casualties among the population and the housing stock. Most houses were empty when hit, but not all, and it was very difficult for the ARP and the other rescue services to know whether the houses were or were not occupied when the bomb hit. Had they gone to the shelter? Were they elsewhere? It was difficult to know and the only reliable information was what the neighbours knew. Many were entombed and buried for days because of lack of information which led the diggers to

234

concentrate on other bombed houses or rubble. Most houses had cellars and these were where survivors would usually be found. To reach them, every brick and piece of debris resting over or in the cellar would have to be removed to clear a passage for entry. This all had to be done by hand and without any protective gloves often with leaking gas, water and electric mains mixed up and escaping in the rubble. A lot of the bombing destroyed everything above ground but left the cellars intact and many families continued to live in the cellar when everything else above ground was gone until they could be rehoused — it was still their home. This use of the cellar as an air raid shelter was common. The public shelters were awful — cold, bare, foul-smelling, overcrowded and with no toilets or means for even making a cup of tea. As a result many preferred the alternative of their own cellar or an Anderson shelter in the back garden. A hole in the ground covered with galvanised corrugated steel with earth on top.

Rosie was a woman around fifty, a little bit retarded, who lived in a shared house on the corner of Bedford Place and Brasenose Road on the way to school. The houses were hit and Rosie who was in the cellar was unharmed. I remember her sitting in the rubble imploring people to dig for people in the debris of the next door house. She did this for two days and for whatever reason no one came and nothing happened. Then on the third day she finally got them digging and a man and a woman were brought to the surface, still alive, and taken off to hospital, Rosie, in tears, kissing them as they were dragged out. Rosie continued to live in the cellar until the end of the war. She had the bare essentials for life and a number of times I ventured into her cellar as I knew her and was curious about how she lived. She had running water and candles and that was about it. The cellar door and the steps down were still intact, though the door had no lock and so it was easy to enter and look around. How many lived like Rosie? Probably lots. I never forgot Rosie who lived for many years after and I often thought that though fate had not bestowed much upon her in the way of gifts, she was blessed, and saved the lives of her two neighbours. If that was the reason she was put upon earth, perhaps it was enough.

Mr Doran was a customer in the Marine. A quiet, good-living man who lived near the school. He had two daughters, Jean and Peggie, and a son Gerard, and asked my father if he had any work for the girls. They were a close-knit family and he wanted to keep them near to home and he knew that they would be safe at work under the eye of Tom and so we got two new barmaids. Peggie was only seventeen, pretty and feminine, and quiet. I fell in love with her immediately and indulged my childhood fancy and we became the best of friends. Jean was a few years older, not as pretty but a great worker with the gift of the gab. She had an answer for everybody and was made for the Marine. Liverpool Irish to the core, she livened up the quietest of days. We got a new barman around the same time, Pat Melia. Pat was a young man exempt from military service because of the loss of a kneecap playing football. Much quieter than Jean, but always smiling and singing. Everybody seemed to sing in those days and I'll always remember Pat singing in the mornings as he polished the glasses:

> Sierra Sue I'm sad and lonely
> Sierra Sue I think of you
> Sierra Sue my sad heart's calling
> It calls for you, Sierra Sue

He had other numbers in his repertoire but I remember that one best. Perhaps because he always sang it whenever we had a party. Pat was with us a couple of years and then went to another job. I don't know if he went voluntarily or was directed, for in those times one could be directed to another job by the Ministry of Labour without warning. Jobs such as munitions manufacture were considered more important than others. A card would arrive directing one to report to another place of work and the current employer would be told to pay the employee up to date, send him his cards and find a replacement. Pat left and we all missed him. He died young a few years later and May, unaware of the fact and out shopping, saw Pat's mother and greeted her, asking how was Pat? She received a cold stare in exchange. Mrs Melia did not know that news of Pat's death had not reached us, and she felt understandably that it had been ignored as we had not attended the funeral. May was shocked when Mrs Melia told her Pat was dead and explained that none of us knew, so Mrs Melia was placated. Such things mattered then, far more than they seem to today. The community was just a large family. This failure in information transmission in such a close community was yet another example of how little everyone knew at the period of what was going on in the war and the rest of the world. The Melias lived a mile away and we'd not heard about Pat's decease — even in a popular meeting place like the Marine where everyone knew him.

Nationally, we were totally dependent on the BBC and newspapers, cut down to four pages owing to paper rationing. Locally, we depended almost totally on word-of-mouth for news of what was happening around us. It must have been similar for all the warring nations. Later the Nuremberg Trials would highlight these difficulties. Who knew and did what sometimes came down to "the likely probability". A hard decision when somebody's life depended on it.

Around the time May's mother died in 1913 and she went to her grandmother, Adolf Hitler arrived in Liverpool, according to the testimony of his sister-in-law Bridget. Bridget was an Irish girl who met Adolf's half-brother Alois in Dublin, where he was working as a waiter. There was a relationship and misbehaviour and a pregnancy followed. To escape the censure of Holy Catholic Ireland they decamped to Liverpool where their son Patrick was born on 12 March 1911 at 102 Stanhope Street, near the city centre. The house was actually in the parish of St Patrick's, one of the city's oldest Catholic churches, and presumably that is where he was baptised. Later according to Bridget's sworn deposition in the US Library of Congress, Alois left them and returned to Berlin where he opened a very successful restaurant which was heavily patronised by Nazi party members. By this time Patrick was grown and he and his mother were now living in the United States. Patrick visited Berlin and his father and uncle and there seems to have been some difficulty in getting back as they were keen for him to remain. He did return however, and later in the war, was conscripted into the US Navy. On demobilisation he was employed in a New York advertising agency as a "Greeter" but never attained any senior position there or elsewhere. Obviously the name Patrick Hitler was a good start point for conversation or introduction. Perhaps his career would have advanced more rapidly if he'd stayed in Berlin with father and uncle.

Nowhere in the many biographies of Hitler is this Liverpool period mentioned. Probably because the future Führer was at the time dodging the army call-up in Vienna for which he was wanted by the police. It would not have been something he'd have liked others to know later. Again, the question of evidence arises. Bridget Hitler, Patrick, Alois and their Berlin visits are all authentic. The story rings true on the "likely probability" yardstick. His second visit — by proxy — would be well-recorded and remembered by all who were there, when his emissaries — the Luftwaffe came. They also flattened his old home in Stanhope Street.

It was clear that both the earlier reconnaissance missions and the bombing itself were well planned and directed. The raids began in the early evening around six and continued for eight to ten hours. There were some anti-aircraft and searchlight batteries outside the centre, but they were totally ineffective and we never saw them bring down a single raider. All the fighter planes were in the south and none were available to repel the attackers. The many warships in the port seemed unable to use their guns, possibly because of regulations concerning port operations. All in all the raids did not constitute any great danger for the German flyers. This was in stark contrast to the RAF raids over Germany when they began later in the war. We started sleeping in the cellar every night and were joined often by others caught far from home and no trams running. Everybody wanted to be with their own when the bombs started falling, but it wasn't always possible and so we were joined by stragglers — nightbound and far from home. Everybody was tired — talk was minimal and we just dozed or slept in the lighted cellar and waited for the bombers to go, the dawn and a new day.

CHAPTER
FIFTEEN

Destroy Liverpool

The importance of Liverpool in the coming conflict had been assessed by Germany long before war began and extensive aerial reconnaissance had provided the Luftwaffe with detailed plans for their future offensive. After the fall of France and the Battle of Britain, the centre of attention for the German High Command became the supply line from America.

Grand Admiral Raeder, Commander-in-Chief of the German Navy (the Kriegsmarine), urged Hitler to destroy Liverpool with a strongly argued presentation in July 1940. The destruction of the port and the ability to receive supplies from America, plus the obliteration of the main anti U-boat capability, would lead to total collapse, and Britain would have to sue for peace. It was a sound strategy and agreed enthusiastically by the German High Command, according to documents discovered after the war, and so it began.

Like the first light of a summer's day, it began slowly, before bursting into the heat of noon. It started with small sporadic raids, then everything warmed up and from 30 August for three nights, 200 bombers of 14 Gruppen hammered the city and the waterfront from end to end. The Custom House was burnt down and Cammell-Laird's was hit. The ill-fated *Prince of Wales* still being built in their yard was nearly sunk by a bomb landing between ship and dock which caused the great ship to spring leaks and take in water. The vessel was saved from foundering by the fire service, which pumped out the water, for the ship was not yet in service and capable of doing the job itself. What was very apparent was the accuracy of the bombing which was concentrated on the docks and other riverside targets like Cammell-Laird. Damage was extensive but inland was almost untouched.

This was our first real taste of what was to come, but there was some confusion because everything went quiet for the next few weeks. At the end of September the raids started again and the much-loved and ancient Argyll Theatre in Birkenhead was burnt down. The raids, however, were light and short — nothing like the late August bombings, and this is how it proceeded up to Christmas, with December being peaceful and without any attacks up until Christmas week. Our presents arrived early on 20 December, delivered by over fifty carriers from the sky. The spirit of goodwill was clearly in the air for they didn't want to leave and stayed with us for nearly ten hours. It was the same for the other nights up to Christmas Eve, then they left, went home for Christmas and New Year and stayed away until mid-January. The damage and fires were widespread and the canal was breached and deposited a barge into the adjacent railway goods yard. Everything was unpredictable — the raids seemed to have no pattern. Heavy attacks would be followed by peace and calm, then they would return but in much lighter numbers, then more quiet, then heavy and prolonged bombing. It produced uncertainty in the people, which was probably intended, and although morale remained high, the uncertainty produced fear and worry which had a cumulative affect — everyone seemed tired and in need of sleep.

This is how life continued in its desultory manner up to May and then it all got serious and desperate again. The Luftwaffe raised the stakes and put all their chips on the table — the game lasted nearly two weeks before they withdrew — we were down to our last and nearly out of the game. The Christmas blitz had been severe, but it was a lighter event than May. Even at distance the pictures are vivid and alive with flames, explosions, spectacle and above all destruction and death.

By now and since mid-1940 we were sleeping most nights in the cellar which had been heavily reinforced with wooden roof supports to prevent collapse and entombment. We had a variety of beds, mattresses, chairs and a couple of electric bulb fires which were needed, for the cellar was for keeping beer cold — below 52°F. This is a bit cool for humanity and it was ironic that we sheltered in the only part of the house without heating, but better cold than dead. We were often joined in the cellar by refugees from the pub — staff and customers caught by the air raid warning sirens and unable to get home before the bombs started. Electric kettles were a rarity and a drink of tea required the hazard of a visit upstairs to get a kettle of boiling water. Though surrounded by drink in barrel and bottle, it was tea we all wanted. We stayed in the cellar until the long, uninterrupted high whine of the all-clear sounded or until morning arrived when we arose and resumed whatever we each had to do.

My bed was a mattress on the floor under a double bed and there I slept soundly and heavily throughout the period. It was dark under the bed which was an advantage as the cellar was lit and I assumed that Fran who was beside me slept soundly as well, but he did not. He worried about the trapdoors to the cellar from Raleigh Street. These were the access for the draymen with their weekly delivery and collection. Full barrels in, empty barrels out. A bomb could come through those doors, thought Fran, and then we'd all be finished. This was a constant concern and it must have affected him greatly, particularly at school. I was totally unaware of his fear until many years later when May told me that he had been affected by the war. When I spoke to Fran about it he confirmed it and told me of his constant nightmare of the trapdoors to the street. Many people had similar worries but few voiced them. It wasn't done, you just got on with things. Maybe it is a genetic thing but I didn't worry at all that I can remember — very like my fatalistic father, "If your name's on the bullet, you'll get it," he'd say. For me the war was exciting and dangerous — so much going on. My curiosity and interest in what was happening around me perhaps overpowered any thoughts of self.

It had been a long and noisy night and then morning and the all-clear finally arrived. Fran put on his cap and

244

looked at May. "Where are you going?" she said. "I'm going to Mass," said Fran, and with that, left. He was soon back. "The church has gone," he said, "it's burnt down". Beautiful St Alexander's and its gilt altar was no more. The first bomb had caused extensive damage but had failed to remove the flowers on the altar, richly decorated for the May celebrations. Incendiaries and fires had followed and the destruction was now complete. The school had been hit in the middle and was now in two parts, a pair of towers pointing to the sky, but the presbytery was untouched. It would be my schoolhouse later on. We sat down to eat our toast, which I covered with beef dripping, for we had lots of it from May's nightly roasts — it's much better than the beef, I thought. Another popular item of diet now long gone. Fran was telling me about the church and school when suddenly there was the loudest bang we'd ever heard. The house shook and the holy pictures fell off the walls. The three of us looked at each other in the silence that followed. What we'd heard was the last cry of the *Malakand* which had been burning for days in the nearby Brocklebank Dock. She was loaded with over 1,000 tons of ammunition and explosives and should not have been in dock. Usually and elsewhere explosives were loaded from lighters in mid-river as a safety precaution but the Mersey flows too fast and strong to allow this. It was an unfortunate restriction and exacted a heavy price. The area around the dock was completely devastated and flattened over a wide area, and the dock itself completely destroyed. It was later filled in with rubble from the surrounds and the remnants of the ship's superstructure were left sticking up to the sky. It was a powerful, if unintended memorial, which was left that way for many years. The ship's master, Captain Kinley, his crew and the fire service made heroic efforts to save the ship but it was not to be — events were against them. An early hit with incendiary bombs had been extinguished, then a shot-down flaming barrage balloon had landed on the ship and finally the inferno created by the burning sheds alongside could no longer be controlled. It was not possible to save the ship and prevent the coming catastrophe and the crew and fire services withdrew and everyone was removed from a wide area around.

The bang we heard was the last of a series of explosions which began soon after she was abandoned and left to die. She burned for weeks and was isolated for months. Nobody knew if we'd heard the last, or if she still held further surprises in her smouldering hull. The *Malakand* was the source of later reports and rumours relating to the disappearance of people who were never accounted for, particularly firemen and a missing tender.

We got the detail and news about the *Malakand* when father returned from the ARP post and Fran and I went out to look around and see the night's damage. The city was like an annexe of Hell. The timber yards were all in flames and firemen were asleep, exhausted on the pavements with the abandoned hoses on the ground pouring out water onto the burning pyres. All the way to the Pier Head it was the same. No trams were running and at Goree we walked through knee-deep piles of coffee beans and cocoa. The warehouse floors had collapsed and the sacks had split, disgorging their contents onto the street. St Nicholas, the mariners' church, was gone and the city centre was an appalling sight. The Central Library and Museum, the Technical School, and Lewis's were among the major casualties and the *Royal Daffodil* ferry had been sunk at the Seacombe landing stage.

We walked on up Byrom Street and Scotland Road and back along Stanley Road — devastation and fire everywhere and then we came to Hermia Street on the other side of the road from Wolsey Street where our grandparents and aunts, Winnie and Emily, lived.

I say we came to Hermia Street, but it no longer existed, neither did Celia Street or Rosalind and Jessica streets. Where there had been houses there were now only bricks and rubble — none of it above head height. It was as if a massive press had come down on the houses and flattened them. We had not seen damage so complete, so widespread and uniform as this. Its cause was the landmine — a new weapon of terror which we knew nothing about. These were silent killers 12ft long and 2ft in diameter which came down by parachute. Their power was frightening and as none of their force was absorbed by burial in the ground on landing, ground level took the full blast. These land mines were actually sea mines for sinking ships, but rendered obsolete by improved means of detection. Any which failed to explode were the responsibility of the Navy, which knew all about them — not the Army.

247

They were digging and looking for people in the rubble, and the public house (the Derby) on the surviving corner of Celia Street and Stanley Road was acting as a temporary morgue. The windows and doors had all gone and inside on tables, counters and floors were the bodies brought out from the debris. Many of them were doubtless customers who little thought their next visit would be their last. It was, and they got no farewell drink or "one for the road". "Time gentlemen please" had been called — but by the Luftwaffe, not the publican. From then the words became an evocation of Hermia Street. The finality of the scene overwhelmed me and I thought of the words on death in the gospels at Mass in St Alexander's.

"You know not the hour or the day, for it cometh like a thief in the night."

Now I understood what that meant.

The Hermia Street devastation was the result of two, or possibly three, landmines and remained in the memory as the most total piece of devastation we ever witnessed.

Most of the dead were in their day clothes but some had died in bed — but how? Very few showed signs of injury and all faces were peaceful with eyes wide open — not contorted in any way. How had they died? "Blast," we were told. But how does blast kill — it seemed to be like a great vacuum cleaner which sucks the life from people? No one could tell me. I touched the hand of a man in a navy blue suit to see if he was really dead. I wanted to touch him on the lips but was restrained by his dignity even in death. His hand was cold and his skin was smooth like a tablet of soap. A tablet was his future.

Fran broke the eerie silence, "They don't look dead, do they?" "No." That was all I could reply, overcome by the sadness of the scene and thinking about the rapidity of the transition from life to death. There was no living person in the shattered pub other than ourselves, and we walked slowly out of the doorless entrance onto the burning, smoky, rubble-strewn streets.

We called in to Wolsey Street which was directly across the road to see our family and all were OK, although only yards away from the devastation. Grandfather was now available for evening work he told us, as the Metropole had gone in the night and also the Rotunda on the way to town. The theatres were falling thick and fast. Grandma gave us a cup of tea and a slice of bread and butter. She always buttered the bread before slicing it and I'd never seen anyone else do this.

We arrived back home and there was sad news waiting for us. The previous night the Doran girls had departed quickly when the air raid siren sounded. They had refused the offer of sanctuary with us in the cellar saying their parents would be anxious about them and off they went. Shortly after arriving home near St Alexander's, the house was hit. Mr Doran and Peggy were killed and the others injured. Again the dead were unmarked — killed by the blast. Jean had gone to hospital and eventually returned to us bringing with her Peggy's green corduroy lumber jacket from her youth hostel walks as a present for me. She knew how fond I was of her and it was something she thought I'd like to have. It was too big for me but clothing was rationed and she said I'd grow into it, and I did, and wore it a lot. It was the first piece of clothing I had with a zip fastener, which was a very new thing and it was much admired by my pals. Jean was a wonderful woman who helped May domestically in addition to her duties in the bar. Every week she polished everything she could lay her hands on, and in particular a copper kettle made by grandfather which shone like the sun. We always knew when she'd been, just by looking at the kettle in the hearth. Her mother went back to Ireland and found a cottage in her native County Down for one shilling a week which made a great impression on me at the time, but then everything in Ireland was cheap, for there was little money and little demand for accommodation. Everyone was working in England or fighting far away in foreign lands.

The bombs had started again and Father came into the cellar. "We've got to get out. Campbell & Isherwoods is on fire and it could set us alight too." Campbell & Isherwood, the electrical contractors, were separated from us by a narrow entry about 3ft wide at the back. They'd been hit by a string of incendiaries and the workshops were now blazing fiercely. "Take these," he said passing us some orange passes to the basement of Blackledges, now operating as an air raid shelter for the neighbourhood. We struggled up the stairs and across the road with the anti-aircraft guns booming and staining the night sky and into Blackledges, then down into the dimly lit basement refuge. The Porters were there — covered in black with

250

big white eyes like a troop of Christy Minstrels. It was bath night and a nearby bomb had blown all the soot down the chimney onto the assembled children around the tin bath in the centre of the kitchen. Being wet, the soot stuck on the naked bodies but nobody was concerned about the niceties of dignity or the naked body — safety was the main concern and everybody was laughing about it, little Mrs Porter in particular. Having no clothes on was not a problem, for being next to the bakery ovens we were all nice and warm. Shortly before the raid ended and dawn broke we all received a reminder of how tenuous our existence had become. The bakery was next to a warehouse which fronted onto Bedford Place and suddenly we were jerked out of our light slumber and into suspense by a bomb hitting the warehouse crashing through the roof and the five floors below and coming to rest on the other side of the dividing wall — only feet away. Everything went quiet. We waited for the explosion but none came and we all said our prayers silently as we all evacuated the building as quickly as we could. Many bombs failed to explode but it was difficult to know immediately if they were faulty or whether they were a "delayed-action" type timed to explode later. Another landed outside the Marine in the middle of the tramlines and only about 10 yards away. Again, it failed to explode. Both were dealt with by the army's bomb disposal teams, but not for several days.

The fire at Campbell & Isherwoods had gutted the workshops, which were a total loss, but fortunately the Marine was safe, standing defiantly — the only remaining building on that side of the burning street and we were able to reoccupy our home again. The pub continued in business right through these, the worst of times. No windows at all and everybody drinking and laughing and singing behind the thick blackout curtains shielding the light from the street when dusk fell.

Back in the Marine, Uncle Jack appeared with a large jug of hot Bovril. "Have some of this, mate," he said, "it'll warm the cockles of your heart." I eagerly accepted his offering but couldn't understand how cockles got into your heart. Cockles were what the man with the tray and the bottle of vinegar sold when he came around the pubs in the evening and there were plenty of them on the shore at Seaforth. I made a mental note to ask him to explain it to me later, but forgot. All round us was news of bombs damage, deaths, heroism — all local — we had no idea of what was happening elsewhere. There was a total preoccupation with getting through the day and the jobs to be done and surviving and thinking about the convoys. Yes, the convoys and their crews heavily drawn from the close-packed surrounding streets with most families having someone at sea. Families like the Kavanaghs — handsome boys and pretty sisters — who were also great singers. Losses at sea were heavy particularly on the Russian convoys which began that year. Seamen who we all knew well just never came in anymore — lost in the icy waters running to Murmansk. Three minutes in the water was enough. They were the bravest of men and the lack of official recognition of the efforts and sacrifice by the Merchant Navy is still resented.

Many ships were old, slow and without any form of protection. Their cargoes were often lethal and in oil tankers the dangers were compounded. In the water, if the crude oil failed to burn, it smothered survivors while petroleum products invariably exploded and incinerated everyone who'd managed to get off the ship. Yet men sailed on these funerary ships throughout — some for nearly six years. Liverpool — heavily represented in their ranks put up a memorial to them at the Pier Head and Russia decorated them all. This was much appreciated by the recipients but no enthusiasm was shown for a similar award by their own country. We were now being assisted by fire brigades from all over Lancashire and Cheshire and further afield which had responded to calls for help when it became apparent that the city's services and capability were being overwhelmed. Warehouses provided the accommodation and mobile canteens their food.

Father had been engaged on his usual nocturnal activities of locating where bombs had fallen and rescuing the victims. From the post in Sheridan Place they could hear every explosion in their sector but sound is far more difficult to trace than light, and in the dark it often took a long time to locate a hit. This was what happened in Howe Street, across the road from the post and running down to the docks on the north side of Harland & Wolff. The houses were tall and terraced and were divided between families. There were no separate entrances or staircases and people shared toilets and kitchens. The bomb here had removed the front wall of the house into the street and on the top floor, unable to escape, was the Gibbs family, most of them together in a large bed on a sloping floor, and in imminent danger of despatch into the street below. The wardens, having located the danger, ascended the stairs, and Tom and Harold Brown being the slimmest and most active, supported the collapsing ceiling and holding onto the door frame and linking hands pulled each one from the listing bed and off to the rescue centre. They had just checked the rest of the house and were outside when the remaining structure collapsed. A close-run thing, but a danger which they were always aware of with blitzed buildings.

The local paper, the *Bootle Times*, gave a full report and the rescue was celebrated. Father and Harold and the others all got medals (OBE), went to the palace and were decorated by the king. It was Tom's only visit to London. His employers, Threlfalls, sent him a letter of congratulation on his award and presented him with a gold watch. Nicest of all, the Gibbs family presented him with an engraved cigarette case. They had little — another example of the generosity of the poorest. Father took all this in his stride — he never made a fuss about anything and we only found out all the details when we read the report in the paper. I think he regarded it all as a bit excessive, for they were doing similar rescue work all the time. Always in danger from collapsing buildings and the enemy overhead — for all this was happening while the raids and bombing were in progress. He put his medal in the safe and I never saw him wear it, though he had many opportunities to do so. I was very proud of him and asked him could I

254

have his medal when he died. He smiled and said yes. I think it pleased him, though he said no more. I got the medal and the cigarette case and Fran got the watch.

By now so many were homeless and sleeping in fields on the outskirts that refugee centres were established in the surrounding areas of Maghull, Formby and Ormskirk. Only a few miles away, but almost totally untouched by the bombing. Here they slept, were fed and rehoused either back home later, with relatives, or outside the area. The utilities were badly affected. Water, gas and electricity supplies were not available in many places and emergency water standpipes were erected where you went with your bucket. It wasn't even possible to bury the dead properly — the funeral services were totally inadequate for the calls of the moment. The mortuaries were full and the clergy were exhausted from their twenty-four-hour days. And there was no petrol for the hearses. So as they'd lived together and died together they were now buried together and on 14 May at Anfield over 1,000 of the dead were buried in a mass grave. Internment in groups, rather than singly, became common.

This appealed to me and I thought that if you had to be buried it was comforting to have lots around you — just like when you were alive. This feeling for togetherness is particularly strong in the city: tribal and probably Gaelic and lost in the mists of time and antiquity and there in the ancient Irish proverb, "It is in the shelter of each other that the people live."

It may even be a factor in the latter-day adoption of, "You'll never walk alone", as the anthem for Liverpool

Football Club. As an old priest said to the reporter as the old tenements were prepared for demolition, "Down there nobody dies alone." The conditions were squalid but the humanity was rich — everybody belonged.

It was now decided that Fran and I should again be evacuated — a not unsurprising decision considering events and the removal of school, church and much else. May and Tom decided that May would take us to Wexford again, but it wasn't easy. We couldn't get out from Liverpool as the service to Dublin had been halted and only passage from Holyhead was possible. Even this was difficult as Lime Street station was closed due to the blockage of the cutting through the sandstone ridge to the station by a bomb. Trains were finishing and starting at Edge Hill, the other side of the ridge and the original city station of the world's first passenger railway. There were no trams and we were saved by Mr Burke, one of Father's ARP colleagues who ran a hackney company on Stanley Road near Bankhall. Petrol was rationed and in very short supply but he could get us to Edge Hill. Even then we needed several detours as the direct route along Stanley Road was closed by a bomb destroying the carriageway above the rail tracks 100ft below. We arrived at Edge Hill and boarded a carriage from a bygone era and we slowly made our way to Holyhead where we arrived in the early evening. You can see Holyhead from Liverpool on a clear day — about 45 miles as the crow flies — but it took us all of four hours. The train terminated at the boat station and then as now the boat and the short crossing to Dublin were the main economic factors in the town's existence.

We had left a world of chaos where the effects of the damage would be felt for a long time. Much had gone forever and other things would be changed beyond recognition in just a few years. In Bootle 95 per cent of all housing had been damaged and 12 per cent totally destroyed. The figures for Liverpool were 62 per cent and 5 per cent. 25,000 were homeless. The city would have open spaces everywhere as bomb sites were cleared and nothing put in their place. A question often asked was why so little was done by either central or local government to replace what had been lost? Even the Crown let the city down. The main post office in Victoria Street, a Crown property, never replaced the upper storeys lost in 1941, the fine truncated edifice standing as a monument and reminder of government inaction. What happened to war reparation payments?

In bombs per square mile in Britain, Bootle would remain unsurpassed. Only some German cities later would receive assaults on a similar scale.

May 1941 signalled the end of the Blitz on the city and things started to function again as repairs to transport, utilities and structures were carried out. Work along the line of docks was by now ceaseless as convoy and submarine activities increased in intensity. The month of May was not only the end of the bombings but also the turning point of the war at sea. In that month the capture of *U-110* and its cipher machine allowed the codebreakers at Bletchley to decipher and read the German naval codes. The result was dramatic as the Admiralty now knew where the U-boats where and where they were going. Sinkings of over 300,000 tons of merchant shipping in May/June were cut by two-thirds in the following period.

By the time that John McCormack, accompanied by the band of the Irish Guards, was singing in the rain to the dockers and seamen at Gladstone Dock in November, the losses were only around one-fifth of the May/June figure. Things were looking up but there was still far to go — the conflict hadn't yet even reached half-time. The concert was one of many strange, now forgotten wartime events and was well recorded at the time. This passage comes from *A Port at War*:

It was decided in high quarters, as an experiment, to see whether dock workers could not be given "Music While You Work". The Band of the Irish Guards came down with them, for one concert, no less world-famous a singer than the late Count John McCormack, singing in the open air, a thing he had always refused to do, for only the second time in his career. And what a day he had! Rain dripped through a tarpaulin cover on to singer, pianist and band alike; above, the Overhead Railway trains roared at intervals; in the middle distance shunting engines went about their business. In front of the platform a sea of cloth caps was flanked by the grey bulk of HMS *Ramillies*. Even in these unfamiliar surroundings, McCormack sang with the sincerity which never deserted him and the serenity of "The Gentle Maiden" sung by this incomparable artist momentarily put even Gladstone Dock under a spell.

258

Though he sang on the radio several times afterwards, this was one of McCormack's last appearances in public.

CHAPTER
SIXTEEN

Sanctuary

We stood on the platform at Holyhead and looked back eastwards towards Liverpool. The sky was red as the city burned from Bootle in the north to Dingle in the south all along the waterfront — 12 miles of inferno — it was now the easiest of targets for the next wave of Luftwaffe attackers.

"I see Liverpool got it again last night," said a man next to us and I looked up at mother as she stood silent, showing no emotion at all. All she wanted to do, but unknown to us, was burst out crying, but she restrained herself, knowing it would upset her young sons who looked to her for comfort. The stationmaster appeared and told us that he'd put down straw mattresses in the waiting rooms and we would all be alright there until the boat to Dublin the following morning. He also produced a large teapot and hot tea and cups a little later and we all fell asleep on the straw surrounded by our baggage and fellow refugees.

The early crossing the next day got us to Dublin in bright sunlight. The trip was fast, owing to an alert that a U-boat was in the area, and there on the quay were Annie and Fran to meet us with the large Ford V8.

Although we'd only been away for a year, lots had changed. Annie and Fran and our cousins were now living in Clarence House which had been refurbished and Monck Street seemed quiet with them gone. I was now old enough to go to the big school with Fran, Pat and Lar. This was run by the Irish Christian Brothers — a lay order founded in 1802 in Waterford to provide schooling for poor boys. State schooling was not begun in Britain until 1870 and only really got underway with the 1894 Elementary Education Act. This introduced new secular schools and education but also provided grants and annual financial assistance to the existing denominational schools, which had been carrying the full burden until then.

The Christian Brothers were hard men who believed in the liberal use of the strap — a stiff black, leather weapon residing in a special pocket in their black cassocks for maintaining both discipline and punishing errors in schoolwork. By this time they had schools in many places in both countries, and back in Liverpool I would become their pupil again later and remain so until I became adult. It has been a popular practice to criticise the order in recent years which in many instances seems both unjust and somewhat unrealistic. Corporal punishment was the method almost everywhere for correcting and disciplining not only children but those in institutions such as the services, prisons or asylums. Viewed from today it seems totally unacceptable but then it was regarded as the norm and proven as a method for correction and instruction.

The brothers lived together at schools like monastics, but they had little in the way of life's pleasures. They were unpaid and unlike monastics, their table was Spartan and no wine, beer or spirits appeared upon it. Likewise tobacco.

No money was allocated for it and so there was no smoking. It was also banned by the order itself because it gave bad example to the boys. All in all they didn't get a lot back for devoting their lives to the teaching of boys from every social class. It was their whole life. Most shared accommodation and their holidays were spent together at a house or hotel near Dublin or Galway. They were not allowed to go home to visit their families, except once every five years for ten days. Many of them had a reputation for brutality, but strangely at the Boca in Wexford it was the lay masters who were the ones to look out for. Lay masters were not issued with a strap, so they used hands and fists instead. Mr Woods, a man in his thirties with a red face and a blue suit, seemed to spend most of his lesson attacking his charges. Sometimes they retaliated and sometimes so did their relatives at the school gates or once or twice in the classroom. It seemed to make little difference to him or them and they continued in this way for many years. I can't remember learning much at all at the Boca, except to avoid Mr Woods. I was there for nearly two years but I enjoyed it very much with Barney and Stikey from the same street and many others who all became friends.

There were some sexual liberties taken with the boys at the Boca but they only came from one small, fat brother who would move around the class looking at the boys' work. Peering down and talking he would lean on the desk and slide his hand in between their thighs. Everybody knew what was going on and it didn't bother the boys very much at all. Fran received the treatment but like the others was unfazed. Nobody complained as they realised they would not be believed, and all males hate fuss. The perpetrator was a subject of amusement for the lads and was not regarded as a serious danger. He was under the full surveillance of the class and provided them with amusement. It was educational and taught the boys a recognition of the sexual perversity of the wider world outside.

Gone with the Wind was showing at the Capitol. Everybody had been talking about this film for a long time and waiting for it to arrive in town. Finally, after three years since production, it was here. Very different from the other films we'd seen, it was four and a half hours long, more than twice the usual length. There were several intervals to allow reels to be changed by the projectionist and we discussed what had happened so far when the lights went up in the breaks. It was also in "glorious technicolor" and most films were still black and white. We got our pennies together and queued and were finally seated on the right in the cheap seats (wooden benches) about six rows from the front. The film has a good storyline and we were enthralled — all of us — the boys and the girls. Fran was so taken with it that he didn't notice Terry Wrack seated behind him. Terry was simple and although about thirty years of age was always with the kids. Somewhere he'd found a razorblade and during the film he applied the blade to the seam of Fran's short trousers. Fran never felt a thing and it was only when he emerged into the street and saw his shorts hanging by the belt and his exposed leg that he knew something had happened. Terry, blade in hand and very proud of his handiwork, followed him out grinning broadly. It was no good saying anything to Terry — just another job for Mary and the sewing basket. Needless to say we all thought it was hilarious — including Fran. We even forgot about Rhett Butler and Scarlett O'Hara for a while in figuring out how Terry had managed to do it unnoticed. My overwhelming memory and impression from the film was the burning of Atlanta scene which reminded me strongly of how Liverpool looked the last time I'd seen it.

Across the river from the house in Monck Street was Ferry Bank. In earlier times a bridge had linked the two, but was long gone, but the promontories remained on both sides of the water. It was a long walk round over the "New" Bridge but there was a ferry for the crossing provided by Jack from the cotsafe. Jack was about fifty and operated a big rowing boat between the two points. In summer, business was brisk because the beach at Ferry Bank was good and very popular and from it one could walk along the strand to Curracloe. The fare was one penny each, including boys and girls, but infants were free. The Slaney runs strongly between the two points and Jack earned his pennies when the stream was in full flow either inward or out, but he never had any difficulty, unlike others less practised on the crossing who would be carried by the strong flood far from their destination. There was a flag at Ferry Bank side which was raised if you needed the boat. Jack sometimes did the trip there (empty) and back with only one or two passengers late in the day. Much effort for little reward.

From Ferry Bank, a breakwater of stones ran parallel with the quay for about half a mile. This was an effective barrier to the worst of the storm waters which battered the coast in winter. Behind it in mid-river were the fishing boats safely at anchor. There was also a man-made island in midstream near the end of the breakwater. This was for taking on and taking off ballast for sailing ships, which needed to be made seaworthy. There was little if any activity there and few ships came, as sail gave way to steam. It was also probably due to the fact that the approaches to the harbour had been silted up over the years. No dredging of the channel seems to have taken place and by this time only small ships and old schooners were using the port. The largest of these were the *Goldfinder, Kerlogue, Crest* and *Cymric. Goldfinder* was a steam collier running between the South Wales coalports and the town and it was the main source of coal supply in the war. She was unloaded into rail wagons alongside the quay by gangs of men very rapidly, and departed empty a couple of days later. All the coal went to Staffords, the town coal merchant (and many other things), and was then distributed. Coal was very scarce in Ireland during the war and none was available for the public. *Crest* and *Cymric* were sailing ships and carried other things

265

beside coal. *Crest* was a wooden ship but *Cymric* was made of steel. All ships arriving were news and as they lay at the quay we were able to examine them closely. They were tiny ships compared with those we were used to seeing in Liverpool but as little happened in the town, their arrival was an event.

The breakwater was black in colour and the stones were covered in a variety of seaweed and mussels. Nobody in Wexford ate mussels — not even the destitute. They were used for crab bait. The idea of eating them was nonexistent. Just over ten years after the war, a physician and lover of music in the town started the Wexford Opera Festival which was an immediate success, mostly due to the stress-free and relaxed atmosphere in which it was conducted and the calibre of the artists attracted by this unusual venue. This brought with it foreign visitors for the first time, for there was little in the way of other tourist attractions. Two visiting Frenchmen had taken a rowing boat to Ferry Bank and on landing and looking around saw the rich colonies of large mussels on the breakwater. Being French they were enthused, and taking the can used for bailing out the rainwater which collects in open boats, they filled it in minutes, put it in the seawater to keep fresh and enjoyed the day on the sands. Returning to White's Hotel in the early evening, they asked the chef to prepare them for their dinner that evening, prior to the Theatre Royal and the night's performance. Now the chef was not certain if this was all a joke and explained to them that "sure, you wouldn't want to be eating them — they'd do you no good at all." Eventually he was convinced, but only when it was agreed that one of the French would attend him in the kitchen and show him how to do it. And that was how "Moules Marinière" entered the menu at White's and all the other hotels in the town. When our Frenchmen sat down that evening and were served the mussels, other diners there for the festival saw their plates and requested the same, only to be disappointed. The next day Lizzie Meyler had a new item on her list. The mussels really were large and this was almost certainly due to the nearby sewer outfall in the river which gave plenty of nutriment for their growth. Like our Frenchmen, Fran had earlier been attracted to the shellfish but for a different reason. Somebody told him that pearls were to be found inside mussels. Not of course in many of them but in just a few, so he decided he would find out if this was true and maybe become wealthy. Collecting a basketfull he brought them back and opened them in secrecy in the bedroom. Mary called out, "tea!" and before going down to the kitchen, he hid them in a drawer and then forgot about them. Some days later Mary was complaining about an awful smell in the room, despite the open window, and there in the drawer under the skylight were the mussels. She threw them out immediately and told the culprit who'd owned up that he had been misinformed. "Pearls are in oysters!". To us they were, and still are, crab bait. I don't remember any of us being converted. Ah! the powers of nurture.

Almost opposite the cotsafe and just beside the Scout HQ there was a small outhouse and Mr Welsh.

Mr Welsh was a young man in his twenties who repaired bikes and fixed punctures. He repaired punctures for us and his lunch each day was a piece of bread and a cup of Oxo — boiling water courtesy of one of the neighbours. He had so little that he cut up old inner tubes to make patches as he couldn't afford to buy standard repair kits. Like Kevin Kehoe, Liam Hayes and Nick Roe he also eventually left for England and the army. His loss was particularly felt as we then had to learn to fix our own punctures, so some good came of it. We all seemed to have lots of punctures, probably because our tyres were all worn and close to the canvas. New tyres were expensive and hard to get. We then started patching the tyres from the inside — it worked. From necessity — progress, another lesson learned.

Clarence House was a delight. It was large and beautifully laid out and we all had lots of room to amuse ourselves. We were mostly left to our own devices particularly during the day when Annie and Fran would be about their business and in the shops. The girls were an alternative attraction and their numbers were swelled even further when our cousins arrived from Liverpool — more refugees from the bombs. Bella, Uncle Jim's wife, arrived with her little girl Marie and produced Joy, another daughter, while living in Monck Street. She was then joined by Lizzie, Tommy's wife with their daughter Pat, so Monck Street became crowded again and Fran and I sought the sanctuary of Clarence House which also offered the great blessing of being "ogre-free" — Johnny being confined to the territory of Monck Street. The arrival of this latest batch of refugees was welcomed by Mary, who liked a full house, especially "family". Bernie liked it also because it brought her playmates close in age, in Marie and Pat. Bella and Lizzie contributed to the household and this allowed additional luxuries on the dining table for Johnny. As they'd each brought him a bottle of the mandatory HP sauce he was not displeased with the arrangements.

Bella's money arrived regularly each week from the shipping company — Jimmy was far away at sea somewhere in the Pacific it was believed — and correspondence was difficult and censored and only possible when landfall was reached. Tommy's money to Lizzie was a "now and then" thing, and May, now back in Liverpool, being informed by Mary that Lizzie hadn't had any for weeks got hold of Tommy her youngest brother.

He just hadn't got round to it was the explanation. "Obviously," said May, "we'll get round to it now, and see you send all the back money too." He did. Tommy was everybody's friend. His difficulty was that being popular he was always in demand and ready to answer the call for a little refreshment. He didn't refuse his cronies because he liked them. He was, as they say, "easily led". At this time he was working in the rigging crew for Harland & Wolff the shipbuilders and he was very good at his job. Totally unafraid at any height he also had the gift of being able to estimate at a glance the fall and position of masts and rigging when they were taken down or raised. His boss, lacking this gift, would often send a search party out to scour the alehouses for "Yer man" if Tommy was off duty.

As there was no one at home, Tommy never went there. No one knows where or when he slept. The repair and rigging crews worked around the clock and everyone worked "all the overtime God sent" to get the ships back out on the water as quickly as possible, as well as for the extra money. Much of the work was for our local hero, Commander Walker and his sloop and corvette squadron, and all the stops were pulled out for them. He was already the most famous U-boat hunter of the war and would die young, exhausted by his efforts on the Western Approaches.

I remember one of Walker's corvettes arriving back in the dock with the bow stoved in, all bent and twisted. They'd rammed and sunk a U-boat which had surfaced in the dark and discovered the threat too late to submerge. I was surprised to view the same ship complete with new bow and ready for the fray once more, about four days later. The repair crews were as heroic as the ships' crews.

In Monck Street, Fran and I were now hag-ridden — the only males in a household of females — young and old with the exception of Johnny and Mr Kirk, who only appeared in the evening. We began to spend more and more time at Clarence House with our cousins. I think I needed this more than Fran, for he was always happy with his own company and didn't seem to need others as much as I did. For my part, I seemed to require enrolment in the human race on a daily basis and I found great pleasure in the company in the big

270

house. What I liked particularly was the variety of things one could do there. There was always somebody who wanted, or was easily persuaded to do the same thing as one wanted oneself. We were all fond of singing and would spend hours learning the words from the popular songbooks and penny sheets available in the shops of the town. We would encourage and perform them for each other and quite unconsciously we all developed as performers ready to give a song at any time if it was asked for. Journeys all featured lots of songs. No false shyness or refusal at all. Some voices were better than others but it didn't matter — everyone did their best and everyone had something they could give to the entertainment. Cards were another great activity — mostly Rummy, Snap, Pontoon, Whist or Cribbage if we could find the crib board, for sometimes it went missing. The girls had knitting and crochet as well. It was the "Golden Age of Knitting". In Britain and everywhere in Europe women were knitting furiously for our gallant soldiers and sailors and clothing was rationed. The knitted balaclava entered fashion and was much in demand for the Russian convoys. Though wool was scarce, old garments and woollens were unpicked to provide a supply and children were very good at this with their quick fingers. This led to sweaters and jerseys in many colours and exotic patterns. Mix and match productions were often put together with great skill. Madge always seemed to be knitting something for someone. She was remarkably fast and rarely seemed to make a mistake which would require unwinding to get back to the faulty row.

She would talk away in time with her needles and every few minutes held the piece up before her eyes to see that she was still OK, and then carry on. Being the eldest, she represented authority when Fran and Annie were out, but she exercised it lightly. Marie and Angela, who was nearest to me in age, were both very handsome — though totally different. They were each of harmonious proportions but Marie was a brunette with very attractive flashing eyes which took in everything and Angela was a real true blue-eyed blonde. Marie was excitable and partly because of this she stammered a lot at this time but she rapidly grew out of it in her teens. She had attitude and a temper, but she could be made to laugh more easily than any of the others. Very much a "people person", she was always good to be with and I spent pleasant times with her, though she was a couple of years older, which often separates at that stage of life. Angela was very different. A cooler more complex customer altogether, and already used to getting her own way with adults and her father in particular — she even charmed Johnny. Because of her smile and her ability to manipulate others she seemed to get away with more, and probably did. She was a little apart from the rest of us — a characteristic shared with her little brother, Frankie. In Frankie's case there was a big age difference which could account for it, but Ange was just different. Bernie, on the other hand, although living in Monck Street, was always one of us. Veronica was probably my favourite at this time. She was a typical Cooney. Red hair, freckles and fazed by nothing. Excited by very little but amused by much. Laconic and a rock of sense. She would become the Martha of the household as they grew — doing the work and looking after others at some cost to herself for she would not marry until late in life. Pat and Lar were opposites. Pat lacked Lar's love of people. Interested in many subjects but particularly himself, he thought deep things and would have made a good academic. Like the rest, both boys liked singing. Lar had the better voice and his frequent renditions of "Kelly the Boy from Killan" and other rebel standards led to his joining me in Johnny's black book. Pat was keen on boxing and we both read everything we could on the subject. We had acquired an old copy of *Ring* magazine, an American publication, and we kept reading and re-reading it. We were proud of the family connection with Jem Roche, the Irish heavyweight champion at the turn of the century. Jem was a Wexford man who lived with our family in Monck Street, where he was reputed to eat a stone of potatoes for his dinner. They seemed to have done him little good, for though unbeaten in Ireland, he found Tommy Burns the World Heavyweight Champion on his European tour, too much. Tommy KO'd Jem in less than a minute when they met in Dublin. It was said the fight was over before the band had finished playing the national anthem. It should have been "God save Jem Roche", one of the locals is alleged to have said as they departed. Whatever happened, "Jem had been in there with the World Champion — which of youse can say the same thing?"

Lar had a sense of humour like Veronica's and a similar ability to laugh at himself. He saw things from other angles — a very attractive trait. Sometimes it was almost psychic and he could detect falsehood quickly. He had his father's disputatious nature, which caused trouble between them as he grew, for in this they were so alike and neither would yield to the other. Lar and I were enthusiastic viewers of gangster movies and we both adopted the speech and style of Messrs Cagney, Raft and Bogart when we were together. This language of our own would continue into later life. He was a lot of fun and we were united by the enmity of Johnny, which made the bonds between us strong.

It was our first Christmas at Clarence House and everybody was there. The dinner was over but we were all still picking at nuts and cake and all the other consumables that appear only at Christmas and vanish for the rest of the year — things like figs, dates and marzipan. There was plenty of drink and tobacco and everyone was having a good time — the adults and the children. All from Monck Street were in attendance and the songs were in full flow. "Best of order please!" The call would immediately produce silence and then the next song or recitation would be announced, listened to attentively and then applauded. It was Johnny's turn, and fortified by many earlier bottles of stout and several large Power's whiskeys and even redder in the face than usual, he stood up. Two bottom waistcoat buttons were undone to relieve the immense pressure of the great belly. He gave forth. I suppose I was more than curious watching and listening to all this

274

as singing was fixed in my mind as being a thing alien to Johnny. I'd never heard him sing a note — ever. His choice of song was strange — an unknown ballad which I'd never heard before:

> There's a bell in Moscow
> There's a bell in Moscow
> I've heard bells chiming
> I've heard bells chiming
> But never like this before

There was no verse, just the chorus, and I've never heard it since, and I'm not sorry. The occasion was impressive, though the performance was not, and I've never forgotten it. Often the case with the bizarre. After several stanzas he sat down to general applause with a smile (a collectors' item but unfortunately not recorded for posterity) and sank another glass of stout in one. After the first songs, tea was made and further refreshments were brought in and everyone began talking and amusing themselves. Angela and I were sitting together. She had been tormenting me for a while. I think it was her way of testing me, which she was always doing and very good at. I would have none of it that night. Other times, yes, but not that night. Johnny, who was nearby, heard or misheard our talk and when I went to leave the room a little later he rose and struck me hard across the face. I left the room shocked and upset. I just wanted to be back in Liverpool, away from this nasty man. Everybody saw what happened but embarrassed, they carried on talking and left it to Annie who got up and came out to me in the corridor. She restored my spirits and consoled me, blaming the drink for Johnny's bad temper and violence. He never offered any apology, either to me, his hosts or anybody else. Ange followed me out and was upset — she couldn't understand his action any more than I could. "He just doesn't like me," I told her, "that's all there is to it." We went back in and sat on the other side of the room to avoid further incidents. Johnny carried on drinking and soon all the waistcoat buttons were released. They had been under duress for some time. It was not a pretty sight.

CHAPTER
SEVENTEEN

Noisy Endgames and the
Page Turns

We were very happy in Wexford but May was missing her children and now that the bombs had ceased and things were quieter, she thought we should be back in Liverpool. Annie and Uncle Fran drove us to Dublin, loaded us up with butter, rashers and most importantly, sausages from Hafner's in Mary Street and put us on the boat. As we left the North Wall and headed east towards Liverpool I had mixed emotions. Ireland had been good to us. How would we find Liverpool? The picture of how we'd left it was strong. The fires still burned in the memory.

All the ferries between England and Ireland were primitive. The conditions in which they transported people had improved little over the years and were in marked contrast to the ferry services across the Channel to France, which were of a much higher standard. There was competition on the routes but each operator was as bad as the other. There was no better alternative. First class was OK but it was very limited in availability and the bulk of the passengers were in second class or steerage. The seating was of wood, un-upholstered and insufficient to seat those travelling and the salons were tiny and totally inadequate. Catering was almost non-existent. Bunks were available on the long Liverpool — Dublin crossing, but were insufficient in number for the demand. The passengers' comfort and status had advanced little since the famine transports a hundred years before. The Liverpool boats carried cattle and these were perhaps considered a priority, more important than people, as the boats often went first to the lairage at Birkenhead to land the cattle before crossing the river to disembark the passengers. All very basic — it would change radically when air passenger services started after the war.

It was a night crossing and we huddled together for warmth beside our suitcases in the depths of the forward steerage accommodation in the bow of the ship. We were surrounded by humanity in all its colours. Women and children soldiers, priests, the market women with their loaded tarpaulined handcarts on the deck above. All seeking shelter from the cold piercing north-west wind blowing strongly across the waters. Despite the lack of comfort, I soon fell asleep and after a while Fran followed. When I awoke the night had wrapped itself like a blanket around the ship and the only noise was the dull revolution of the ship's engines and the snores and moans of our fellow travellers, now all asleep. The air in the hold was foul, and I rose without waking the still-sleeping Fran and went on deck. Morning was on its way and in the early light I could see Anglesey on our right-hand side as we steamed up the Welsh coast as the day grew gently brighter. Roughly an hour later we were at the Bar lightship and started the right turn into the Mersey Estuary, marked by lightships and buoys all the way to the landing stage on Liverpool waterfront. As we turned into the channel I was joined by Fran. "Look at that!" he said as we passed a wreck aground on a sandbank, down at the stern and leaning heavily over to one side. The channel needed no markers, for it was lined with the remains of all the ships which had died on the way in and out, like tombstones in a graveyard of the sea. Most were recent — casualties of mines and torpedoes since the outbreak of war but a few, more ancient, were reminders of the perils of poor navigation in a busy estuary. In the Mersey, ships' masters always tried to beach a sinking ship on a sandbank to prevent blocking the channel, but this was rarely an option where mines or torpedoes were involved. Any obstruction in the confines of the narrow channel had to be cleared with explosives by the Royal Navy who were at work on the port (left-hand side) as we steamed slowly past. The Liverpool waterfront is visible from well out at sea, dominated by the tall towers and mythic birds of the Royal Liver Buildings and as they came into view I felt for the first time that love and longing to be there — back in the womb of the city, an ailment affecting all its children and the returning wanderer in particular. Thus occupied by wrecks, the sight of the Waterloo and Seaforth sands where we played, and happy anticipation, we landed and there was Father in a bowler hat, black overcoat and rolled umbrella talking to the armed sentry on the landing stage but inside the barrier.

279

Everyone else waiting to greet and collect their friends and relatives was on the other side. First they had to pass customs and security. This didn't seem to apply to us and was not a surprise as Father always seemed to regard restrictions as things which were for other people, but not for Tom. We staggered down the gangway with our cases and the barrier was opened and we departed for the nearby no. 17 tram. Father received a full salute as we left and acknowledged it with a raised umbrella. I was eager to see how the city looked. Had everything returned to normal? Was it like it used to be before the bombing started? No fires were burning and some of the debris had been cleared, otherwise everything was the same or so it seemed, but it was not. The war and the world had moved on and we would be moving with it.

We had been away a year and a half. Fran started at St Mary's in Crosby — a Christian Brothers grammar school about four miles away — the same order which we'd had in Wexford. The school was well established and preparing itself for a massive expansion, which would follow the new Education Act then in progress in Parliament. For me it was rather different. There was no St Alexander's — my school mates had all gone — evacuated to Wales and elsewhere — and the school was bombed and in ruins. The surviving church presbytery where the priests lived was now the schoolroom for the few remaining pupils and there I joined them, and Miss O'Donaghue. She was in her fifties — average height and slim. She was of a tranquil disposition and never raised her voice. Neatly dressed and bespectacled she lived with her sister who was also a teacher and both were unmarried. We took to each other immediately and as I was now ten years old and the scholarship exam (the later eleven-plus) was beckoning, she gave me a lot of attention. This was fortunate as I'd really been away from school for three years. We couldn't really count the Irish schooling as the syllabus was very different. I'd learnt things which were useful, such as how to avoid the attentions of authority, and Mr Woods in particular, and I'd come on tremendously in subjects such as Gaelic, fighting and hymn-singing. Unfortunately none of these were examination subjects in the British education system. The core subjects were English composition, arithmetic and general knowledge. The scholarship exam took place over two full days of written examination papers. It was very competitive and there was only one chance offered. Success offered entry to grammar school and higher education — the chance to escape the hard life of one's parents. The latter wanted it too — maybe more than their children — for they knew how hard it was to rise in the world.

At this time great change was afoot and the coalition government was in the process of enacting what became the 1944 Education Act. This would provide financial assistance for children and the youth from eleven until they had finished at university — if examinations were passed at several stages. The testing was to take place at around eleven, sixteen and eighteen years of age.

It was all very competitive and schools only entered for examination those with a real chance of success. The grammar schools up to this time were all fee-paying, though most offered a very limited number of scholarships or bursaries, to those who had passed their own entrance examination. Now the state was offering to pay the school fees and give grants for school materials like books, stationery and uniform. These had previously put grammar schools out of reach of working class parents and their children. Now they would be open to everyone — in theory, that is, for grammar school capacity was limited, the war was on and everything was scarce — particularly teachers. In Liverpool the Catholic hierarchy made a brave decision. They stated early that they would find a grammar school place for any scholarship boy or girl. This was a great incentive. It was then made even better by the government's statement that the legislation would be anticipated and anyone passing the scholarship in 1943 would be paid for from then at the grammar school.

The Archbishop of Liverpool, Richard Downey was a far-seeing man, aware that the perception of Catholics in England could be defined by two words — Irish and poor. The new Education Act could change all that in a generation — not only the perception, but the reality. Education overcomes all barriers — economic and social. We would all get our chance and all the grammar schools in the archdiocese would be enlarged to take the increased numbers. Archbishops have dictatorial powers and so it came to pass and quickly. The efforts required were monumental, particularly in the fields of personnel and investment. The grammar schools would be changed beyond recognition. Like the continent of Europe they now prepared for invasion — in this case by a horde of boys and girls from the toughest and roughest streets of the city. All streetwise and all bright. They would present a formidable challenge to the schools, which had up till then operated sedately with small class sizes and fee-paying pupils — all good boys and girls. There would be casualties — on both sides. Inevitable when cultures collide.

Everything was now clear — the places were waiting — all we had to do was pass the exam. We were fortunate and I do not believe that the boys and girls at other denominational schools in the area got the same chance, for there were widespread reports later of local education authorities failing to find grammar school places for children in similar positions. A sad waste for the nation as well as the children.

The rooms in the presbytery were small and we had about twelve in the class — different ages and different abilities. It was lovely and cosy with the fire burning in the grate and our milk warming on the hearth. With all the difficulties, the state had looked after its children well. We always had our milk and the government issue of concentrated orange juice and rosehip syrup. At break, having no playground, we went out onto St Johns Road and bought hot buns at Nickson's the baker on the corner of Hamlet Street. In class, "Miss" had us all progressing at a different pace. John Swift was attempting the scholarship too — just the two of us were thought to have a chance. Of the others I remember Quinn, who lived in Hertford Road near Grandfather and Alice. Looking at his composition one day I saw he'd spelt bottle as bootle. I thought this was strange as living in Bootle the name was all round him yet he couldn't recognise it. Maybe he was dyslexic — a condition awaiting diagnosis and recognition in the future. I still think it odd that someone should be noted and remembered for a spelling mistake. He was a nice lad, one of two brothers and worthy of a better point of reference.

Then there were Porgie and Ruddy. Porgie was a strong lad about a year or so older — good at sport, though there was little of it as we had no bats, balls or other equipment. We became great friends and much later he had a part-time job as a butcher's boy bringing us meat on his delivery bike. It had a steel basket on the front and the plate formerly advertising Holdens Butchers fixed to the frame below the crossbar, but now painted-over in case invaders were able to verify they were in Bootle! All such evidence of location had to be removed. Ruddy was something else — as bold as Porgie but smaller and younger. Leaving school one day he fell out with Craven — there was a short exchange of blows and Craven decided he wanted none of it and took off. He was pursued by Ruddy but not immediately and by the time Craven reached his front door (always open) and slammed it shut the pursuer was some yards behind. Ruddy was cross and decided retribution was in order and pulling out his organ he proceeded to piss through the letterbox. This was in full view of Craven and his mother who were looking on smugly through the side-glass of the bow window of the front room. Mrs Craven wasn't much in favour of all this and knocked on the window for him to desist. Ruddy looked at the window and switched his attack from the letterbox to the window glass. Now boys have the ability to piss long and strong and develop this ability in competition with each other — both vertically (walls) and horizontally (pavements). Ruddy was up there with the best — literally, and the window got it all. Mrs Craven kept knocking, but was hardly visible through the monsoon of Ruddy's deluge. When the rains ceased he adjusted his dress as the notices in the public toilets advised and walked away — home to his tea. Mrs Craven didn't complain or report him to the school.

When we came back from Ireland the air raids had ceased but their effects lay all around us. Many bomb sites were still covered with rubble but the majority had by now been cleaned and levelled. All around us spaces, damaged houses and workshops in various states — missing floors, no doors, windowless, no staircase, no roof, the variety was endless for nearly all of the Bootle housing stock had received some damage and all the streets were empty. There were no cars and everyone was at work winning the war. It was a vast playground, free from adult intrusion and perfect for war games, particularly in the holidays. Policemen had been sent off to join the army and those that remained were aged or unfit and had more important things to do than chase small boys all day. We could do almost what we liked in the wrecked houses and workshops — and we did.

One day I went home with Porgie who lived across the tracks and he introduced me to Laurie Rice and all his gang who lived between the railway line and Stanley Road and the Kings Park. They were totally different from my playmates on the other side of the tracks and from a socially better-off background. Many of the damaged properties had been evacuated at the outbreak and had suffered more damage subsequently. Over the tracks on Derby Road there were few evacuees, no empty houses and no opportunity to cause further structural damage. A growing boy is aware of, and delights in, his increasing strength which needs an outlet — usually found in sport. But there was no sport for us. Our energy built up and we took it out on property. Wreckage was all around us and all the work of adults, so we had no thought in our minds that maybe we shouldn't be wrecking what was left. The Luftwaffe had shown us what they could do, and right now "Bomber" Harris was attempting to flatten most of the German cities, and he knew he had to go some to beat what they'd done to Liverpool and Bootle.

The great man also had what the constabulary refer to as "previous", having been an early dropper of hand bombs on Arab villages in Iraq in the 1920s when he commanded 45 Squadron. He'd been at it a long time. We felt he'd approve of our activities and our puny efforts at imitation of his nightly 1,000 bomber raids on German cities. The play formula was simple — war. We got together and divided into two groups — each believing the other to be Germans. Fran had joined the play when I told him there was combat and he immediately assumed leadership of one group. I, of course, had to be on the other side. The drill was easy. A house (enemy headquarters) on Kings Road was selected. This one had a tower and other features which would make the battles more interesting. One side was then allocated the house and the other became the assault force. Victory was achieved when the control room was seized along with the wireless (a car battery removed from a left-behind Morris Cowley in the garage yard).

The defenders were allowed a full day to prepare defences (blocking up doors, etc.) and both sides collected ammunition (pieces of plaster from the walls which were old and fragmented easily) and the next day at an agreed time the headquarters was entered, fortifications positioned and after slowly counting to one hundred, a whistle was blown by the defenders and battle commenced.

There were nine of us — aged from ten to fourteen, including a new arrival — Jim. He was living temporarily in Crosby away from the bombs, though only three miles away, but he came from further up the road. Laurie, one of the gang, was his friend and he'd dragged him along for the action. Jim was a gentle boy and a little reluctant to join in, recognising accurately a touch of the desperado in this gang.

"I can't play 'cos I've got to get back to get the bread."

"Never mind the bread, you'll love this game — you can get the bread later," said Laurie. Then Fran produced a master stroke and clinched his recruitment.

"You can have this helmet," he said placing it on Jim's head. The fit was not bad — a bit big but it would do the job and it was a real army steel helmet after all.

"And you'll need these." A pair of machine gunner's goggles were handed over together with an army gas mask shoulder bag filled with broken plaster.

"That's your ammunition." So Jim became a mercenary and joined Fran's attackers.

"We're going now and don't start counting until we're at the door," I said and we left them standing on the pavement as we crossed the quiet, deserted street and entered our HQ.

The front door had been removed from its hinges earlier, courtesy of the Luftwaffe. We placed it back in position and shored it up with timber. Then we climbed the stairs without handrails to the top floor — the tower and the HQ "control room".

The rules of combat were established and worked better than those made in that place in Switzerland — the rule makers all being fighting men. Bricks no bigger than a quarter, plaster maximum 3in × 3in, wooden swords and sticks, film smoke bombs only and no chemicals. Fireworks and explosives were OK.

Agreement was not universal on material to be used in catapults: urine, faeces (human/canine/feline) or dead dogs. The latter had been used successfully to repel a previous attack up the stairs. Agreement was still awaited on dead dogs, but there was a new weapon — a lavatory pan — surely outside the rules.

I'd removed it some days earlier, and struggling, I lifted it up and placed it on the sandstone window sill.

Departure of the tenants had been immediate following the bomb three doors up — very immediate it seemed for the lavatory pan remained unevacuated. There was no running water and the contents had dried and hardened. It was large and cold and white and bore the maker's name — Shanks. The seat and cover made of dark mahogany with big brass hinges. A formidable deterrent.

The attackers were experienced and had found a large piece of plywood which they held over their heads as they rushed the front door. Defensive fire was heavy and some of the exposed fingers on the shield sustained painful damage. The shield was dropped and the attackers turned and fled back to the safety of the other side of the street. The hail of plaster and brick slowed and ceased by the time they regained the relative safety of the opposite pavement. The opponents eyed each other — there was little said. The lavatory pan precariously balanced on the sill was now arousing fears as sucking their bruised and bleeding fingers, the vanquished considered the next move.

"Well we've got one more than our kid so I think three of us should rush the door while the other two throw everything we've got at them. That'll stop a lot of stuff as they'll have to dodge and take cover. Ian and Charlie are our best throwers and they've only got the room in the tower to aim at."

Ian and Charlie agreed immediately as it took them out of the front line.

"OK, that'll leave Joe and me and Jim to push the door down and once in we're safe."

Jim was not convinced.

"What about that?" he said pointing to the bogpan on the ledge.

"He won't drop it on us," said Fran, "it's just to frighten us." It was a long way up and the pan was large and white — at least on the outside. Jim was still not convinced. "He may be your kid but he looks a bit wild to me."

"He won't drop it!" said Fran and they ran towards the door.

"Get off or we'll let youse have it," Laurie shouted.

Fran and Joe pushed at the door and it fell in — they were safe — for the moment.

As I pushed the pan off the ledge my eyes met Jim's — he was in the direct line of fire. I expected him to move, and quickly, and I was alarmed as he seemed mesmerised — unable to move. Maybe it was the goggles. At what seemed the final moment he stepped neatly aside. The lavatory pan came down and hit the pavement. The paving stone cracked from corner to corner and patterned like a Union Jack. The white porcelain and its contents showered everywhere in a million fragments. It was spectacular. The invaders turned and fled and we couldn't stop laughing. An attack repulsed.

When Jim got home and went for the bread his mother wanted to know where he'd been. "Your jersey is full of bits of white and smells terrible."

"I met some boys and we played in this bombed house."

290

"It must have been a strange game you played to get your jersey into this state."

"It was," said Jim.

These games we played day after day in the holidays. We had a wide choice of battlefields and anarchy reigned. Amazingly, no one suffered serious injury. We were having a wonderful time and suddenly it got even better. With all the troops stationed everywhere preparing for the invasion of France, the army decided it would start training for the house-to-house and street fighting which it was going to encounter in the coming conflicts in Europe. Britain's bombed cities were an ideal training ground for these exercises with ruined empty houses and buildings necessary for the exercises available and waiting, and nowhere more suitable than Liverpool. The activity was tightly controlled and quite impressive, and realistically took place as the normal life of the city continued, as it would in Europe, for even in war life must go on. The troops were of great interest, particularly for the new equipment and weaponry they were showing which we hadn't seen before, like the Sten Gun and the blank ammunition they were using, but it was the Thunderflash which excited us. This was a firework more powerful and louder than any previously manufactured and made especially for army exercises. We were entranced. It arrived inserted in an oval of soft wall plaster shaped like a grenade which showered the plaster widely when the Thunderflash core exploded. We had to get some of these and we did. A few months later they started to appear in a few shops and our tests confirmed that they were the genuine article and the equal of our earlier military acquisitions. Once they entered our armoury we began using them in a variety of weapons. We could throw or drop them on each other which caused immediate scattering and sometimes they exploded in mid-air. Laurie Rice was an early casualty when one blew up inches from his right ear. He was deaf on that side for some days and his hair was singed and all spiky like a hedgehog. The Thunderflash was well-named, for it was extremely loud and produced a flash of flaming light when it went off. We started to study how long it took from lighting to detonation and on average it was about 4 to 5 seconds. Immediately before the explosion, the fuse burning became stronger and it was time to let go. It was a bit like Russian Roulette and there was competition between us — who would hold on the longest? The power of the firework was immense and to increase the effect even further, I decided to explode one in a closed container, for I had read in the paper that explosions in enclosed spaces were more violent than in the open. That sounded good to me and worth trying. There was an empty 10-gallon round steel drum in the garage of our HQ and I dropped this on the attackers a few days later. They scattered as it hit the pavement with a bang and then bounced and rolled gently down the incline of the street — and then it went off. There was a complete panic with everyone running in different directions and now a little distance away they looked at the drum now at rest with smoke pouring out of the narrow cap opening. I was delighted with both the volume of the bang and the fact that I'd kidded them with my secret weapon. I hadn't even told my comrades in arms until the last moment when I said, "Watch this!" as I dropped a lit Thunderflash into the drum and then dropped it out of the window. Later, on the way home for tea, Fran said, "That was sneaky."

"But it was good," I replied and Fran nodded — he was already working on how we could use this new advance in technology, and we didn't have to wait long.

Such power could be used for artillery, he suggested, and we decided to test the idea after much discussion sitting on the top floor in HQ.

We took a piece of steel drainpipe from a nearby bombsite and made a cannon. The land in front of our HQ on King's Road was open and contained the railway lines, the Leeds & Liverpool Canal and led to Derby Road, and the streets running into it from both sides. It was a fair distance of 300–400 yards in width, we estimated, and would make a perfect firing range for testing our gun.

We mounted the drainpipe by banging it into the ground and angling it towards Derby Road and the river — supported and fixed in position by bricks on all sides. We had decided to use a bottle for our projectile, mainly because it fitted neatly into the barrel and we knew this was important. A close fit was essential to get velocity and distance. We dropped the Thunderflash down the barrel and then the bottle, bottom first, and waited. It seemed longer than the average 4 or 5 seconds and then an almighty bang and a sheet of flame about 8ft long from the narrow barrel as the bottle was launched across the tracks, but it kept going, beyond the railway and over the canal until it smashed into the gable end wall of the warehouse in Bedford Place, depositing a shower of glass fragments on a poor horse below walking the canal towpath pulling a barge. A bit to the right in our set up and we might have hit the houses in Princes Street or Harland & Wolff's workshops, or even the Marine. We were awestruck and decided we would refrain from further artillery exercises.

The only negatives in our Thunderflash adventures were the 2d cost (money was tight) and we were drawing attention to our activities, which we didn't want. The drum incident and loud explosion brought a number of people to the site, including a policeman looking for a delayed-action bomb explosion. There was nothing to see and we all said we knew nothing about the bang. We didn't cease our activities and experiments with fireworks and gunpowder, but after any of our particularly loud explosions, we evacuated the scene and moved elsewhere to allay suspicion.

The fourth Christmas of the war drifted upon us and although there was not a lot for people to give each other, there was optimism in the air — better than all the gifts. It had been a bad year in many areas but the Yanks were now with us and everybody was convinced about victory — but when? — that was the question. It was much safer on the convoys now and they were getting through to Russia, which was occupying most of the German war effort and attention. The Christmas parties that year were memorable and I was now called upon regularly. There was a special liking for war songs, naturally. Songs about heroism, true love, keeping going, home fires, waiting. It was an opportunity which the songsmiths seized avidly and new compositions were produced in quantity. May encouraged the inclusion of a selection of them in our repertoire, sound in her judgement of the mood of the time. "Bless 'Em All", "There'll Always be an England" and "Coming in on a Wing and a Prayer" were added and proved popular. In retrospect I suppose it is a stirring thing when a small boy sings patriotic songs, whatever, they were the ones most requested. All the other singers who were adult and both male and female sang the usual standards which I preferred, and my own favourite remained the first song May taught me "The Miners Dream of Home".

Father was a fine singer but with a small repertoire. His "Rose of Tralee" was always well sung despite smoking sixty Capstan a day (untipped). He was also adept at playing the spoons, which always got plenty of applause. The parties provided great variety in entertainment and I was fascinated by some of the turns which presented themselves. Wally Woods, a 6ft 2in blond, wavy-haired policeman and a member of Bootle's finest was ever-present and his monologue of "The Green Eye of the Little Yellow God" was mandatory. It was a polished performance and though written as a serious work, Wally played it for laughs and got them. Monologues and recitations were popular and "Dangerous Dan McGrew" often put in an appearance. The parties were a great success and the children of course loved them. They provided a great opportunity to get to know adults, uncles and aunts better (particularly if you performed) and were a great confidence-builder. Many of the guests were seamen or soldiers and they brought talents and songs we'd not heard before. Everybody had a good time. May catered for and fed the crowd and with the pub below we never ran out of drink. Father paid for everything — he was a generous host.

Growing up on such a busy main road I early developed an ability to cross safely, moving in and out between moving vehicles in both directions with confidence. One day I was returning to school from lunch and standing on the side of the road waiting to cross, but it was difficult. The traffic was very heavy in both directions, slow-moving but tightly packed — no gaps. Suddenly there were three heavy bumps and I was now fenced in by three massive bales of cotton which imprisoned me in a triangle of space on the pavement. They'd fallen from a moving lorry. It was a miraculous escape — any one of them would have crushed me as each weighed 500lb and my triangle of space was minimal. I was only inches away from each bale. There was no space to slip out of the triangle so I climbed over the bales and finally crossed the road and went back to school. I don't remember anyone speaking to me about it and I'm not sure the driver was even aware he'd lost the bales. Overloading and a failure to secure loads was not unusual at the time, and the pressure to get things moved quickly resulted in the shedding of much merchandise along the road. Sometimes it was a benediction and very welcome like the load of frozen lambs which fell off. Here we were one of the beneficiaries — courtesy of Paddy Porter.

"There y'are boss," he said, as he removed the frozen carcass from his shoulder, dropped it on the counter and then walked out. May cooked it for the coal heavers who had lamb for a change instead of beef in their sandwiches. It proved popular and a repeat was requested. May explained it was a one-off without revealing the source. Paddy was much amused and said he preferred beef anyway.

Fran had settled in St Mary's and came home one afternoon with a classmate. His name was McIlroy and when I came in he was sitting at the kitchen table about to have tea. But strangely he was still wearing his school cap and raincoat though it was a warm day. He was a fat boy and we always remembered him afterwards for putting his belly on the table when he started to dine. When tea was poured he moved his chair close to the table and released the belly by unbuttoning his raincoat and jacket whereupon it dropped on the table like a blancmange. I was fascinated. He lived in a small house in Cobb Avenue close to the recently burnt-out matchworks of Bryant & May. Fran's influence was judged to be highly detrimental by his grandmother, who ruled the household and had observed him on his visits and to escape it he was taken out of St Mary's and sent to the Jesuits at Saint Francis Xavier's in the city centre. In adult life he emigrated to South Africa, which was probably blamed on Fran, also. He could affect people that way, though it all seemed a bit extreme. Close to where he lived were Sturlas and Tolls, two shops on Litherland Road. Credit Drapery was a business which was big in these times. Sales agents issued credit cheques for stores such as Sturlas which allowed the holder to buy clothing and household goods and furniture in the issuing stores to the value of the cheque. Sturlas was a small department store and had a big business in this area. Credit on hire purchase as it was then called was not widely available and strictly controlled by law. The cheques enabled families to obtain badly needed items such as beds and clothing and they were repaid over time by weekly payments collected by the agent on her visits from house to house — much like the insurance man. The agent was usually a woman who could quickly and accurately assess the likely reliability of repayment. She talked to her customers who gave her quality status reports on neighbours also possibly seeking cheques. A good report would result in a call. Bad debt was rare, partly because the arrangement was personal as well as financial. May had availed herself of cheques during the penurious days in Timon Avenue when Tom was in hospital and they had helped a lot, but after our rise in fortunes following our move to the Marine, she didn't need them. The agent was a lady named Mrs Woodcock, always referred to by my father as "Mrs Timberdick". He never used bad language and very rarely rude words, but the name amused him. She was a small, down-to-business woman who always dressed smartly in black. Quite jolly, talkative and probably very good at her job. She was a major source of information on all sorts of things and ever alert for anyone needing a cheque. Sturlas was a Jewish company like most of the others that offered this service including Swifts and the Provident, the largest of them. The Provident (what a suitable name), was different however, in that it had no shops — it was a pure moneylender and operated nationally. Banks — the gentile variety — had yet to make the acquaintance of the working class and they preferred to borrow from their customers rather than lend.

For the working class they were a great benefit and without them hard times would have been harder. Tolls, the other store, I knew little about and I remember them for the words "The Hut" which followed their name on the signboards and advertising. They had a store in Strand Road where we shopped regularly, but I can't recall ever going in.

In terms of the enemy, and the Germans in particular, there was little vehemence or hatred when the war started and even to the end this would continue. An abridged version of Hitler's life story *Mein Kampf* in thick magazine style was published early on, and sold well with all proceeds going to the Red Cross. We had a copy, and I went through it without too much difficulty. It had lots of pictures and perhaps I was able to read it because of Hitler's use of a very limited vocabulary, 650 words approximately, according to reputable sources. He spoke as he wrote, and part of his power it is said, lay in his use of language. He only used words everybody understood, and emphasised points by repetition. Perhaps the long lead-up to the war and the attempts to avoid it, particularly by Chamberlain, induced a familiarity and feeling in the country that the Führer was a reasonable man who just wanted to reunite Germany and give her back the dignity lost after the first war and the economic nightmare of the 1920s.

He had many supporters in Britain, including royalty and nobility, as well as those in lower orders. In politics in Britain his followers were led by Oswald Mosley, who was very active. He nearly became a major political figure, but Britain distrusts extremists and that did for him. Nevertheless many were not unfavourable to the creeds of Hitler and his ally Mussolini, simply because at distance they had stimulated their countries and got everyone back to work. Britain was lagging well behind — people couldn't understand why we weren't on the up as well. Among the friends of Germany was William Joyce, an early lieutenant of Mosley, who later broke with him and fled to Germany as war broke out. Joyce, who was born in New York of an Irish father and English mother and (according to local tradition in Liverpool), went to school locally at Merchant Taylors in Crosby. The school is in a suburb of the city roughly a mile from the end of the line of docks. He commenced broadcasts to Britain in early 1940 and quickly won a large audience — bigger than the BBC. I have since read that his broadcasts were banned by the government but have no recollection of such a prohibition. If true, it was totally ignored and as the words "Germany Calling, Germany Calling" came out over the airwaves, everybody sat back and listened. He was a superb broadcaster and his plummy enunciation of "Jar-meny" led to the *Daily Express* calling him Lord Haw Haw — the name stuck. Haw Haw's programmes were a mixture of propaganda, questions and advice on such things as how to treat injuries received in the bombing. His tone was that of a friend speaking to the misguided and unfortunate, and he displayed an amazing knowledge of local trivia such as the time at which local clocks had stopped (probably from the Luftwaffe reconnaissance photography) and were showing incorrect time. This was clever and led to the widespread belief that there were German spies and agents everywhere, and the government reacted strongly with continuous campaigns that "Walls have ears" and "Careless talk costs lives". It was destabilising and in that area was successful. Liverpool was much mentioned and his references indicated a good knowledge of the area — his own it was believed. The Caradoc, a pub at the gates to Gladstone Dock, was in the script which would go something like "You're drinking in the Caradoc as I speak, but where is the Ark Royal?" It was a good question, but the answer was before our eyes for the bow of the great ship was towering over the end of the graving dock a hundred yards away. We had seen her building in Laird's yard across the river and watched as she slipped silently out of the Mersey one dark foggy morning early in 1940. She was going at speed with destroyers fore and aft. "Gosh, she's big!" said Fran. She was iconic and great deeds lay before her. Joyce's popularity tailed off as the war went on and the air raids diminished. Brave, misguided and heavily prejudiced, he was executed as a traitor at the end of the war on the basis of an expiring British passport. A decision now regarded as legally unsound — like others of the time but war is rarely just.

Miss O'Donoghue was a wonderful teacher to whom I owe much. She had been at the school over thirty years and she stayed behind to help look after us stragglers when the school was evacuated. She was small and neat in everything with a gentle manner to which the roughest boys responded very well. We were all very fond of her. In the short period with her I made rapid advances and despite the difficulties, it seemed a happy time for all of us in the little room in the presbytery. Each of us was at a different stage in the syllabus and she gave her time and tuition as it was needed to both the bright and the not-so-bright. There was no punishment and no bad behaviour — yet her pupils came from the toughest of homes. She and May were similar, I thought, in how they handled people. I liked them both for similar reasons and wanted to please. Happily progressing, we approached Easter 1943.

It was the day for the scholarship exams. They were being held at Breeze Hill School which was very new and about a mile and a half away on Bootle's highest point. It was a sunny spring morning but there had been heavy showers and the sparks were flying from the carthorses' steel shoes as they struck the flint of the wet granite sets as they toiled and slipped up the steep incline of Miller's Bridge. Miller's Bridge was always very busy. The "bridge" crossed both the railway and the canal. On one side was the park where three years earlier I'd fallen off the swing and on the other were tall houses with semi-basements and interesting shops and businesses underneath. One of these was the public bakehouse where one could take bread or meat for baking or roasting. Many people had no cooker or oven and it was much used. I thought of my wild uncle Bill every time I walked up the hill. He had married a girl named Annie Connolly and they lived in one of the tall houses up there. One day there was an argument and she told Bill that everything in the place was hers and to get out. Bill's total property was the alarm clock and seizing it, he threw it out of the window and left. It was that sort of relationship. He was my grandfather's younger brother and was widely loved, particularly by his brother (and Annie). He died in Southampton as a result of fighting with his friend Corcoran during which he struck his head on concrete. He died from a blood clot on the brain some days later. Corcoran later perished on the *Titanic*. The family version of the story was somewhat different and being a professional listener, I knew all the details. Annie, Bill's wife, was almost certainly alive at the time but there was no contact with the rest of us. Fran it seems, however, had met her as out walking one day with Uncle Tom (Bill's younger brother) they called into a house on Miller's Bridge and had a nice tea with a lady and a pleasant chat for a couple of hours. Tom loved humanity and it would be in keeping with his nature that he stayed in touch. I only learned this later and I used to wonder if she still lived on the bridge. The pieces of the alarm clock on the pavement and road had left a strong impression and I expected to see the debris every time I walked up the bridge and in this contemplative mood I arrived at the school.

Everything was tightly organised. No going to the toilet during exams, so go now. No talking and no looking at other boys' work (we were segregated and the girls were in the next hall). Read the questions and remember that when the bell sounds you've got ten minutes to finish and correct before the papers are collected. And that was it. The papers contained no surprises and Miss O'Donoghue had prepared us well. I don't know if an interview was part of the exam, but they did take place. The interview was the most interesting part and I quite enjoyed it. The panel of (I think) three (two men and a lady), were very kind with us and as a result of my performances before audiences I was not nervous at all. Then we all went home to wait — the purgatory of doubt and inactivity.

School continued until the end of the summer term and Swiftie and I hoped that September would bring us to St Mary's where our elder brothers already were. They were fee-paying — we would be the first "free" scholars if we were successful. Our brothers would still have to pay. It seemed unfair but was understandable as it would have increased the costs to the government fivefold. Then it happened. About three or four weeks later I entered our classroom and Miss O'Donaghue was beaming. As soon as the roll was called she stood up and announced that Swiftie and I had both been successful and to give us a clap — and the class responded. Canon Kelly and Father Taylor came in from the adjoining rooms and shook our hands and told us we were a credit to the school and we could all have the afternoon off. Miss O'Donaghue gave us both a lovely new rosary each, bought with her own money from the Catholic Repository. These were shops which sold religious items such as rosaries, candles, holy books and mass cards as well as regular merchandise. At lunchtime we went home with the glad tidings and May and Father were delighted, though not over-effusive — none of us liked fuss. I met Father Rigby at the gate. He had gone completely grey as a result of the blitz in a matter of weeks, despite being only in his early thirties. May got out the utensils and soon my favourite lemon cake was baking in the oven. She was very happy and I knew it, though little was said. I had made May and my dad happy and it gave me a warm feeling.

It would be St Mary's in September with Fran, and by then we'd also be in a new home. May's prompting of Tom to apply for a better house in a nicer area had succeeded and in a couple of months we'd be moving to the Lion and Unicorn in Waterloo. Only a mile or so from the new school and a nice, quiet residential area. Everything was in a state of flux and change and with the optimism with which the gods bless the young, we were now just waiting for it to happen. It would all be very different. A new life. The constants would remain however — May, Father and Liverpool. Unchanging like the granite of the city streets.

Also available in ISIS Large Print:

Goodbye, Wigan Pier

Ted Dakin

"My escape from a school that taught me very little was a euphoric occasion and because of the headmaster's ruling that only short pants should be worn by all pupils, my first pair of long ones was an added bonus."

Ted Dakin returns to his childhood in Wigan, with more stories of the people and places he grew up with. He tells of boxing matches ruled over by his vindictive headmaster, Owd Hector Wainwright; of men stealing coal from the trains; and of his first job in a saddlery. Full of the characters of his youth, like Dolly Varden and her predictions, Fag-Ash Lil and Dunkirk veteran Ginger Dyson, Ted's stories are full of the warmth and wit of a Wigan lad.

ISBN 978-0-7531-9510-9 (hb)
ISBN 978-0-7531-9511-6 (pb)

The Grocer's Granddaughter

Rose Parish

"The English are often referred to as 'A Nation of Shopkeepers', and my family were certainly among them."

As the child of a family running a busy village shop, the author developed the ability to be "a fly on the wall" watching, listening and establishing lasting memories. She has drawn up a very special picture of life in the Worcestershire village of Ombersley during the 1940s. This is a pithy account of village life as it was, offering a view decidedly unlike a picture-postcard image. The full stratum of village life is reflected, drawing attention to a variety of ideas and attitudes; poverty, wealth, a common work ethic, crime, tragedy, sorrow and pleasure are all there in the village mixing pot.

ISBN 978-0-7531-9482-9 (hb)
ISBN 978-0-7531-9483-6 (pb)

Clap Hands for the Singing Molecatcher

Roderick Grant

When I was three I was stung 172 times by a swarm of angry, demented bees. And as my mother said later when my head, face and neck had returned to a reasonably normal shape, "It was all your own fault".

In this evocative memoir, Roderick Grant recalls the laughter, tragedy and drama of a boyhood spent in Morayshire in the late 1940s and 1950s. Against the backdrop of some of Scotland's most beautiful scenery, he not only re-creates the experiences that moulded his early life but also paints a vivid picture of a remote country community, close knit in its isolation from the changing post-war world.

ISBN 978-0-7531-9490-4 (hb)
ISBN 978-0-7531-9491-1 (pb)

A Derby Boy

Anton Rippon

"Eventually, getting on for midnight, I appeared, just in time for Christmas. I've always liked a party and obviously didn't want to miss this one"

Anton Rippon is a Derby boy through and through. Born just before Christmas 1944, his entrance into the world was hastened after his mother fell over a milk churn in the blackout. A Derby Boy is a collection of Anton's reminiscences of childhood, teenage years and his introduction to the bustling world of work. Nostalgia abounds with tales of family, schooldays, trips to theatres and cinemas, shops and streets, pubs and clubs, sporting life and national events.

Tales of mad butchers and dodgy coalmen, eccentric schoolteachers and odd publicans, illegal gambling and irate undertakers combine with his family's often tragic story to open up a new perspective on life in Derby over four generations.

ISBN 978-0-7531-9484-3 (hb)
ISBN 978-0-7531-9485-0 (pb)